The Politics of Environmental Control
in Northeastern Tanzania, 1840–1940

University of Pennsylvania Press
ETHNOHISTORY SERIES

Lee V. Cassanelli, Juan A. Villamarin, and Judith E. Villamarin, Editors

A complete listing of the books in this series appears at the end of this volume.

The Politics of
Environmental Control
in Northeastern
Tanzania, 1840–1940

James L. Giblin

ʊ/ɦɦ

University of Pennsylvania Press

Philadelphia

Publication support was provided by the University of Iowa Vice President for Research

Library of Congress Cataloging-in-Publication Data

Giblin, James Leonard.
   The politics of environmental control in Northeastern Tanzania,
1840–1940 / James L. Giblin.
      p.   cm. — (University of Pennsylvania Press ethnohistory series)
   Includes bibliographical references and index.
   ISBN 0-8122-3177-5 (alk. paper)
      1. Agriculture—Economic aspects—Tanzania—History.   2. Famines—
Tanzania—History.   3. Environmental policy—Tanzania—History.
4. Tanzania—Economic conditions—To 1964.   5. Tanzania—Politics
and government.   I. Title.   II. Series: Ethnohistory series
(Philadelphia, Pa.)
HD2128.5.G5   1992
338.1'09678'27—dc20   92-28388
                                                          CIP

FOR BLANDINA

Contents

List of Illustrations   ix
List of Abbreviations   xi
Acknowledgments   xiii

Introduction   1

Part I: Environment and Economy in Late-Precolonial Uzigua   13

1. Agronomy and Trade   15

2. Cattle, Control of Bovine Disease, and Patronage   29

Part II: The Politics of Patronage in the Late-Precolonial Chieftaincies   43

3. Merchant Capital and the Chieftains   45

4. Emulating the Chieftains: Patronage in the Spiritan Missions of Uzigua   60

5. Ambition and Obligation in Late-Precolonial Politics   70

Part III: Famine, Disease, and the Decline of Patrons Under German Colonial Rule   83

6. The Colonial Economy and Its Impact on Patrons and Dependents   85

7. Colonialism, Infanticide, and the Destruction of
Precolonial Political Authority   102

8. Colonialism, Famine, and Epizootic, 1884–1914   121

**Part IV: British Administration, Obstacles to Peasant
Production, and Ecological Crisis**   133

9. Indirect Rule and Peasant Production in Uzigua   135

10. Famine, Depopulation, and Epizootic, 1916–1940   153

Conclusion: Historical Interpretation and Ujamaa in Handeni
District   177

Sources   185
Index   205

Illustrations

FIGURES

1. Mandera in the 1880s   36

2. Site of ancestor veneration and medicines   63

3. Precolonial Healer with infant   110

4. Mohamedi Mjewe with his wife   118

5. The Teutloff house at Kwediboma   147

6. Parakuyu Maasai men at Kiberashi   175

MAPS

1. Uzigua and surrounding territories   16

2. Late-precolonial Uzigua   51

3. Uzigua under German rule   89

4. Expansion of tsetse belts under Indirect Rule   169

Abbreviations

AA	*Annales Apostoliques de la Congrégation du Saint-Esprit et du Saint Coeur de Marie*
AOSE	*Annales de l'Oeuvre de la Sainte-Enfance*
APF	*Annales de la Propagation de la Foi*
ARPC	Annual Reports of the Provincial Commissioners on Native Administration
BC	*Bulletin de la Congrégation du Saint-Esprit*
BRALUP	Bureau of Resource Assessment and Land Use Planning, University of Dar es Salaam
DOAG	Deutsch-Östafrikanische Gesellschaft (German East Africa Company)
DOAR	*Deutsche Östafrikanische Rundschau*
DKb	*Deutsches Kolonialblatt*
Jahresbericht	*Jahresbericht über die Entwicklung der Deutschen Schutzgebiete*
LMC	*Les Missions Catholiques*
PRGS	*Proceedings of the Royal Geographical Society*
RKA	Reichskolonialamt (Central State Archives, Potsdam)
TIRDEP	Tanga Integrated Rural Development Project
TNA	Tanzania National Archives
UMCA	Universities Mission to Central Africa
USPG	United Society for the Propagation of the Gospel

Acknowledgments

Despite the hardships they were enduring, many persons in Tanzania treated me with hospitality and kindness in the early 1980s. Among them were Asumani Mhandeni, Saidi Kigoda, Leonard Mhina, Juma Kahungo and his family, Amani Sumra and his family, Hassani Simba, Mwanamkuu Sefu and the late Amos Kazubi at Kwediboma; Tunzo Saidi at Mgera; Marco George at Handeni; and Ignas and Abdu Kaduma in Dar es Salaam. At the University of Dar es Salaam I was assisted by Professors I. N. Kimambo and A. M. H. Sheriff. Missionary records were kindly made available by the Rt. Rev. A. Mkobo, the Bishop of Morogoro, and by Fathers Fritz Versteijnen and Harry Tullemans.

Among the archivists who assisted me were Ian Pearson at the United Society for the Propagation of the Gospel; the Rev. Richard Wersing, Dorsey Archivist, Duquesne University, who provided many items from the *Bulletin de la Congrégation du Saint-Esprit*; the Rev. Henry J. Koren of the Spiritan Archives, USA, who loaned me Spiritan records on microfilm; and the staffs of the Tanzania National Archives and the Central State Archives, Potsdam. The Inter-Library Loan offices of the Memorial Library, University of Wisconsin, and the University Library, University of Iowa, obtained many sources for me. For constant assistance at the University of Iowa I must thank John Bruce Howell.

At various stages of this project I benefited from the comments of Charles Ambler, Tom Beidelman, Lee Cassanelli, Jonathan Glassman, Paul Greenough, David Henige, Keith Marshall, Tom Spear, Michael Twaddle, Allen Roberts, Richard Waller, and Luise White. The influence of Steven Feierman and Jan Vansina is evident on every page. For his willingness to devote much time to meticulous reading, and for his encouragement and criticism, I am deeply indebted to Stephen Vlastos. As research assistants, Sung-hwa Cheong and Mike Pfeifer provided invaluable help. Kay Irelan prepared the maps. The research was supported by the Social Science Research Council, a Fulbright-Hays Award, and grants from the University of Iowa, the Center for International and Comparative Studies at the University of Iowa, the American Council of Learned Societies, and the National Endowment for the Humanities. Although I could not have completed this project without the assistance of these individuals and organizations, they are in no way responsible for the statements, judgments, and errors contained in this work.

Introduction

Among the poorest farmers in Tanzania are the 200,000 villagers in the northeastern district of Handeni. Although information on the relative condition of Tanzania's districts has rarely been published in recent decades, there is little reason to suppose that Handeni's standing within the nation has improved since 1967, when its per capita Gross Domestic Product, which stood fifty-ninth among sixty-one districts, was only 41 percent of the national average.[1] Most of Handeni's residents can neither purchase sufficient food and clothing nor accumulate reserves of cash, grain, and livestock in anticipation of the droughts that occur frequently. Only a handful of peasants in each village, moreover, are able to afford cattle and the drugs which protect livestock from insect-borne infections. Their inability to accumulate money and other resources leads both to annual pre-harvest hunger, which leaves many farmers ill and gaunt, and to periodic famine.[2]

In the early 1980s, severe transport difficulties were a contributing cause of scarcity. As fuel shortages forced trucks and buses off deteriorating roads, Handeni residents became used to making thirty-mile journeys by foot (while the more intrepid traveled one hundred miles or more on homemade wooden bicycles) and watched food supplies dwindle in markets, state-run stores, and the district's few failing private shops. Distribution was not the principal problem, however, for even when food was available many farmers could not afford to buy it, just as they could not purchase other basic goods and services such as school uniforms and primary health care. Government policies that prevented farmers from earning money were primarily responsible for scarcity, because stipulations that crops be sold at low official prices to state buying agencies and a ban on the

1. L. Berry, ed., *Tanzania in Maps*, p. 161.
2. On seasonal scarcity and illness, see Robert Chambers, Richard Longhurst, and Arnold Pacey, *Seasonal Dimensions to Rural Poverty*, esp. pp. 45–52, 218–224; and James P. Goetz, "A Study of Childhood Disease in Tanzania," pp. 182–186, which documents increased bronchitis, pneumonia, diarrhea, and "severe protein-energy malnutrition" during the pre-harvest rainy season in a district which adjoins Handeni.

hiring of wage labor prevented farmers from raising money through crop marketing and wage-paying jobs.[3] Many farming households depended, therefore, on remittances from relatives working outside the district.[4]

Poverty, hunger, and restrictive government policies were nothing new in the 1980s, however. All have prevailed in Handeni since the early colonial period, and all have had greater impact on the district than the transition from colonial rule to national independence. Indeed, even the boldest initiative of the post-colonial government, the resettlement of the farming population in Ujamaa villages during the 1970s, did not fundamentally alter the conditions and administrative practices that had developed under colonial rule, because Ujamaa villagization was inspired by the same constricted perceptions of economic development and peasant economy, and accompanied by the same narrowly-conceived policy options, as those that had predominated under German and British colonial administrations. Like its colonial predecessors, the Tanzanian state during the Ujamaa period wavered between compulsory cultivation of marketable crops and restrictions on trade. By turns it required the growing of designated cash crops, food crops, and both types of crops simultaneously, as it shifted between policy alternatives that reflected two other legacies of colonial rule: pessimism about the prospects for development in Handeni's environment and the conviction that all villages and households must produce enough food to meet their own needs.

Tanzanian government officials of the 1980s were as doubtful about the likelihood of material improvement in the Handeni environment as the former British administrator who, visiting the district in the early 1970s after a fourteen-year absence, was impressed anew by "the physical environment [which] still exercises a dominating influence. . . . Rainfall is still erratic, topography hinders road maintenance, the scattered nature of Handeni settlements impedes communication."[5] Because they regarded sparse precipitation, poor soils, and tsetse flies as almost insurmountable obstacles, and assumed that districts and villages should be self-sufficient (just as colonial administrators had believed that "tribes" ought to remain

3. Recent government policies in northeastern Tanzania have been described as impeding "accumulation by capitalist farmers, without creating any viable alternative form of organization of production" (John Sender and Sheila Smith, *Poverty, Class and Gender in Rural Africa: A Tanzanian Case Study*, pp. 137–138).

4. Deborah S. Rubin, "People of Good Heart: Rural Response to Economic Crisis in Tanzania."

5. David Brokensha, "Handeni Revisited," p. 167. For similar comments, see Clarke Brooke, "Types of Food Shortages in Tanzania," p. 343 and Hassan Omari Kaya, *Problems of Regional Development in Tanzania*, p. 169.

essentially self-enclosed units—see Chapter Nine), Tanzanian officials believed that farmers could survive in Handeni's environment only by producing enough food to satisfy their own needs.[6] A development strategist reformulated this view in 1983 by arguing that because "malnutrition and seasonal or periodical hunger characterize the life of the peasant in Handeni," self-sufficiency is the *sine qua non* of progress: in Handeni "with its low density of population and the large distances between settlements, each village has to become as much as possible self-reliant in food."[7] More recently, another study of Handeni took the same position in contending that colonial and post-colonial developments "led to the loss of the self-sufficiency that was the feature of the pre-capitalist mode of production."[8]

Peasants: Subsistence Oriented or Market Oriented?

Given the daunting problems associated with scarcity of water, unreliability of rainfall, and widespread tsetse infestation in Handeni, the attribution of poverty and food deficits to environmental factors and lack of self-sufficiency would perhaps appear unobjectionable. This is not, however, the view of many Handeni farmers, who share neither the administrators' fatalism about environmental adversity nor their enthusiasm for household, village, and district self-sufficiency. Intensely interested in crop marketing and wage-paying employment, yet bitterly critical of colonial and post-colonial governments, Handeni's farmers fit uncomfortably into the categories, such as the "impoverished," "accumulating" and "ornery" peasant types, found in historical studies of African peasants.[9] Although peasants in Handeni are unquestionably poor, many men and women wish

6. For pessimistic surveys of Handeni's soils, see S. A. Hathout and S. Sumra, "Rainfall and Soil Suitability Index for Maize Cropping in Handeni District," and Tanzania, Ministry of Water, Energy and Minerals, *Tanga Water Master Plan*, vol. 4, *Soils*.

7. Tanzania, Tanga Region, Regional Planning Office, "Handeni District Development Strategy: First Draft," mimeographed (Tanga, October 1983), pp. 22 and 34. Officials of the Tanzanian government as well as the Tanga Integrated Regional Development Project (which is active in Handeni) frequently stressed the need for "sustained self-reliance and self-supply of food" (Sender and Smith, *Poverty, Class and Gender*, pp. 119, 124 ff, 169, 172).

8. Suleman Alarakhia Sumra, "Primary Education and Transition to Socialism in Rural Tanzania: A Case Study of an Ujamaa Village in Mswaki, Handeni District," p. 317.

9. Frederick Cooper, "Peasants, Capitalists, and Historians: A Review Article," p. 302 and Allen Isaacman, "Peasants and Rural Social Protest in Africa," pp. 14–15. Terence Ranger contrasts "entrepreneurial" peasants who "responded to colonial market opportunity" with those who "managed to stand relatively aloof" in "Growing from the Roots: Reflections on Peasant Research in Central and Southern Africa," p. 113.

that they could emulate the few Handeni farmers who have managed to accumulate wealth despite government restrictions, and most of them, in the opinion of district administrators, are "ornery." Seeming recalcitrance on the part of peasants stems not from a desire to avoid market relationships and development, however (though officials have often interpreted it as such), but rather from rejection of government policies that limit access to markets.

Indeed, because Handeni's farmers have not resisted incorporation into a market economy, they cannot be considered part of Goran Hyden's "uncaptured peasantry."[10] Nor do they demonstrate the dichotomous "market" and "non-market," "capitalist" and "non-capitalist" tendencies that have long been a staple topic in African studies. Recent forms of this discussion have analyzed peasants and peasant modes of production that resist, coexist with, or become articulated with capitalism.[11] Historians of South Africa, for example, contrast Christian converts who were "highly incorporated in the colonial economy" with a majority of peasants who "displayed a cautious or selective traditionalism."[12] Numerous studies of other areas, which hold that precolonial African cultivators devoted themselves primarily to the production of use-values, grant only secondary significance to market production and exchange in the history of rural societies.[13] Like Goran Hyden, some authors take the argument further, insisting that the lingering influence of precolonial subsistence orientation disposes modern African peasants to resist market integration, production

10. Contending, however, that Handeni peasants "used their 'exit' option as soon as they could" is Goran Hyden, *Beyond Ujamaa in Tanzania: Underdevelopment and an Uncaptured Peasantry*, p. 60.

11. For example, Martin A. Klein, "Introduction," in Martin A. Klein, ed., *Peasants in Africa: Historical and Contemporary Perspectives*, pp. 9–43. The articulation thesis is developed in P. P. Rey, *Colonialisme, néo-colonialisme et transition au capitalisme: exemple de la "Comilog" au Congo-Brazzaville* and *Les Alliances de classes: sur l'articulation des modes de production*. A study that avoids assumptions about dichotomous market and non-market tendencies is Angela P. Cheater, *Idioms of Accumulation: Rural Development and Class Formation Among Freeholders in Zimbabwe*.

12. William Beinart and Colin Bundy, "Introduction: 'Away in the Locations,'" in William Beinart and Colin Bundy, eds., *Hidden Struggles in Rural South Africa*, pp. 11–12, 30. Also, Colin Bundy, *The Rise and Fall of the South African Peasantry* and J. B. Peires, *The Dead Will Arise: Nongqawuse and the Great Xhosa Cattle-Killing Movement of 1856–1857*, pp. 315–316.

13. For example, Robert W. Shenton, *The Development of Capitalism in Northern Nigeria*, p. 138, Abdi Ismail Samatar, *The State and Rural Transformation in Northern Somalia, 1884–1986*, p. 10, and Jonathan Musere, *African Sleeping Sickness: Political Ecology, Colonialism and Control in Uganda*, p. 46ff, 100. See also James C. Scott, *The Moral Economy of the Peasant: Rebellion and Subsistence in Southeast Asia*, p. 60. For criticism of this tendency in studies of modern African peasants, see Sara S. Berry, "The Food Crisis and Agrarian Change in Africa: A Review Essay," pp. 32–33.

of agricultural commodities, and wage labor,[14] a position that they may maintain despite considerable evidence of precolonial trade and production for market. Michael Watts's justly influential study of northern Nigeria, for instance, describes dogged "peasant resistance to commoditization" arising "from the persistence of an economy of use-value production in which work and consumption were united in the family." Thus even though he acknowledges precolonial grain trade of "great practical virtue," and "vast, ramifying networks" controlled by merchant capital, his study contends that precolonial commerce was not a "residual element in a predominantly peasant economy."[15] He tends, therefore, to emphasize the passivity of colonial peasants, who either are "swept up into the commodity boom" or remain "obdurately uninterested in wage labor."[16]

While Watts shares with other authors the inclination to assume that precolonial rural communities were essentially self-sufficient, he nevertheless challenges another quality found commonly in historical writing about rural Africa—the tendency to underestimate the importance of politics. Unlike the bulk of peasant studies, which, as Allen Isaacman notes in a recent review of peasant historiography, have "most often ignored or marginalized peasants as political actors," Watts's work incorporates politics into his analysis of precolonial subsistence security.[17] He has been joined in recent years, moreover, by a number of historians who study rural political history, but their treatments continue to be influenced by the tendency to think in terms of self-enclosed peasants; as Isaacman shows, they often characterize rural politics as the defense of peasant "autonomy" against encroaching states and market economies.[18] Few studies, however, consider that farmers may have used political means to *enter* markets.[19] And despite Isaacman's insistence that analysis of rural politics must be rooted in an understanding of work processes, still fewer studies connect political activity with work that affects ecological conditions.[20] Indeed,

14. For example, Maureen Mackintosh, *Gender, Class and Rural Transition: Agribusiness and the Food Crisis in Senegal*, particularly pp. 38 and 44.

15. Quotes from Michael Watts, *Silent Violence: Food, Famine and Peasantry in Northern Nigeria*, pp. 312, 108, 134–135, 64; see also pp. 188–189.

16. Watts, pp. 221 and 223.

17. Isaacman, "Peasants and Rural Social Protest," p. 5 and Watts, esp. pp. 119 ff.

18. Isaacman, pp. 49–58

19. A study that seeks to reconcile political initiatives to profit from crop marketing, however, with concepts of peasant "autonomy" and "exit options," is Stephen G. Bunker, *Peasants Against the State: The Politics of Market Control in Bugisu, Uganda, 1900–1983*.

20. The path-breaking exception is Steven Feierman, *Peasant Intellectuals: Anthropology and History in Tanzania*.

even the finest treatments of African environmental change neglect the politics of environmental control.[21]

The assumption that the legacy of precolonial subsistence orientation discourages market involvement and the associated tendency to overlook rural political life are both manifest in studies of rural Tanzania.[22] Although the most prominent work on Tanzania to stem from the subsistence-orientation assumption is Hyden's argument about the "economy of affection,"[23] the idea also emerges in other forms, most recently in books by Deborah Fahy Bryceson and by John Sender and Sheila Smith.[24] Bryceson sees a Tanzanian tendency to retreat from market uncertainties into "face-to-face" patron-client relationships, while Sender and Smith, who are critical of Hyden, nonetheless take a somewhat similar position by arguing that market-oriented peasants must resist "pressure to conform to 'traditional' practices."[25] Sender and Smith support this contention by asserting that men of the Usambara region, which adjoins Handeni, discourage their wives and daughters from doing wage labor. In Handeni, however, where wage-earning opportunities for women have always been scarce, this thesis cannot be tested.[26]

Handeni has itself inspired similar comment on peasant unwillingness to trade, grow cash crops, and perform wage labor. Missionaries, administrators (including post-colonial Tanzanian officials who are usually not natives of the district), and scholars[27] have tended to regard Handeni farmers as subsistence-oriented and reluctant to enter wage labor. Such views can be traced to the early colonial period, when a German official

21. For example, John Ford, *The Role of the Trypanosomiases in African Ecology: A Study of the Tsetse Fly Problem* and Michael Mortimore, *Adapting to Drought: Farmers, Famines and Desertification in West Africa*.

22. A study that overlooks the political dimension of environmental change is Helge Kjekshus, *Ecology Control and Economic Development in East African History*. The politics of ecology control *are* discussed, however, by Juhani Koponen, *People and Production in Late Precolonial Tanzania: History and Structures*. For examples of the emphasis on subsistence production, see Deborah Fahy Bryceson, "Peasant Cash Cropping versus Self-Sufficiency in Tanzania: A Historical Perspective," especially pp. 39–40 and *Food Insecurity and the Social Division of Labour in Tanzania, 1919–1985*, particularly pp. 31 and 74; Ralph A. Austen, "The Official Mind of Indirect Rule," pp. 601–602.

23. "In the economy of affection, economic action is not motivated by individual profit alone, but is embedded in a range of social considerations . . . . This economy of affection is being maintained and defended against the intrusions of the market economy." Hyden, *Beyond Ujamaa in Tanzania*, p. 19.

24. Bryceson, *Food Insecurity*.

25. Sender and Smith, *Poverty, Class, and Gender*, p. 87.

26. Sender and Smith, pp. 65–67.

27. See Michaela von Freyhold, *Ujamaa Villages in Tanzania: Analysis of a Social Experiment*, p. 61 and Hyden, p. 60.

dismissed the "notoriously stubborn and indolent" men of Handeni as ill-suited for wage-paying employment.[28] The attitude that Handeni farmers were "indolent," "lazy," "improvident," and heedless of the advantages of crop sales and wage labor pervaded German and British administrations.[29] This outlook was absorbed by African government employees, including one primary school teacher who complained in 1935 that villagers in western Handeni "had neither respect for authority nor purposefulness."[30] Thus administrators blamed the farmers of Handeni for their own poverty and hunger. They "do not trouble to more than scratch the soil before planting," observed a British official in 1923; they "do not take kindly to paid labour," concluded an administrator in 1951. "Except when at work on his own shamba [cultivated plot]," remarked a district official, the Handeni cultivator "is a rather lazy and unreliable employee where manual labor is concerned."[31]

Also common among government officials and missionaries has been the belief that the predominantly Zigua-speaking farmers of Handeni are hobbled by fear of witchcraft and spirits. As Chapter Seven shows, such ideas originated in the 1880s when European missionaries began to argue that infanticide among the superstitious "Zigua tribe" was the chief cause of regional depopulation. Similar notions resurfaced in the 1970s, when Tanzanian administrators blamed peasant opposition to resettlement in Ujamaa villages on irrational fear of witchcraft and superstitious unwillingness to leave locations associated with ancestor cults. For their part, however, Handeni peasants see no conflict between beliefs in ancestors and their desire to trade, accumulate and modernize. Instead, their accounts of the past portray exchange and accumulation, as well as propitiation of ancestors, as sources of community health and welfare. Yet they also regard the maintenance of community welfare as a political process that requires particular qualities of political leadership. Thus many Handeni farmers believe that the colonial and post-colonial developments— including Ujamaa villagization—that transformed political authority, cost them opportunities to trade, and weakened ties between the living and dead, are all causes of modern scarcity.

28. RKA 123/129, report of Siegel (August 16, 1912).
29. BC 24 (1907–1908): 515. A recent study which discusses peasant "indolence" and subsistence orientation is Ronald E. Seavoy, *Famine in East Africa: Food Production and Food Policies*, esp. pp. 217, 220 and 225.
30. Mgera Primary School Journal, entry of January 28, 1935.
31. Quotes from Pangani District, Annual Report (1923) and Handeni District, Annual Reports (1950–1951), TNA. Also, Handeni Sub-District, Annual Report (1925), TNA.

Handeni as a Case Study in Famine and Environmental Crisis

Unlike the administrators who assume that Handeni is ensnared in a timeless struggle with environmental adversity, many peasants believe that environmental conditions became worse from the mid-1890s through the 1930s. This book reflects their view by arguing that the period between 1894 and 1940 is a distinct era, one dominated by a prolonged sequence of famines, epizootics, and waves of depopulation for which there is no evidence of any precedent. Indeed, precolonial evidence suggests that Handeni was not "frontier territory," as John Iliffe characterized early-nineteenth-century Tanzania.[32] Rather it was a region where farmers painstakingly developed a mode of agriculture that took advantage of its natural endowments, gradually transformed its vegetation communities into easily cleared parks, controlled trypanosomiasis and theileriosis (East Coast fever) with more success than would their colonial and post-colonial descendants, and, most importantly, created political institutions that responded to environmental and health conditions. Chief among these institutions was patronage, which governed relations between precolonial clients—who performed labor service, paid tribute, and pledged loyalty—and patrons, who provided various resources, including food reserves, arable land, seed and livestock.[33]

Colonial rule broke the power of patrons, however, and, between about 1890 and 1930, allowed patronage to be replaced by short-term labor relations, which unlike precolonial patronage did not provide workers with long-term access to food reserves. In periods of colonial scarcity, therefore, destitute farmers were left with no alternative but migration, a resort that disrupted agriculture, interrupted control of the vegetation that

---

32. John Iliffe, *A Modern History of Tanganyika*, p. 8; also, Richard Waller, "Ecology, Migration, and Expansion in East Africa." Critical of this view are Koponen, *People and Production*, and Carol Jane Sissons, "Economic Prosperity in Ugogo, East Africa, 1860–1890." Probably the most prominent challenge to this interpretation, nevertheless, remains Kjekshus, *Ecology Control and Economic Development*. Cautioning against the tendency to overstate precolonial security from famine, however, and to assume that complementary exchanges of food develop "spontaneously," is Johan P. Pottier, "The Politics of Famine Prevention: Ecology, Regional Production and Food Complementarity in Western Rwanda."

33. This usage assumes that patronage does not necessarily redistribute wealth obtained from the state or external markets. For a similar position, see S. N. Eisenstadt and L. Roniger, *Patrons, Clients and Friends: Interpersonal Relations and the Structure of Trust in Society*, esp. pp. 48–50. The distinction between the "patron" who "controls the resources he distributes directly" and the "middleman who controls them indirectly," is discussed in Sandra T. Barnes, *Patrons and Power: Creating a Political Community in Metropolitan Lagos*, p. 8.

harbored disease-bearing insects, and led ultimately to outbreaks of cattle disease. Thus, in contrast with late-precolonial farmers, by the 1930s many cultivators kept virtually no livestock and left the region, at least temporarily, with the onset of severe subsistence shortages.

Although change in political authority, patronage, and labor relationships played a critical role in the emergence of chronic scarcity during the colonial period, the possibility that an adverse shift in climate may have contributed to this development cannot be ruled out. The study of East African climate change suggests, in fact, that an abrupt decline in precipitation between about 1895/1900 and 1920 followed a period of unusually wet conditions.[34] Yet because the period of anomalously low rainfall covers only the first half of the 1890s–1940s era of crisis in Handeni, this chronology indicates that at the least, non-meteorological factors probably perpetuated subsistence insecurity in Handeni. A more important reason for hesitancy in applying this chronology to northeastern Tanzania, however, is that it is derived chiefly from fluctuations in the levels of Lakes Nyasa, Tanganyika, Victoria, and Turkana, which are all located many hundreds of miles from Handeni. Although it is true that, given the scarcity of data for most of the region, interregional extrapolation of this kind is unavoidable in the construction of East African climatic chronology, it remains an imprecise method, as comparisons of drought and famine across much shorter distances reveal. Between Handeni and nearby portions of eastern Tanzania and southeastern Kenya, for example, there are significant discrepancies in the record of drought and famine.[35]

While the debate about climatic and historical explanations of African famine continues,[36] the evidence from Handeni points, as it does in other

34. Sharon Elaine Nicholson, "A Climatic Chronology for Africa: Synthesis of Geological, Historical and Meteorological Information and Data," pp. 119–120, 156–157, 227–228.

35. See Thomas J. Herlehy, "Historical Dimensions of the Food Crisis in Africa: Surviving Famines Along the Kenya Coast, 1880–1980" and Gregory H. Maddox, "Leave, Wagogo, You Have No Food: Famine and Survival in Ugogo, Tanzania, 1916–1961."

36. Among studies which attribute famines to drought and climatic adversity are Jill R. Dias, "Famine and Disease in the History of Angola ca. 1830–1930" and Alexander de Waal, *Famine That Kills: Darfur, Sudan, 1984–1985*, for example, p. 68. Southern Africa has produced a debate about climatic and social causes of famine. In "Drought, Famine and Disease in Nineteenth-Century Lesotho," p. 85, Elizabeth A. Eldredge argues that the "impact of drought in nineteenth century southern Africa was determined by prevailing sociopolitical and economic circumstances," while Diana Wylie, in "The Changing Face of Hunger in Southern African History, 1880–1980," places considerable weight, as the present study does, on changes in patronage and dependence. Studies that emphasize climatic change are Charles Ballard, "Drought and Economic Distress: South Africa in the 1800s" and M. D. D. Newitt, "Drought in Mozambique, 1823–1831."

instances, toward political, economic and social conditions as the principal causes of scarcity.[37] It testifies, moreover, to a dynamic relationship between famine and environmental change, because while famine caused decline in control over cattle infections, the resulting loss of livestock increased the likelihood of famine.[38] If, therefore, famines are both the results of political changes associated with the decline of patronage, and at the same time contributing causes of long term ecological deterioration, then subsistence crises in Handeni reveal links between political history and environmental adversity.

* * *

This study is divided into four parts. Part One (Chapters One and Two) discusses precolonial agriculture, trade, methods of controlling cattle diseases, and the role of livestock in precolonial society. It argues that, because frequent drought prevented precolonial villages and residential groups from achieving self-sufficiency, farmers depended on trade and the production of exchangeable wealth, particularly livestock.

Part Two (Chapters Three, Four, and Five) treats the late precolonial era from approximately 1840, when the expansion of Zanzibari merchant activity in northeastern Tanzania led to the emergence of a new political regime, until the German colonial conquest in 1889. Chapter Three examines the commercially-oriented chieftains who ruled between 1840 and 1890, and concentrates on the role they played in the Zanzibar-dominated system of trade. Chapter Four uses records of Catholic missions, a source that requires some discussion of missionary activities and outlook, to analyze relations of production under the late-precolonial leaders. The primary means of accumulation and redistribution, this chapter argues, were

37. See Watts, *Silent Violence*; Megan Vaughan, *The Story of an African Famine: Gender and Famine in Twentieth-Century Malawi*; James McCann, *From Poverty to Famine in Northeast Ethiopia: A Rural History, 1900–1935*; Mesfin Wolde Mariam, *Rural Vulnerability to Famine in Ethiopia, 1958–1977*; and Wayne K. Durrill, "Atrocious Misery: The African Origins of Famine in Northern Somalia, 1839–1884," pp. 287–306. The basis of much of this work is the "loss of entitlement" theory of Amartya Sen, presented in *Poverty and Famines*, which has been criticized, nevertheless, by David Arnold in *Famine: Social Crisis and Historical Change* for begging "questions as to why certain sections of society were placed in such dependent and precarious relationships."

38. The works already cited do not assess the long-term ecological consequences of famine. A study that does this, however, is Mortimore's *Adapting to Drought*. The relationship between famine and disease is discussed by Marc Harry Dawson, "Socio-Economic and Epidemiological Change in Kenya, 1880–1925."

extra-household labor relations under patrons.[39] Hence labor outside the household, which has great importance in the modern peasant communities of northeastern Tanzania,[40] is shown to have also been a vital aspect of the late precolonial economy. Chapter Five examines stories of the past from Handeni that reveal precolonial tensions between individual ambition and mutual responsibility, and suggests that these tensions shaped the politics of patronage and environmental control under the chieftains.

Part Three (Chapters Six, Seven, and Eight) covers the period of German colonial rule in Uzigua, 1889–1916. Chapter Six surveys the economic changes of the early colonial period, including reorientation of trade, the imposition of colonial taxation and labor demands, and the transformation of relations between patrons and dependents following the abolition of slavery. Chapter Seven shows why peasant accounts from Handeni link the decline of precolonial leaders and the disappearance of patronage with infanticide, and why peasants believe that these developments are related to modern scarcity. Chapter Eight compares the last precolonial famine of 1884–1886 with crises of the German period and concludes that, unlike their predecessors, colonial famines led to depopulation, the spread of disease-bearing insects, and epizootics.

Part Four (Chapters Nine and Ten) concerns the pre-Second World War period of British rule. Chapter Nine focuses on change in local political authority under the administrative system of Indirect Rule, which was instituted, this chapter suggests, partly to end shortages of plantation labor.[41] The emphasis in this chapter, however, is on the "untraditional" nature of appointed chiefs, who derived power and legitimacy not from precolonial sources of political authority but rather from their ability to act as intermediaries within the political structure of Indirect Rule.[42] This chapter also describes the concern with "tribal" self-sufficiency that led the British to restrict trade and rural accumulation. Chapter Ten, continuing

39. For similar emphasis on extra-household economic relations, see McCann, *From Poverty to Famine*, p. 69, Vaughan, *The Story of an African Famine*, p. 60, Mackintosh, *Gender, Class, and Rural Transition*, pp. 28–30, and Charles H. Ambler, *Kenyan Communities in the Age of Imperialism: The Central Region in the Late Nineteenth Century*.

40. Sender and Smith, *Poverty, Class and Gender*, p. 126.

41. Hence the Handeni evidence does not support the argument that Indirect Rule reflected "anti-settler paternalism" (Austen, "The Official Mind of Indirect Rule," p. 579).

42. A considerably different concept of Indirect Rule, which emphasizes the "traditional" roots of authority held by appointed chiefs, is presented by Karen E. Fields, *Revival and Rebellion in Colonial Central Africa*, and by Terence Ranger, who comments that "colonial rule in Northern Rhodesia" relied partly on "traditional religious beliefs which gave authority to chiefs within systems of Indirect Rule" ("Religious Movements and Politics in Sub-Saharan Africa," p. 19).

the analysis of ecological deterioration begun in Chapter Eight, discusses research performed during the 1930s that confirmed the causal connection between famine and epizootic in Handeni.

At the beginning of the Second World War, an abrupt shift in colonial policies modified conditions in Handeni. After 1940, scarcity would be associated with population growth, monetization, increased reliance on wage labor, heavy sales of staple food crops, and dependence on purchases of food imports. Nevertheless, the roots of many post-1940 problems, including unresponsive political structures, mistaken administrative policies, vulnerability to subsistence scarcity and an adverse disease environment, lie in the preceding era. Furthermore, because Ujamaa villagization reintroduced policies and conditions that in some respects were quite similar to those of the interwar years, the pre-1940 period retains particular immediacy in Handeni District. The concluding chapter attempts to place peasant interpretations of the 1890s–1940 era in the context of the 1980s, the period when they were collected, by showing that they reflect the painful experiences of Handeni farmers during and after Ujamaa villagization.

Part I

Environment and Economy in
Late-Precolonial Uzigua

1. Agronomy and Trade

The Regional and Environmental Context

Handeni District lies within Uzigua, the area bounded by the Indian Ocean, the Pangani River to the north, the Wami River to the south and the Maasai steppe to the west. Today Handeni's 13,209 square-mile confines contain the bulk of Uzigua, while Pangani, Bagamoyo and Morogoro districts incorporate the remainder. Before colonial and post-colonial states created administrative divisions, however, nothing distinguished Handeni from the rest of Uzigua. Likewise, there was relatively little difference between Uzigua and the rest of the larger region that extends southward from the Usambara Mountains and Bondei, through Uzigua, and as far as the Zaramo hinterland of Dar es Salaam and the Kaguru and Luguru Mountains. Although the scale of political organization was much larger in the Kilindi Kingdom of Usambara than in the decentralized areas further south, most of nineteenth-century northeastern Tanzania shared a common culture and economy. Throughout this area, kinship, marriage, friendship, mutual confidence in healers and diviners, shared myths and names of putative descent groups, political alliances, patronage, reciprocal exchanges, and trade tied together farming and pastoral communities.[1]

Appreciation of the region's precolonial cultural and economic unity is hindered, however, by twentieth-century ethnic and linguistic classification. Although there are few differences between the speakers of the Zigua language who live in Handeni and, for example, either the Zaramo-speakers near Dar es Salaam or residents of the Kaguru Mountains, Europeans began trying to distinguish various "tribes" and "tribal" characteristics

1. For names of putative descent groups found widely throughout the region, see Godfrey Dale, "An Account of the Principal Customs and Habits of the Natives Inhabiting the Bondei Country"; Thomas O. Beidelman, "Kaguru Descent Groups (East-Central Tanzania)"; "Historia ya Wazigua" (anon., n.d.) in Handeni District Book, vol. 1, TNA; and Martin Mnyendo (Gombero, September 22, 1983). Similar forms of local identity and regional spheres of activity in central Kenya are discussed by Charles Ambler, *Kenyan Communities in the Age of Imperialism*.

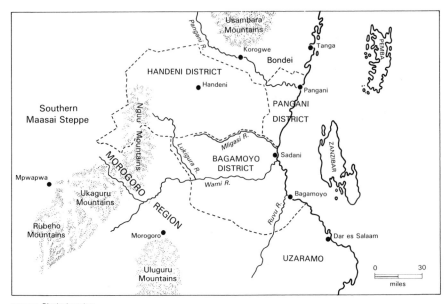

Map 1. Uzigua and the surrounding territories of northeastern Tanzania.

- - - - - District boundary

in the region even before the institution of colonial rule in Tanzania (see Chapter Seven). Linguistic classification is in some respects as misleading as ethnic categorization. Conventional classification includes two highly similar, mutually comprehensible language varieties "Zigua" and "Nguu," rather than the single language that comprises them, among the Northeast Coast Bantu languages.[2] Yet the speech of most farmers in Handeni varies only very slightly on minor points of vocabulary and pronunciation. The insignificance of the distinction is reflected in the practice of "Nguu"-speakers who, when traveling to Dar es Salaam or other areas of Tanzania where the "Nguu" are less well known than the more numerous speakers of "Zigua," simply refer to themselves by the term "Zigua."

The paradox of language and ethnic classification in northeastern Tanzania is that, besides obscuring similarities, it has also concealed diversity, by implying that the area is divided into linguistically and culturally homogeneous zones. Indeed, the concept of ethnically "pure" homelands led colonial officials of the 1920s, who believed that Maasai pastoralists should not live among a majority of Bantu-speaking farmers, to expel the

2. Derek Nurse and Thomas Spear, *The Swahili*, p. 41.

Maa-speakers from Handeni District (see Chapter Nine).[3] Yet nineteenth-century Uzigua was home to several linguistic and occupational groups, just as it is today. Then as now, Maasai pastoralists, who in 1975 constituted about 3 percent of Handeni District's population of 130,000,[4] were Uzigua's largest linguistic minority. Handeni's Maasai share traditions of common origins, but they are divided into two groups, the Kisongo and Parakuyu, who practice somewhat different forms of pastoralism.[5] Whereas the Kisongo enter Uzigua seasonally from the steppeland west of Handeni in search of dry-season grazing, the Parakuyu live throughout the year in proximity to farmers, sharing water sources, grazing their cattle in cultivated fields after harvests, and purchasing grain, medicines, and beer from cultivators, whom they sometimes employ as wage laborers. Unlike the transhumant Kisongo, moreover, Parakuyu communities practice some cultivation in addition to keeping cattle. Besides the pastoralists, an additional group of Maa-speakers in Handeni are the small number of hunter-gatherers usually called the Ndorobo.

Just as Maasai identities are shaped by the ways in which pastoralists utilize slightly different environments, distinctions among nineteenth-century farmers also derived in part from microenvironmental differences, particularly those between the lowlands of eastern Uzigua and the Nguu Mountains. The terms "Nguu" and "Zigua" were erroneously converted in colonial usage into "tribal" and language names; in precolonial society they denoted highland and lowland environments and identified communities distinguished not by language and culture but by residence in different environmental niches.[6] (Community identities stemmed primarily from political relationships rather than environmental differences—see Chapter Five.) Other terms indicating residence in particular environments, such

3. The tendency to think of culturally homogeneous regions has also led researchers to assume that Maasai pastoralists arrived in the region only recently. This assumption is discussed and rejected in Peter Rigby, *Persistent Pastoralists: Nomadic Societies in Transition*, pp. 53–55.

4. *Tanga Water Master Plan*, vol. 5, *Socio-Economics*, p. 19; L. Vejmola and N. Ngobei, "Water Supply and Range Management Improvements for the Nomadic Population and Livestock in the West Handeni Area," pp. 1–3.

5. "It is the dependence upon some vegetable foods which distinguishes Baraguyu from Masai" (Beidelman, "The Baraguyu," p. 256). Beidelman demonstrates that cultural distinctions between Parakuyu and Maasai develop from different systems of production in his "A Note on Baraguyu House-Types and Baraguyu Economy." This view is disputed, however, in Daniel Kyaruzi Ndagala, "Pastoral Livestock-Keeping and Rural Development in Tanzania: the Case of the Wakwavi," p. 21.

6. Steven Feierman, in *The Shambaa Kingdom: A History*, Chapter 1, shows that these identities derive from "indigenous categor[ies] for understanding the natural environment" (p. 17).

as "Ruvu" for villagers in the Pangani River Valley and "Sambaa" for inhabitants of Nguu mountain tops, were also current in precolonial Uzigua.[7] Because colonial officials did not recognize these groups as separate "tribes," however, the terms fell into disuse during the British period when the government reorganized local administration along "tribal" lines. Realizing that very small "tribal" units would cause administrative inconvenience, British officials effaced subtle distinctions by amalgamating various areas into the "Zigua" and "Nguu" "tribes" (see Chapter Nine).

Although precolonial cultivators recognized a number of microenvironments, the most pronounced differences are those between the eastern lowlands and the Nguu highlands. Most of eastern Uzigua is a plain which rises gradually from sea-level near the coast to about 1000 meters at the foot of the Nguu Mountains. The isolated hills, or "inselbergs," that rise dramatically from the plain are its most noticeable feature. The wooded eastern lowlands are separated from the Maasai steppe to the west by the low barrier of the Nguu Mountains, which stretch along a roughly north-south axis. Although elevations throughout most of the range do not exceed 1500 meters, slightly greater precipitation in the highlands, where mean annual rainfall is 800 to 1200mm, less risk of drought, and lower nighttime temperatures favor a wider range of crops, including rice, tobacco, coffee and fruits, than are grown in the eastern lowlands, where mean annual precipitation is 700 to 1000mm. In the highlands, moreover, abundant water permits irrigation in small valleys that are startlingly luxuriant by comparison with the nearby lowlands. In the eastern lowlands, on the other hand, the salinity of much groundwater and absence of permanent surface sources force women to carry water as much as five miles during dry seasons and purchase water brought even longer distances. (An additional difference between lowlands and highlands is that the malaria-bearing mosquitoes found in the hotter eastern woodlands do not infest the Nguu Mountains.)

Both highlanders and lowlanders must cope with the region's primary form of environmental adversity, the unreliability of rainfall. Uzigua has a bimodal regime of heavier "long" rains from February or March through April or May and lighter "short" rains in November and December. Farmers cannot rely on the short rains, as precipitation records over a thirty-seven year period confirm in showing that monthly rainfall (there are no records of daily rainfall over extended periods) failed to reach 100mm in

7. Maingwa W. J. Kallabaka, "The March Towards Ujamaa: Ten Years After," p. 22.

both November and December twenty-one times. The same data also reveal that droughts occur frequently in long rains seasons, for in that thirty-seven-year period precipitation failed to reach 100mm eleven times in at least two of the three crucial long rains months (March, April, and May). Indeed, a study of forty-seven years of precipitation concludes that Handeni's susceptibility to drought is "moderate to high," because the probability that rainfall will exceed 1000mm in any year is only 25 percent and the probability that it will exceed 700mm is only 68 percent.[8] The erratic timing of rainfall is another problem, particularly for farmers who depend on maize, for while heavy early rains may ruin maize plantings and force growers to sow again, a more frequent cause of reduced maize yields is belated rains, which delay planting and push the stages of silking and pollination that require moisture well into the dry season.[9]

Patterns of Settlement and Cultivation

Precolonial farmers settled in the relatively few areas where they found adequate water and soil moisture, leaving drier areas uninhabited. Throughout Uzigua, they worked a combination of gardens along watercourses that could be farmed for many years in succession, and larger upland plots which they left fallow after growing sorghum, maize, and beans for three or four years. In this and other ways, their agronomic system was governed by the need to use all available moisture and guard against drought-induced crop failure. The drawback to the concentration of farming communities in relatively well-watered but scattered locations, however, was that it allowed insect-borne cattle infections to remain prevalent. Because wide stretches of woods, thicket, and grassland could not be settled permanently for lack of water, they were occupied by disease-bearing insects and wildlife.

In the lowlands, farming settlements clustered in the areas endowed

8. *Tanga Water Master Plan*, vol. 2, *Geography, Climate, Hydrology*, p. 27, vol. 6, *Agriculture*, pp. 52–54, and Technical Report no. 18, "Daily Rainfall Figures from Selected Stations in Tanga Region," vol. 2 (July 1976); Tanga Integrated Rural Development Project (TIRDEP), "Meteorological and Hydrological Data for the Tanga Region"; monthly rainfall records from Handeni between 1923 and 1963 are in Handeni District Book, vol. 4, TNA. Precipitation records from Handeni do not note the number of days in which rain fell. Monthly rainfall of 100mm is taken as the rough minimum for cultivation, following the rule that rainfall during a growing season must exceed half of potential evaporation: M. J. T. Norman, C. J. Pearson and P. G. E. Searle, *The Ecology of Tropical Food Crops*, pp. 21–32.

9. J. D. Acland, *East African Crops*, pp. 125–126.

with comparatively moist soils, particularly the slopes and depressions surrounding the "inselbergs," where cultivated fields, often winding ribbon-like along ephemeral watercourses, yielded plentiful crops in years of sufficient rains.[10] Farmers worked gardens and large sorghum and maize fields, for example, near the seasonally flowing Msangazi River.[11] Cultivation on alluvial soils was also common south of the Wami River, where "streams were tolerably frequent, the water being sometimes brackish, and on their banks Indian corn [sorghum], tobacco, groundnuts, sweet potatoes and a few bananas were grown."[12] Stretches of both the Pangani and Wami river valleys, moreover, were densely populated. Villagers who lived on small islands in the Pangani River planted slopes overlooking the river in sorghum, while farmers of the Wami Valley worked moist soils that they rarely had to leave fallow.[13]

Highlanders also made intensive use of valley bottoms and soils along watercourses. In the small but well-watered valleys of Nguu, farmers tended sugar cane, plantains, tobacco, and orange trees on low ground, and planted hillsides in sorghum, maize, and beans,[14] a pattern that the missionary James Last noted while visiting Northern Nguu in 1881–1882. "Both sides of the Luiji Valley," wrote Last, "were thickly populated, there is, in fact, one long string of villages from Sagassa to Mgera [about thirty miles] in the north of Nguu. There is a fair amount of land cultivated, chiefly Indian corn [sorghum]; but sugar cane and bananas also abound."[15]

In addition to maize, sorghum in several varieties was the staple in

10. RKA 215/22–24; TNA G8/773.

11. Ernst Marno, "Bericht über eine Excursion von Zanzibar (Saadani) nach Koa-Kiora," pp. 357, 362–364, 366, 371, 376–378, 385–386, 391; Étienne Baur, "Dans l'Oudoé et l'Ouzigoua," p. 57; Rochus Schmidt, *Geschichte des Araberaufstandes in Ost-Afrika*, p. 176; RKA 215/22–24; J. P. Farler, "Native Routes in East Africa from Pangani to the Masai Country and the Victoria Nyanza," p. 740; Franz Stuhlmann, "Bericht über eine Reise durch Usegua und Unguu," p. 169; Oscar Baumann, *Usambara und seine Nachbargebiete*, p. 273; "Station Petershöhe in Useguha," p. 298.

12. Charles T. Wilson and R. W. Felkin, *Uganda and the Egyptian Soudan* 1, pp. 32–33; Anton Horner, "Voyage dans L'Oukami," p. 415, and "L'Oukami (Afrique Orientale) IV," p. 623.

13. Stuhlmann, "Bericht," p. 172; G. A. Fischer, *Das Masai-Land*, p. 6; Cado Picarda, "Autour de Mandera," p. 185.

14. Nyangasi Mohamedi Munga (Kilwa, September 12, 1983). Also, Pogwa Rashidi (Handeni, August 14, 1982); Elders of Magamba (Magamba, September 30, 1983); Ernest Mkomwa (Kwa Masaka, September 29, 1983); Yusufu Kaberwa (Mswaki, May 28–29, 1983) and Omali Gumbo (Kwinji, May 5, 1983); also, Marno, "Bericht."

15. Quote from J. T. Last, "A Journey into the Nguru Country from Mamboia, East Central Africa," p. 151; also, Last, "A Visit to the Masai People Living Beyond the Borders of the Nguru Country," pp. 520ff; Stuhlmann, "Bericht," p. 161; RKA 215/22–24; François Coulbois, "Seconde tournée dans le vicariat apostolique du Zanguebar," p. 595.

the 1880s. Planted in January, February, and March and harvested in late July and August, sorghum was the principal long rains crop. Although farmers preferred the taste of sweet white sorghum, they also valued bitter red sorghum for its greater invulnerability to birds, and in addition planted other varieties that would bear grain for several years. They intercropped maize with sorghum to obtain a preliminary grain supply before the harvest of the slower maturing but more drought-resistant sorghums. Men and women worked together to dig rows of holes and fill them alternately with a combination of sorghum and maize seeds and with maize seeds alone. During both short and long rains seasons they made successive plantings of maize, but waited for the flowering of the euphorbia called *Mwata* or *Mwasa* before sowing their short rains crop. Farmers of southern Nguu, who relied more heavily on maize than did villagers in the drier lowlands, planted maize continuously from November through June to produce a succession of early yields in advance of the main August sorghum harvest.[16]

By intercropping, making repeated plantings, and supplementing sorghum and maize with a variety of cultigens, farmers tried to minimize the risk of crop failure. One European who was impressed in the 1870s by their skills exclaimed, "I am more than ever struck with the population of this [Wami Valley] route, and the abundance of everything in the shape of food," while his companion described the highlands as a "country [that] possesses abundance. The corn grows to a height of sixteen feet, and sugarcane runs wild."[17] Rice was the supplementary crop favored in particularly well-watered highlands and riverine neighborhoods, but everywhere farmers grew a variety of legumes, of which the most common was the velvet bean (*Mucuna utilis*; Zigua *ngwala*) that after being planted with sorghum and maize would produce beans for two years.[18] Farmers also interplanted pumpkins (*Cucurbita spp.*), whose seeds they dried and stored as a reserve food, with grains,[19] and in addition grew a variety of tubers— cassava, yams, arrowroot, sweet potatoes, and taro—though not always in great quantity. Among other cultivated foods were cucumbers, sugar cane, spinach, tomatoes, onions, okra, and bullrush millet. For sale, farmers

16. Msulwa Mbega (Gombero, September 21, 1983); Mzee Samzimba (Kwediboma, September 1, 1982); Baumann, *Usambara*, p. 273; Mhonda Mission Journal, 1879–1888.
17. Roger Price, *Private Journal of the Reverend Roger Price*, pp. 58–59; Joseph Mullens, "A New Route and New Mode of Travelling into Central Africa," p. 239.
18. Other legumes included *choroko* (*Phaseolus mungo*), *kamuli*, *kunde*, lentils, lima beans, and pigeon peas.
19. Mzee Sekiteke (Kwediboma, March 8, 1983).

grew tobacco, simsim, and ginger as well as the beans of the castor-oil plant, whose extract had many uses, including softening bark cloth. With the exception of various plantains and papayas tree crops were confined primarily to the Nguu Mountains, where oranges and tangerines flourished, and to the coconut palm groves of the Pangani Valley.[20]

These risk-minimizing practices filled the calendar with tasks that included the clearing of trees and heavy bush, preparing the soil with broad, short-handled hoes, repeated plantings of grains and other crops, weeding, and harvesting. Men did most of the clearing while women gathered cut vegetation into heaps for burning; in other field work, however, both women and men participated, though women had primary responsibility for the back-breaking task of weeding. To women, moreover, fell the laborious chore of preparing dried grains and legumes for storage. During the eight-month sorghum growing season, children helped adults protect fields night and day from monkeys, birds, and wild pigs, though by clearing contiguous plots farmers deprived field pests of the bush in which they would otherwise have been able to hide near standing crops.[21] Even though the pace of work was more relaxed for a month or two after the August sorghum harvest, farmers nevertheless enjoyed no season of inactivity because during that time they conducted extensive burning of bush, thicket, and grasses around settlements to prevent the encroachment of wildlife and disease-bearing insects.

Precolonial Trade

Trade linked every community with neighboring and distant settlements, various microenvironments within Uzigua, specialists throughout northeastern Tanzania, pastoralists of the Maasai steppe and, via the ports of the Swahili coast and the international entrepôt of Zanzibar, Europe, India and the Persian Gulf. Uzigua's trade was first described in writing by the British mariners Smee and Hardy, who in 1811 reported that Uzigua

20. Msulwa Mbega, Gombero; Mzee Sekiteke, Kwediboma; Stuhlmann, "Bericht," pp. 153, 156–157; Stuhlmann, *Mit Emin Pascha ins Herz von Afrika*, p. 25; J. T. Last, "The Tribes on the Road to Mpwapwa," p. 662.; Last, "A Journey," p. 151; Last, "A Visit to the Masai," pp. 520–521; Picarda, "Autour de Mandera," pp. 186 and 236; Fischer, *Das Masai-Land*, p. 5; Farler, "Native Routes in East Africa," p. 739; Baumann, *Usambara*, p. 273; Mhonda Mission Journal, 1881–1883; Mandera Mission Journal, 1881–1883; Marno, "Bericht," passim; RKA 215/22–24 and 6475/130; Charles Sacleux, *Dictionnaire Français-Swahili*, appendix; Walter H. Kisbey, *Zigula-English Dictionary*.

21. Mzee Samgome (Kwediboma, February 25, 1983) and Msulwa Mbega, Gombero.

supplied livestock, ivory, and slaves to the Swahili ports of Pangani, Kipumbwe, and Sadani in return for cloth, beads, copper wire, and iron goods.[22] Indeed, trade was so conspicuous in Uzigua, where, as in Usambara, "social solidarity [was] created through exchange,"[23] that the Europeans who developed notions of Tanganyikan "tribes" and "tribal" proclivities would speak of an inherent Zigua propensity for commerce.[24]

Exchange need not have been regarded as a "tribal" inclination, however, to be appreciated as a vital source of security in drought-prone Uzigua. Farmers not only obtained staple foods and other goods, such as cloth, iron tools, salt, and meat, through trade, but also devoted substantial effort to the production and gathering of tobacco, ghee, simsim, honey, livestock, medicines, and other salable goods.

Situated between the Indian Ocean and the Maasai steppe, Uzigua's residents were well placed to exchange the complementary products of different environments. Along the western steppe-woodland frontier, cultivators constantly engaged in transactions with Maasai cattle-keepers. The ports of the *Mrima*, as the stretch of Swahili coast adjacent to Uzigua was known, attracted traders from all parts of the region. Zigua-speaking communities also participated in the segmentary trade networks that connected *Mrima* towns with the distant Tanganyikan interior, and provisioned traders who passed between *Mrima* ports and western interior regions. By the early nineteenth century, as Smee and Hardy learned, Uzigua's trade connections with Zanzibar and the *Mrima* seaports immediately opposite the island had become well established through the export of slaves, grains, and ivory. Indeed, Pangani and the other ports that transshipped the products of the Uzigua hinterland furnished "the most beautiful ivory and the best grain, resins, wax, simsim and millet" in the Swahili world.[25]

Much of Uzigua's export trade was conducted by small groups that came to the coast from as far away as the Nguu Mountains. "When there is little or no work to be done in the gardens," observed the missionary

22. "Report of Thomas Smee" (September 25, 1811) and "Report of Lt. Hardy with Accompaniements," India Office Marine Records, Misc. v. 586 (a microfilmed copy was generously made available to me by Professor A. M. H. Sheriff); Smee, Hardy, and Wingham, "Observations During a Voyage of Research," pp. 23–61.

23. Feierman, *The Shambaa Kingdom*, p. 50.

24. For example, Stuhlmann, *Mit Emin Pascha*, p. 25.

25. Quote from Charles Guillain, "Côte de Zanguebar et Mascate, 1841," p. 520. Also, Guillain, *Documents sur l'histoire, la géographie et le commerce de la Côte orientale d'Afrique* 3: 305, 312–314, 331; Captain Thomas Boteler, *Narrative of a Voyage of Discovery to Africa and Arabia* 2: 176–184; Johann Ludwig Krapf, *Reisen in Ostafrika* 2: 280.

James Last in 1879, "they go down to the coast in parties of twelve to twenty men, carrying their corn to sell. By this means they get cloth and a variety of things such as they need at home. . . . These Wanguru are continually going to and fro between here and the coast." Everyone in northern Nguu, it seemed to Graf Joachim von Pfeil in 1888, had done some trading at Pangani, for constant contact with the *Mrima* had spread coastal styles of dress and knowledge of Swahili.[26]

The trading parties sold a great variety of goods at the coast, including sorghum and maize from eastern Uzigua, livestock, grain, tobacco, and ghee from the Pangani Valley, and rice and tobacco from the Nguu highlands. Farmers from the lower Wami Valley, for example, took rice, sorghum, maize, honey, ghee, rubber, antelope horns and skins, simsim, tobacco, chickens, and cattle to the *Mrima*, where they purchased cotton cloth, brass wire, beads, knives, soap, firearms, and gunpowder. Another item acquired at the coast was salt, even though alternative sources were available at salt beds in the Pangani Valley and northwestern Nguu.[27] The trading parties of Uzigua also sold captives, including enslaved natives of Uzigua as well as chattels brought to the region from Ukimbu, Singida, Tabora, Maasailand, and other areas of western Tanganyika, and thereby helped Uzigua gain a reputation as a major supplier of Zanzibar's slave market.[28] Several periodic markets in or near the coastal towns absorbed the produce of the Uzigua hinterland. One market held every nine days just inland from the town of Pangani attracted 2000 to 3000 buyers and sellers of rice, maize, sorghum, cassava, bananas, tobacco, simsim, honey, and livestock.[29]

After 1840, however, the small-scale traders encountered formidable competition from Zanzibari merchants, whose large caravan ventures

26. Last, "The Tribes," pp. 660 and 662. Also, Stuhlmann, "Bericht," p. 168; Richard F. Burton and J. H. Speke, "A Coasting Voyage from Mombasa to the Pangani River," p. 207; Graf Joachim von Pfeil, "Beobachtungen Während Meiner Letzten Reise in Ostafrika," p. 7.
27. "Salt Production Among the Wasambaa," pp. 102–103; Étienne Baur, "Lettre," p. 356.
28. Baumann, *Usambara*, p. 274; Last, "A Journey," p. 153; Picarda, "Autour de Mandera," pp. 186, 227, 248–249; Charles New, "Journey from the Pangani, via Wadigo, to Mombasa," p. 318; Richard F. Burton, *Zanzibar: City, Island and Coast* 2: 145; Fischer, *Das Masai-Land*, p. 5; Stuhlmann, "Bericht, pp. 157 and 172; Alexander Keith Johnston, "Notes of a Trip from Zanzibar to Usambara in February and March 1879," p. 546; "Station Petershöhe," p. 299; Stuhlmann, *Mit Emin Pascha*, p. 25; Smee and Hardy, India Office Records; A. Germain, "Note sur Zanzibar et la Côte orientale d'Afrique," p. 545.
29. Farler, "Native Routes," p. 731; Johnston, "Notes of a Trip," p. 557; Boteler, *Narrative* 2: 205; Burton and Speke, "A Coasting Voyage," p. 199; Baumann, "Der Unterlauf des Pangani-Flusses," pp. 60–61.

wrested away much of the traffic in the most highly valued goods, ivory, and slaves. The transfer of ivory and slaves into the sphere of the large caravans was assisted by the chieftains who emerged in Uzigua at this time (see Chapter Three). Consequently, after 1840 the small traders concentrated on shipments of bulky foodstuffs, a trend encouraged by Zanzibar's increasing demand for grain, for although Zanzibar had been self-sufficient in foodstuffs before the clove era, after the conversion of much arable land to clove production during the 1830s and 1840s, grain became its primary import.[30] Thus by exporting maize, sorghum and rice in years of abundance, and by importing foodstuffs from *Mrima* towns in years of scarcity, the small trading parties incorporated Uzigua into a vast Zanzibar-centered system of food production and supply.[31]

The factor that limited grain exports, of course, was lack of transportation. Because men head-loaded maize and sorghum in quantities of not much more than thirty kilos, a single trip to a coastal entrepôt earned only relatively small amounts of cloth and other goods. Hence the Uzigua residents who stood the best chance of profiting from coastal grain sales were those who, because they lived within about fifty miles of the coast, could take sorghum and maize to *Mrima* ports often. The extent of grain shipments to the *Mrima* from villages further inland is uncertain, although farmers in the valleys of northern Nguu indeed grew high-priced rice expressly for export.[32] Short-distance movements of foodstuffs between different ecological niches, however, particularly those between the highlands of Nguu and Bondei and the eastern lowlands, were commonplace throughout the region.[33]

Indeed, most of the grain trade probably consisted of exchanges by

30. F. Albrand, "Extrait d'un mémoire sur Zanzibar et sur Quiloa," p. 69; Guillain, "Côte," pp. 537, 541–542; Guillain, *Documents* 3: 313; Richard F. Burton, "The Lakes Regions of Central Equatorial Africa," p. 446; Great Britain, Foreign Office, *Commercial Reports Received at the Foreign Office from Her Majesty's Consuls* (1882); François Coulbois, "Le Sultanat du Zanguebar," p. 384.

31. Guillain, *Documents* 3: 312–313; Burton, "Lakes Regions," pp. 398 and 446; *Commercial Reports Received at the Foreign Office* (1865), pp. 175–176; Admiralty Office Records, o.1 5/23, no. 3 (Loarer), 1849 (made available to me by Professor A. M. H. Sheriff); Johnston, "Notes of a Trip," p. 546. On grain trade in the Mombasan hinterland, see Thomas T. Spear, *The Kaya Complex: A History of the Mijikenda Peoples of the Kenya Coast to 1900*, pp. 92 and 95. The integration of southern Somalia into the Zanzibari-dominated economy as a grain-exporting region is described in Lee Cassanelli, *The Shaping of Somali Society*.

32. Picarda, "Autour de Mandera," pp. 236 and 248; Fischer, "Native Routes," p. 6; Last, "The Tribes," p. 662; Baumann, *Usambara*, p. 273; Nyangasi Mohamedi Munga, Kilwa.

33. Letter of J. P. Farler (Magila, Low Sunday, 1877), USPG, Central Africa Mission, *Occasional Papers* (1877); Mhonda Mission Journal, February 7 and March 20, 1884; Mohamedi Lusingo (Mafisa, July 1, 1983).

villagers who travelled only short distances to local periodic markets, where women found their primary trading opportunities. Richard Burton saw women and men from the Uzigua lowlands and Usambara Mountains converging on one such weekly market in 1857 to sell cassava, sorghum, maize, pumpkins, plantains, poultry, sugar cane, and pottery. At another market in the Pangani Valley, cultivators, pastoralists, and hunter-gatherers exchanged grains, meat, and other goods.[34] Although trading activities were divided along gender lines, with women remaining in local markets while men conducted long-distance enterprises, women nevertheless succeeded in obtaining imported goods. Fashion in the 1870s and 1880s dictated, in fact, that women have imported cloth, beads, and wire and wear jewelry in quantities that fascinated Europeans. In the Nguu Mountains, related James Last,[35]

> as elsewhere, [women are] very fond of ornaments. These consist of beads of various kinds and colors worn round the loins and neck; sometimes they accumulate to a weight of 18 to 20 lbs. They are also very fond of wearing iron, brass and copper bracelets, wristlets, anklets and collars. These vary in size, according to the means of the wearer. . . .

The local periodic markets also facilitated trade between farmers and Maa-speaking pastoralists and hunter-gatherers. Cultivators sold the Maasai grains, beer, vegetables, tobacco, medicines, weapons, tools, and other craft wares in return for cattle, milk, hides, and ivory.[36] These transactions diversified sources of food reserves and increased the interdependence of cultivators, pastoralists, and hunter-gatherers who, besides relying on the same healers, performing rituals together, and sharing water sources, also cooperated in the export of cattle, ivory, and slaves.[37] Maasai pastoralists either sold the ivory they obtained from Ndorobo hunters directly to coastal traders, or provided it to Zigua-speaking partners who resold it to

34. Burton, *Zanzibar* 2: 199–200; Feierman, *The Shambaa Kingdom*, p. 130; Alexandre Le Roy, "Au Kilimandjaro," p. 164; Dale, "An Account," p. 204.
35. Last, "A Visit to the Masai," p. 518; also, Dale, "An Account," p. 204; RKA 217/7; Marno, "Bericht," p. 368; Anton Horner, "De Bagamoyo à Mhonda (Oussigoua)," p. 190 and "L'Oukami (Afrique Orientale) VI," p. 21.
36. Mohamedi Mkande, Ibrahim Kigobwa and others (Mafisa, July 1, 1983); Pogwa Rashidi, Handeni; Kombo Sabo (Kwediboma, September 26, 1982); Elders of Mgera (Mgera, August 19, 1982); Paul Reichard, *Deutsch-Ostafrika: Das Land und seine Bewohner*, p. 292; Beidelman, "The Baraguyu."
37. Mohamedi Lusingo, Mafisa; Mohamedi Semsambia (Kilwa, September 11, 1983); Rajabu Sefu Mwenkumba (Kwa Mkono, December 21, 1982); Leiluli Namania, Tangano Orleerewi, Kari Orleerewi (Gitu, June 24, 1983).

caravans and coastal merchants.[38] In the trade of captives and cattle, more-over, farmers took the same role. "The Wa-Humba [Parakuyu Maasai] find a ready market for their captives amongst the Nguru people," wrote Last in 1883, "who again dispose of their slaves to the Swahilis and coast people (Wa-Rima)."[39]

Among the most important items traded between farmers and pastor-alists were iron goods. The Maasai "are dependent on the surrounding natives," commented Last, "not only for their weapons, but also for the working up of the metal ornaments of the women." To preserve supplies of iron for the manufacture of spears and arrowheads, claimed Last, some cultivators used ebony hoes.[40] Although iron may have been relatively scarce, Uzigua nevertheless had at least two sources: the Itumba portion of the Kaguru Mountains near southern Nguu and the region of Ukimbu about 300 miles to the west, which sent traders directly to Uzigua in order to exchange iron hoes and slaves for foodstuffs, tobacco, and livestock. The knowledge of iron working, residents of modern Ukimbu believe, was first brought to them by smiths from Itumba,[41] a region of remarkably specialized communities that gave "most of their time to working iron," wrote Last, "and almost completely neglect cattle-keeping and agriculture. On this account they are very poor, for though they have to work night and day, all the produce of their labour has to go for food. . . . These men are almost exclusively engaged in working iron, that is, smelting and work-ing up the metal into hoes."[42] At these villages, trading parties from Uzigua purchased both hoes and the iron ore that smiths would fashion into weapons and jewelry for the Maasai.[43]

In addition to the Itumba iron workers, another category of special-ists with whom Uzigua residents dealt were migrant hunters, particularly

38. Reichard, *Deutsch-Ostafrika*, p. 292; Last, "A Visit to the Masai," p. 525; James Christie, *Cholera Epidemics in East Africa*, p. 209; John L. Berntsen, "Pastoralism, Raiding and Prophets: Maasailand in the Nineteenth Century," p. 265; Baumann, *Usambara*, p. 274.

39. Last, "A Visit to the Masai," p. 520; "Station Petershöhe," p. 298. A parallel seg-mentary system brought ivory from the Parakuyu Maasai in the Kenyan hinterland to Mom-basa: Guillain, *Documents* 3: 383.

40. Last, "A Visit to the Masai," pp. 521, 531; Mohamedi Lusingo, Mafisa; Leiluli Na-mania, Tangano Orleerewi, and Kari Orleerewi, Gitu.

41. Aylward Shorter, *Chiefship in Western Tanzania*, pp. 17–18. Mohamedi Lusingo, Asumani Mwanamauka and Omali Mwanamauka (Mafisa, July 1–2, 1983).

42. Last, "A Visit to the Wa-Itumba Iron-workers and the Mangaheri, near Mamboia, in East Central Africa," pp. 586–587, 590–591.

43. Mohamedi Lusingo, Mohamedi Mkande, Ibrahim Kigobwa and others, Mafisa; Juma Ali Matebe, Salimu Mkunda, Mohamedi Saidi Gota, Ramadhani Mswagala, Mwen-juma Mdachi, Omari Mohamedi Gumbo (Gitu, June 24, 1983).

Kamba men from Kenya and Makua visitors from southern Tanzania and northern Mozambique. To these professionals was left the dangerous pursuit of elephants in the last precolonial decades.[44] Itinerant hunters became more numerous in Uzigua after 1840, not only because demand for ivory was growing overseas but also because the new Zigua-speaking trading chieftains, who wished to control supplies of ivory (see Chapter Three), found that they could easily obtain ivory from the migrant hunters who depended on them for food. Besides monopolizing supplies of ivory, their second goal in restricting elephant hunting to the specialists was probably to avoid uncontrolled hunting and the extermination of elephants.[45]

Conclusion

The farmers of late precolonial Uzigua relied on a complex agronomic system and trade to guard against crop loss during droughts. Indeed, short- and long-distance trade was no less important than farming, because self-sufficiency was impossible in rain-poor Uzigua. The patterns of settlement and cultivation that allowed exploitation of scarce water and soil moisture, however, also left one of the primary exchangeable resources, livestock, vulnerable to insect-borne infections. Cattle were under constant threat from the disease-carrying insects that infested the uninhabitable woodlands around villages. If farmers were to keep and trade livestock, therefore, they had to protect their stock from the diseases transmitted by insects. The following chapter, accordingly, examines the role of disease control in late precolonial animal husbandry.

44. Picarda, "Autour de Mandera," pp. 258–259; Last, "A Visit to the Masai," p. 520; Price, *Private Journal*, p. 81.
45. This may also have been the case in nineteenth-century southern Mozambique: Edward A. Alpers, "State, Merchant Capital, and Gender Relations in Southern Mozambique to the End of the Nineteenth Century: Some Tentative Hypotheses," p. 38.

2. Cattle, Control of Bovine Disease, and Patronage

Farming communities depended upon livestock, but because their goats, sheep, and cattle were vulnerable to diseases borne by the insects and wildlife that occupied unsettled woodlands, farmers had to regulate the transmission of these infections if they were to practice animal husbandry. They accomplished this task by clearing bush and thicket to keep away animals and insects. Yet their overall success in raising livestock testifies both to their control of disease transmission and to the effectiveness of patronage, trade, and agronomic diversification. They provided the majority of late-precolonial cultivators with access to food reserves, so that even during droughts and crop failures they could continue clearing and working the land. The issues of patronage and control of bovine infections are impossible to separate: disease control depended on redistribution by patrons, and a disease-free environment allowed patrons to accumulate wealth in livestock.

The Epizootiological Background

The following treatment of the insect-borne infections trypanosomiasis and theileriosis builds on the argument formulated for trypanosomiasis by John Ford.[1] Ford contended that precolonial African societies prevented trypanosomiasis from causing heavy mortality, but not by avoiding all contact with the tsetse flies (*Glossina spp.*) that transmit trypanosomal infections. Instead, he argued that these societies controlled infection by creating conditions conducive to *limited* contacts between tsetse and wildlife, humans, and livestock. *Glossina* act as vectors of trypanosomiasis when they take blood meals from wildlife, humans, and livestock. As they feed,

1. John Ford, *The Role of the Trypanosomiases*.

Glossina may ingest blood parasites called trypanosomes. Because many of their wildlife hosts (particularly bush pig and bushbuck in Uzigua) are highly resistant to trypanosomal infection and therefore may carry virulent parasitic strains in their bloodstreams, tsetse may ingest trypanosomes that are dangerous to humans and domesticated animals with less resistance. These *Glossina* when feeding on humans and livestock may inoculate them with these dangerous trypanosomes.[2] Ford believed, however, that as long as humans and livestock were infected only periodically they would build up resistance to trypanosomiasis. Indeed, all his work rests on the assumption that humans and cattle can develop immunological resistance to trypanosomiasis.

In Ford's view, precolonial societies maintained the conditions that allowed people and livestock to acquire immunological resistance through occasional infection by using fire and clearing to confine, but not altogether destroy, the vegetation that provided refuge for *Glossina*, bush pigs, bushbuck, and other wild mammalian hosts of trypanosomes. Tsetse, which cannot tolerate high temperatures for long periods, require shade, moisture, and proximity to their mammal hosts. Areas of dense vegetation, especially those near settlements, are their favorite habitats, for this is where bush pigs and other animals that forage by night in cultivated fields rest in the cool shade of trees, bush, and thicket. Ford visualized landscapes (precolonial Uzigua's mixture of fire-derived parkland and dense bush is an excellent example) in which these tsetse-infested woods and thicket adjacent to or isolated within cleared zones would be the locations where livestock and humans would occasionally contract tolerable, resistance-building infections.

A crucial though underappreciated corollary of Ford's thesis is that tsetse do not prevent settlement. Unlike many authorities who have held that *Glossina* deprive Africans of vast lands, Ford believed that precolonial societies could control tsetse and trypanosomiasis in areas that were suitable for settlement. In territories that lacked necessary resources, however (the missing ingredients in much of Uzigua, of course, are water and soil moisture), farmers could neither settle nor control vegetation. Ford called these uninhabited, tsetse-infested, and wildlife-filled zones "*Grenzwildnisse*," that is, frontiers between settlements where travelers, hunters,

---

2. There is no evidence from Uzigua, however, of human trypanosomiasis, which is generally absent in the zone stretching through eastern Tanzania (including Uzigua) and Mozambique that is infested by *Glossina morsitans*. Ford (pp. 478–480) attributed its absence to the region's relatively small cattle population and lack of a domestic bovine reservoir of trypanosomes, but the issue merits further study.

honey-collectors, women gathering foods, men seeking construction materials, herders, and stock moving towards grazing, water holes, and markets found their immunological resistance tested and strengthened by intermittent exposure to tsetse. Because cultivators in precipitation-poor regions such as Uzigua could not settle and eradicate *Glossina* everywhere (indeed, for lack of soil moisture, only six percent of Handeni's land is classified as arable[3]), they had to coexist with trypanosomiasis by building immunological defenses through infrequent contacts with tsetse.

The second major insect-borne bovine infection in Uzigua is theileriosis, a disease which, despite the fact that its virulent epizootic form known as East Coast fever exacts heavy cattle losses throughout eastern and southern Africa, has received almost no attention from historians.[4] The transmission of theileriosis has been less thoroughly studied than that of trypanosomiasis, moreover, because means of controlling it with tick-killing agents, or acaricides, were developed without extensive epizootiological knowledge early in this century. While some aspects of theileriosis epizootiology consequently remain unclear, one critical element, the existence of bovine resistance, has long been established. Another well-understood factor in theileriosis transmission is the role of the brown ear tick, *Rhipicephalus appendiculatus*, which, as the counterpart of tsetse in trypanosomiasis, carries parasitic protozoa of the genus *Theileria* both between cattle and from some wildlife, especially wild buffalo (*Syncerus caffer*), to cattle.

Together with the historical evidence from Uzigua presented below (see also Chapters Eight and Ten), these parallels with trypanosomiasis suggest that just as precolonial societies controlled trypanosomiasis, they were also capable of controlling theileriosis. Farmers apparently maintained theilerial infections at resistance-building levels by limiting the number of ticks and buffalo near pastures. Burning, clearing, and cattle browsing kept short the grasses that provide a particularly favorable tick habitat when they grow long. Hunters, meanwhile, forced most buffalo away from settlements, although some animals were nevertheless attracted to the fresh, palatable grasses that sprouted after the burning of pastures. These activities eradicated neither ticks nor buffalo, but did limit their numbers. Thus while theilerial infections continually circulated between wildlife and cattle, they did not become intolerable.

3. *Tanga Water Master Plan*, vol. 2, *Agriculture*, p. 20.
4. See James L. Giblin, "East Coast Fever in Socio-Historical Context: A Case Study from Tanzania." A recent work that investigates early twentieth-century research on theileriosis is Paul F. Cranefield, *Science and Empire: East Coast Fever in Rhodesia and Transvaal.*

This argument presumes that in northeastern Tanzania both enzootic theileriosis and East Coast fever are caused by the same parasite, *Theileria parva*, and that East Coast fever is simply the form taken by the infection when it passes among cattle that lack immunological defenses. Ford made a similar assumption in arguing that the difference between endemic and epidemic trypanosomiasis derives from the circulation of the same trypanosomal species through resistant and non-resistant populations respectively. It must be noted, however, that some studies reject this approach and contend that enzootic and epizootic theileriosis are infections of different theilerial species.[5] Recent research asserts, nevertheless, that because the *Theileria* which cause East Coast fever and those which cause enzootic infections are "morphologically and serologically indistinguishable" there is "no biological justification" for their classification as different species or subspecies.[6]

Control of Bovine Infections in Precolonial Uzigua

Farmers managed vegetation, and thus controlled bovine infections, mainly by setting bush fires. Even outside settled areas, their burning influenced vegetation communities by allowing the development of "*miombo*," a primarily fire-derived ecological formation dominated by *Brachystegia* and *Isoberlinia* trees.[7] Closer to settlements, fierce dry-season burns eliminated bush and thicket and left only fire-resistant trees that could be felled later to open up land for cultivation. Farmers maintained parklands by performing frequent and extensive burning to allow the regrowth of fresh

5. For example, Cranefield, *Science and Empire*.
6. T. T. Dolan, "Theileriosis: A Comprehensive Review," p. 20; A. D. Irvin and W. I. Morrison, "Immunopathology, Immunology, and Immunoprophylaxis of *Theileria* Infections." See also Giblin, "East Coast Fever."
7. *Tanga Water Master Plan*, vol. 2, *Geography, Climate, Hydrology*; D. Conyers et al., "Agro-Economic Zones of North-Eastern Tanzania." On *miombo* as derived vegetation, see particularly F. Malaisse, "L'Homme dans la forêt claire zambézienne," p. 38; UNESCO/ UNEP/FAO, *Tropical Forest Ecosystems*, p. 602; J. R. Welch, "Observation of Deciduous Woodland in the Eastern Province of Tanganyika Territory," pp. 557–573; and S. B. Boaler and K. C. Sciwale, "Ecology of a Miombo Site, Lupa North Forest Reserve Tanzania. III: Effects on the Vegetation of Local Cultivation Practices," pp. 577–587. Also on *miombo*: C. F. M. Swynnerton, "Preliminary Memorandum on the Position in Handeni," July 23, 1934, Secretariat File 11299, v. 1, TNA; Swynnerton, "Some Factors in the Replacement of Ancient East African Forests by Wooded Pastureland"; G. Milne, "A Soil Reconnaissance Journey Through Parts of Tanganyika Territory"; Nils Celander, *Miombo Woodlands in Africa: Distribution, Ecology and Patterns of Land Use*; E. M. Lind and M. E. S. Morrison, *East African Vegetation*, pp. 80–93; and B. D. Burtt, "Some East African Vegetation Communities."

pasturage, prevent bush from swallowing up paths, and keep away wildlife and insects. Indeed, not infrequently their fires sent European travelers who were uninformed of plans for controlled burning scurrying away from advancing flames.[8] Yet with the first rains, landscapes blackened by soot and ash burst into color as leaves and the bright green grasses, called *halati* by nineteenth-century residents of the Pangani Valley,[9] reappeared. For one missionary, the areas maintained by clearing and cattle grazing as well as by burning seemed to "surpass in splendor the best English parks, so fresh and charming they appear."[10]

Fires, clearing, and grazing created a healthy environment for livestock, particularly in the Pangani and Wami River valleys and other heavily settled locales. Pangani Valley communities held large cattle herds, grazed them on riverbanks (places which, without constant clearing, would have been filled with bush, thirsty wildlife, and concentrations of *Glossina*) and penned them on river islands at night.[11] In the densely populated and extensively cultivated neighborhoods of the lower Wami Valley, cattle-tending villagers used fire and clearing to confine tsetse and bush pigs to isolated pockets of bush.[12] When cattle strayed close to the infested thickets and woods (some of which were preserved as sites of ancestor veneration), tsetse challenged them with resistance-strengthening infections. Thus livestock-holding cultivators coexisted with trypanosomiasis and theileriosis, but only in relatively well-watered neighborhoods where, because they held vectors and wildlife at bay by checking the spread of vegetation, their livestock achieved resistance against infection. The farmers' ability to overcome disease-carrying insects was recognized by one of the first European visitors to the lower Wami Valley, who wrote that its[13]

> fertile level, its numerous villages and broad cultivation, and the general population along the [Wami Valley] route, explain the difference in this matter

8. Cado Picarda, "Autour de Mandera," p. 185; Staatsarchiv der Freien und Hansestadt Hamburg, Bestand 622-2, Wissenschaftliche Nachlässe des Dr. Franz Stuhlmann, B.I., part 2: "Reise von Bagamoyo nach Usegua und Unguu"; Ludwig Karl Gommenginger, letters of January 7 and September, 1883 in Th. Hück, *P. Ludwig Karl Gommenginger*, pp. 196–197 and 215.

9. W. H. Kisbey, *Zigula-English Dictionary*.

10. Gommenginger, letter of January 7, 1883, in Hück, *Gommenginger*, pp. 196–197.

11. G. A. Fischer, *Das Masai-Land*, p. 6; Picarda, "Autour de Mandera," p. 197; Oscar Baumann, *Usambara*, p. 272; Franz Stuhlmann, "Bericht," p. 157; Charles Wilson and R. W. Felkin, *Uganda and the Egyptian Soudan* 1: 32–33; Le Roy, "Au Kilimandjaro."

12. Stuhlmann, "Bericht über eine Reise durch Usegua und Ungu," pp. 148, 157; Picarda, "Autour de Mandera," p. 197.

13. Joseph Mullens, "A New Route and New Mode of Travelling into Central Africa," p. 241.

[of tsetse infestation] between the jungly, mountainous and ill-peopled district to the south, and the more open, dry and cultivated route to the north of the Wami River.

This observer was wrong in assuming that *Glossina* preferred dry conditions, but it was an understandable mistake considering that because control of tsetse was impossible in uninhabitable areas travelers were more likely to encounter *Glossina* in drier woodlands than in more moist, heavily-settled areas. Indeed, in extensive, thinly-settled portions of Uzigua, neither vectors nor wildlife were under control.[14] In the densely-wooded country south of the Wami, for example, a dispersed population kept no cattle.[15] The upper Wami Valley was particularly dangerous for cattle, especially west and north of the confluence of the Wami and Lukigura rivers where uninhabited woods provided a famous hunting ground.[16] This was one of several areas in nineteenth-century Uzigua that contained large numbers of buffalo, the major undomesticated reservoir of *Theileria*,[17] for indeed this was a classic example of a *Grenzwildnis*, an uninhabited woodland associated with sickness, "where dangerous things are located, sorcery charms, uncontrolled forces, wild animals, witches."[18]

Livestock and Redistribution of Wealth

Among the many uses of cattle, their role in trade was the one most likely to be noticed by travelers. The early account of Smee and Hardy, for example, mentioned livestock exports, saying that Uzigua and the Usambara Mountains were together "a most fertile country, abounding in cattle," many of which were sold in *Mrima* towns.[19] Outsiders were less likely to

14. Alexandre Le Roy, "Au Kilimandjaro," pp. 197–200; Graf Joachim Von Pfeil, "Beobachtungen während meiner letzten Reise in Ostafrika," pp. 1–9; Stuhlmann, "Reise von Bagamoyo"; RKA 215/22–24; USPG, UMCA Archives, letter of Bishop John Hine; *BC* 16 (1891–1893): 727–728.

15. Wilson and Felkin, *Uganda*, pp. 32–33.

16. Stuhlmann, "Bericht," pp. 158; Étienne Baur, "Dans l'Oudoé et l'Ouzigoua," p. 64; Marno, "Bericht," p. 373; Anton Horner, "De Bagamoyo à Mhonda," p. 190; Picarda, "Autour de Mandera," p. 201; "Einem Berichte des Bezirkamtmanns v. Rode über seine Beteiligung an dem Zuge des Oberführers Freiherrn V. Manteuffel," pp. 377 and 379; RKA 217/7.

17. Picarda, "Autour de Mandera," p. 200, Horner, "De Bagamoyo à Mhonda," p. 189, and Gommenginger, letter of September 1883, in Hück, *Gommenginger*, p. 219.

18. Steven Feierman, *The Shambaa Kingdom*, p. 48. He shows that the association of unmanaged bush and woodland with danger is deeply rooted in the culture of northeastern Tanzania.

19. Smee and Hardy, India Office Records, and Smee, Hardy and Wingham, "Observations during a Voyage of Research," pp. 23–61.

perceive the importance of cattle in politics and patronage, however, even though exchanges of livestock played a vital role in strengthening political loyalties and patron-client relations both within Zigua-speaking communities and between farmers and Maasai pastoralists. Transfers of livestock, which sometimes involved the placement of villagers' cattle with Maasai herders in the vector-free steppeland, helped cultivating settlements to maintain the close relations with the Maasai that both provided them with access to milk and hides and allowed pastoralists to obtain iron and craft wares, medicines, grain, and other cultivated foods, access to dry-season water sources, and the right to graze their cattle in stubble-strewn fields after harvests. The grazing Maasai herds helped keep grasses short and tick numbers limited near villages, for goats, sheep, and cattle were so effective in preventing the growth of vegetation, remarked one Handeni resident, that women in villages that had large herds walked long distances in search of firewood.[20] Farmers received the assistance of pastoralists, moreover, in burning rank, unpalatable grasses to promote the growth of fresh pasturage, and also made use of the manure deposited by Maasai cattle.[21]

Livestock were no less important in the patronage relations and domestic politics of farming communities. In their competition with mothers' brothers for the affection and loyalty of children, for example, fathers derived advantages from owning stock that could be promised as inheritance to sons and daughters and used to pay bridewealth for sons.[22] Modern residents of Uzigua say that in the past bridewealth normally included the transfer of livestock in at least two installments, the first consisting of a small bull or three goats and the second a heifer or six goats.[23] Hence bridewealth payments did not involve cattle in large numbers as they did in the agro-pastoral societies of Southern Africa where cattle-keeping was considered the primary male undertaking.[24] By the same token, however,

20. Ali Mohamedi Masomo (Mgera, August 19, 1982). Although precolonial accounts frequently mentioned herds of sheep and goats (for example, Mullens, "A New Route," p. 239), it is impossible to estimate the relative importance of cattle and small ruminants in nineteenth-century Uzigua. In 1975, however, Handeni District contained almost twice as many goats and sheep as cattle: *Tanga Water Master Plan*, vol. 6, *Agriculture*, p. 24.

21. Mhonda Mission Journal, September 8, 1878.

22. Pogwa Rashidi, Handeni; Mohamedi Mjewe (Kwediboma, September 27, 1982); Mohamedi Chambo, Mwejuma Mbwego and Athumani Mwegango (Kiberashi, May 17, 1983). Records of local court cases from the early 1960s show that women expected to inherit their fathers' livestock, particularly those that had been obtained as bridewealth from their husbands: Handeni District Files M5/1, "Complaints," and 3/6 "Mswaki: Legal."

23. Ernest L. Mkomwa and Godfrey Nkwileh, "Jadi, Mila, Desturi na Historia ya Wazigua"; Pogwa Rashidi, Handeni; Mohamedi Mjewe (Kwediboma, September 16, 1982); Omali Gumbo, Kwinji.

24. See, for example, Jean Comaroff, *Body of Power, Spirit of Resistance: The Culture and History of a South African People*, pp. 67–74.

AUTOUR ·DE MANDÉRA

(ZANGUEBAR)

Figure 1. Mandera and vicinity in the 1880s: a settlement cluster surrounded by *Grenzwildnis*. The map shows a radius of about five miles around the Mandera Mission. Source: *LMC* 18 (1886): 188.

marriage transactions also did not fit the pattern of Central African societies that, according to Adam Kuper, excluded livestock from bridewealth and regarded hunting, rather than cattle-keeping, as the archetypical activity of men.[25] Instead, in the farming communities of northeastern

25. Adam Kuper, *Wives for Cattle: Bridewealth and Marriage in Southern Africa*, pp. 21–25.

Tanzania, where the responsibility of males and rulers was defined neither as cattle-tending nor as hunting but rather as the duties of accumulating wealth and providing meat that could be fulfilled *both* by hunting and by herding, bridewealth ideally involved small but significant transfers of livestock.[26]

Zigua-speaking communities dramatized the symbolic and practical importance of cattle, goats, and sheep in rituals that associated livestock with political authority and portrayed their possession as one of the primordial characteristics of their society. During the major ceremonies honoring the dead, for instance, the celebrants evoked the lost world of the ancestors not only by wearing bark-cloth (which is believed to have been the usual garment before the adoption of imported cotton cloth) and by making libations of beer brewed from sorghum (the "*chakula cha kiasili*" or "original food"), but also by slaughtering a sheep.[27] Ancestor veneration associated livestock with authority because the killing of the sheep was customarily performed by a political leader who in conducting the ritual demonstrated his ability to mediate between the living and dead. Possession of livestock was once again associated with leadership at post-burial feasts where, according to an account from modern Handeni (see also Chapter Five), rival leaders vied to show whose authority over the deceased had been paramount, and, if possible, supplied a cow or goat in fulfillment of a patron's obligation to provide meat.[28]

Ritual reflected the fact, therefore, that possession of cattle was one of the "primary distinguishing attributes" that enabled rulers to obtain clients.[29] Because livestock, unlike perishable grain, could be kept for long periods in anticipation of scarcity, wealthy stock owners, who might have 100 to 200 cattle, attracted clients for whom a relationship with a cattle-holding patron was insurance against destitution. Thus the majority of villagers, who held at most a few animals, as clients gained some of the benefits of stock ownership, including milk from stock-owning patrons and manure from the animals that they were allowed to pen on their farms, perhaps in return for gifts of beer.[30] "Some people had no cattle," explained one Handeni farmer, "that's why livestock owners distributed

26. Feierman, *The Shambaa Kingdom*, pp. 33–34 and 54–64.

27. Asumani Nyokka (Kwediboma, August 18 and 30, 1982); Haji Luwambo (Kwediboma, August 26, 1982); Pogwa Rashidi (Kwediboma, September 2, 1982); Mohamedi Mjewe (Kwediboma, September 19, 1982): Thomas McVicar, "Wanguru Religion," p. 18.

28. Mkomwa and Nkwileh, "Jadi," p. 19.

29. Marno, "Bericht," p. 364; also, Baur, "Dans l'Oudoé et l'Ouzigoua," p. 42.

30. Rajabu Sudi (Manga, October 10, 1983); Mohamedi Semsambia, Kilwa; Mohamedi Mjewe (Kwediboma, September 19, 1982).

cattle to be tended by others."[31] This arrangement not only permitted clients to manure their fields, particularly the plots where men of the Nguu highlands grew tobacco, but also gave them a chance to build a small herd, since every third calf born in the care of the borrower customarily became his or her property.[32] Because distribution of livestock in this manner frequently strengthened relations between patrons and clients who lived in different environmental zones, moreover, clients also gained greater security against localized droughts and crop failures.

Many farmers depended on patrons not only for livestock but also for staple foods, because the output of their own farms could not satisfy their needs. Competition for scarce prime agricultural land probably helped ensure that weaker villagers did not attain self-sufficiency, for they would have had difficulty in gaining rights to both the moist plots that reliably produced short-rains harvests and the fallow whose bush and thicket were easier to clear than mature tree cover. Whether or not such competition was the primary cause, however, significant inequalities in landholding certainly existed, as records concerning German land expropriation at several locations in Handeni District indicate. These records show that although the average size of thirty-seven expropriated farms was 2.13 hectares, 57 percent of them were smaller than one hectare, while 5 percent of them were larger than 5.5 hectares. One-quarter of the dispossessed farmers held 60 percent of the land for which the Germans paid compensation, while another one-quarter of them held only 8.5 percent of the land. The size of expropriated holdings varied considerably, moreover, ranging between 0.75 and 6.25 hectares, for example, at Kwediboma in western Handeni District.[33]

In addition to the small size of the sample, however, several other factors dictate caution in drawing conclusions from this evidence. In particular, the records do not indicate how many individuals depended on the expropriated fields or whether the compensated landholders had plots elsewhere. Nevertheless, it is certainly not implausible to assume that the majority of farmers did in fact work less than one hectare, for this has also been true in Handeni during recent decades.[34] Thus, if the evidence

31. Salimu Kisailo (Kwa Maligwa, May 19, 1983). Also, Mdoe Nyange, Kiberashi; Mhonda Mission Journal, May 30, 1883; E. B. Dobson, "Land Tenure of the Wasambaa," pp. 19–20.

32. Mdoe Nyange, Kiberashi; Mohamedi Mjewe (Kwediboma, September 19, 1982).

33. TNA G8/773, G8/776, G23/205, G55/54, G55/55, G203/153.

34. Government reports show, for example, that twenty-six Handeni District villages cultivated only 0.9 hectares per able-bodied farmer in 1974: Handeni District File A.3/4/IX, "Agriculture: Monthly Reports." Another survey done in the same period showed that Han-

produced by land expropriation can indeed be taken to reflect the pattern of land holding across Uzigua, modern conditions of agriculture suggest that the majority of farms could have supported only the smallest domestic groups. Farmers working less than one hectare would have had to achieve yields of sorghum and maize considerably higher than modern maize yields in order to produce the 900 kg consumed annually by three adults, for in modern Handeni maize yields are about 766 kg per hectare.[35] Hence, even if precolonial yields exceeded modern output, as many Handeni farmers contend, it would nevertheless appear that many of the nearly six of ten farmers who worked less than one hectare probably did not produce enough grain to meet their own requirements, and that many more probably could not have stored enough reserves to last through seasons of shortage.

Although these data are obviously inconclusive, when considered together with evidence that precolonial farmers commonly worked for food in the fields of more affluent neighbors (see Chapter Four), they suggest that many cultivators had to supplement the staple food produced on their own plots. Of course a wide variety of alternative foods were available, including milk, wild vegetables and roots gathered by women, meat brought home by hunters, and various foodstuffs obtained in trade, but the cattle-owning patrons were the most common source of subsistence reserves. Their clients, many of whom cultivated only small plots and held but a few livestock, worked on the patrons' farms and tended their cattle in return for food to carry them through the periods, particularly the hungry preharvest months, when their reserves were exhausted.

Costs and Benefits of Patronage: Enslavement and Control of Bovine Disease

Patronage enabled farming communities to avoid epizootics because cultivators who obtained sustenance from patrons kept fields and pastures

---

deni villages cultivated only three-quarters of a hectare per household: Suleman Alarakhia Sumra, "An Analysis of Environmental and Social Problems Affecting Agricultural Development in Handeni District," p. 130. Research done by Sumra and others in individual villages produced similar results. At Mswaki in the early 1970s, for instance, 48% of households surveyed worked an average of 1.8 hectares, and the village cultivated only one-third of a hectare per person: Sumra, "An Analysis of Environmental and Social Problems," pp. 136 and 151. At Segera, one-half of the farmers worked fields of less than two hectares, and one-quarter worked less than one hectare: Michaela von Freyhold, *Rural Development Through Ujamaa*, vol. 2: *Case Studies From Handeni* and G. Tschannerl et al., "Handeni Water Supply: Preliminary Report and Design Criteria."

35. Data on modern crop yields are from Sumra, "An Analysis of Environmental and Social Problems," pp. 130, 135–136.

cleared and close-cropped despite periodic droughts and crop failures. The cost of maintaining community welfare could be personal tragedy, however, since access to patronage meant accepting subordinate or servile status. Both of these qualities of patronage are reflected in the scant evidence of pre-1880s famine in Uzigua. By contrast with the colonial-period famines, which led to depopulation, interruption of vegetation management, and outbreaks of cattle disease, late-precolonial crises apparently did not cause heavy losses of population and breakdown of control over bovine diseases (see also Chapter Eight). However, slave trading appears to have increased during pre-1880s famines.

In Handeni District, the most widely known stories of famine before the 1880s concern the episode called *Kidyakingo*, a disaster that reduced its victims, say oral accounts, to eating cattle hides. Neither external corroborating evidence, however, nor elements within the brief accounts from Uzigua allow the dating of *Kidyakingo*, although traditions from the Pare Mountains led Isaria Kimambo to suggest in 1969 that it may have occurred ten generations before.[36] The problem of dating is complicated by the tendency of storytellers to insert references to "*Kidyakingo*" into their tales whenever famine serves a rhetorical purpose.[37]

Aside from the traditions of *Kidyakingo*, there are no other accounts of famine until 1884–1886, when the first subsistence crisis to be recorded in writing struck Uzigua (Chapter Eight). But there are two instances of large-scale migration from Uzigua which may have been connected with famines. The first of these movements occurred about 1800, when slaves left Uzigua for southern Somalia, where a small Zigua-speaking diaspora still resides.[38] The second exodus probably occurred shortly before a revolt by Zigua-speaking slaves in Zanzibar about 1820. The fate of these captives is linked to famine in an account collected by Richard Burton in 1857, for Burton was told that they had been exchanged for grain before being taken to Zanzibari slave plantations.[39] Possibly also related to this episode

36. I. N. Kimambo, *A Political History of the Pare of Tanzania*, p. 37.

37. For example, Yusufu Kaberwa, Mswaki. In the Mombasa hinterland, a famine occurring in 1859–1862 was called "Kingo" (Spear, *The Kaya Complex*, p. 112).

38. Carl Claus Van Der Decken, *Reisen in Ost Afrika* 2: 303, 309; Vinigi L. Grottanelli, "The Peopling of the Horn of Africa," pp. 74–75; Bakari bin Mdoe, "Notes on the Wazigua Colony in Somaliland," trans. S. B. Jones (December 6, 1934), TNA 22587. The Zigua-speaking communities of Somalia are discussed in Lee V. Cassanelli, "Social Construction on the Somali Frontier: Bantu Former Slave Communities in the Nineteenth Century."

39. Richard F. Burton, *The Lake Regions of Central Africa* 1: 124–126; Frederick Cooper, *Plantation Slavery on the East Coast of Africa*, pp. 202–203; Picarda, "Autour de Mandera," p. 226.

is another story from Handeni about a prominent chief of eastern Uzigua who sold a great number of captives to Zanzibar in return for food.[40]

Although these movements may have occurred because famine victims either surrendered their own freedom or exchanged slaves in the coastal towns for food, they may also have been unrelated to subsistence crises. Oral accounts may have connected them with famine simply to provide a justification for slave dealing. On balance, nevertheless, the evidence suggests that Uzigua probably suffered famines occasionally in the early nineteenth century, and that one way of surviving them was the exchange of captives for foodstuffs. The descriptions of Uzigua contributed relatively regularly by European travelers after 1811 give no sign, however, of a calamitous, decades-long sequence of crises comparable to that which disrupted control of diseases during the colonial period. Instead, they show that farmers kept cattle throughout the nineteenth century. Not until the 1890s did the region suffer demographic reversals on a scale great enough to interrupt vegetation management. Because the institution of patronage which governed the redistribution of wealth appears, therefore, to have played a central role in maintaining trypanosomiasis and theileriosis enzooticity, the following three chapters turn to the politics of patronage, and particularly to political developments in Uzigua after 1840.

40. Yusufu Selemani, Abedi Juma, Mohamedi Waziri, Mohamedi Nasoro and Idi Sefu (Manga, October 10, 1983).

Part II

The Politics of Patronage in the Late-Precolonial Chieftaincies

3. Merchant Capital and the Chieftains

After 1840, Zanzibari merchant capital and a regime of commercially-oriented chieftains shaped the precolonial politics of patronage and environmental control in Uzigua, for at that time, new leaders began co-operating with the Zanzibari and *Mrima* merchants who wished to increase exports of ivory and slaves. Although they became heavily reliant on their mercantile partners for imports and credit, these chieftains nevertheless attracted widening circles of dependents, diversified their subordinates' access to subsistence reserves, and helped maintain a favorable bovine disease environment. However, they also extracted tribute and labor service, enslaved weaker neighbors, and distributed their resources selectively to favor loyal clients and punish unsubmissive subjects. Thus it was the chieftains who provided the benefits and imposed the costs of patronage in late-precolonial Uzigua.

The Penetration of Merchant Capital

The emergence of the chieftains coincided with intensive planting of cloves and increased demand for plantation labor on the islands of Zanzibar and Pemba in the late 1830s and 1840s. Hence the need for servile labor as well as rising ivory prices encouraged Zanzibari merchants to explore commercial possibilities in the Tanganyikan mainland, particularly in Uzigua and other areas that coastal traders had hitherto rarely visited. Merchants connected to the Bombay ivory and cloth markets financed mainland trading ventures not only because they were interested in obtaining ivory, but also because, as the holders of mortgages on clove plantations, they wished to secure slave labor for Zanzibar.[1] They provided the substantial capital

1. On the economic and political importance of the Bombay merchants, see Frederick Cooper, *Plantation Slavery on the East Coast of Africa*, pp. 47ff, 139–143; C. S. Nicholls, *The Swahili Coast*, pp. 204, 207ff, 214, 348, 354–355; Abdul Sheriff, *Slaves, Spices and Ivory in Zanzibar*, pp. 65–67, 83ff, 105ff, 126, 146–147; Charles Guillain, "Côte de Zanguebar," pp. 543–544.

outlays required by major caravans for the purchase of trade goods and advances to porters, who might number as many as one thousand in a single expedition.[2]

The *Mrima* coast and its hinterland were attractive fields for commercial expansion, not least because the Nguu Mountains and the southern Maasai steppe furnished valuable grades of ivory. In politically decentralized Uzigua, moreover, traders encountered no restrictive state policies. Trade with Uzigua and southern Maasailand also appealed to merchants because it promised more rapid return on investment than did the long-distance undertakings that extended as far as Lakes Nyasa, Tanganyika, and Victoria. Indian and Omani merchants enjoyed an additional advantage on the *Mrima* because the Omani government of Zanzibar barred European, American, and other foreign traders from the area. These considerations outweighed even the onerous Zanzibari customs schedule, which placed its heaviest duties on goods from *Mrima* ports and Uzigua.[3]

As commerce in Uzigua increased, merchants from Zanzibar became increasingly influential in the *Mrima* ports, particularly Pangani and Sadani. In the 1850s most of Pangani's population of 4000 appeared, in fact, to be indebted to the town's twenty Indian merchants. The Pangani merchant houses dispatched large caravans towards the Nguu Mountains (a trip of about eleven days), Maasailand (twenty days distance from the coast), and Kilimanjaro throughout the year. Sadani caravans, which traveled primarily to Nguu and southeastern Maasailand, were usually absent for about six weeks.[4]

In addition to outfitting caravans, the merchants also commissioned agents to operate seasonal trading posts in the Nguu Mountains. As caravans from the Tanganyikan interior approached the coast, these agents welcomed them in the highlands, provided them with food after their long trek across the sparsely inhabited steppe, and either advanced them credit for the last leg of their journey to the *Mrima* or spared them the necessity of continuing on to the coast by purchasing their ivory and slaves outright. The agents acquired provisions for their customers not only from nearby markets and chieftains but also by employing slaves who produced rice for

2. Richard F. Burton, *Zanzibar: City, Island and Coast*, vol. 2, pp. 145–147 and 270.

3. Sheriff, *Slaves, Spices and Ivory*, pp. 121–125 and 172ff.

4. Johann Krapf, *Reisen in Ostafrika*, 2: 279; Burton and J. H. Speke, "A Coasting Voyage from Mombasa to the Pangani River," p. 202; Speke, *What Led to the Discovery of the Source of the Nile*, p. 12; Burton, *Zanzibar* 2: 145–147, 270; J. P. Farler, "Native Routes in East Africa," p. 739; James Christie, p. 245; *Kolonial-Politische Korrespondenz* 2 (August 9, 1886).

export to Pangani as well as food for the caravans. They also formed alliances with local leaders and with their support practiced "oppression and robbery." "Having a few followers," remarked the missionary James Last about one Swahili agent named Bwana Hamadi, "whenever he saw a good chance of success he would attack a weak village, take as many of the inhabitants as he dared to sell as slaves, and put the rest under rule."[5] The primary function of the agents, nevertheless, was to steer coastward-bound caravans toward particular *Mrima* merchants and towns, for as they neared the coast, caravan leaders had several ports from which to choose a destination. The representatives of a merchant house secured a caravan's business by advancing loans of food and other goods repayable in ivory and slaves once the caravan had reached the port in which the merchant resided.[6] Agents encamped in the Nguu Mountains were perfectly placed to influence the caravans' choice of destination, because the route across the southern Maasai steppe split into two roads in the highlands, with one route heading directly east to Pangani and Tanga and the other southward towards Sadani and Bagamoyo.

Although the agents sometimes became rivals of Zigua-speaking leaders, the chieftains usually benefited from their activities because, by providing goods on credit, the agents equipped caravans with the means of paying tolls in Uzigua, and thus enabled the Zigua-speaking leaders to profit from commercial traffic. Before the establishment of the camps and routinization of the toll system, caravans from interior regions, unwilling to surrender any of their slaves and ivory before reaching coastal markets, often fought with toll collectors as they crossed Uzigua.[7] Such conflicts plagued the ivory trade during the 1840s, 1850s, and 1860s and forced the Omani state of Zanzibar to intervene, first by stationing tiny and ineffective garrisons in the Pangani Valley and later, in 1863 and 1864, by making "politic distribution of 10,000 German Crowns amongst the Negro chiefs of Uzegura, whose disputes respecting the right to levy 'blackmail' on the ivory merchants traversing their territories ended in a complete blockade

5. James Last, "A Journey into the Nguru Country from Mamboia, East Central Africa," pp. 153–154. Also, Rashidi Mwenjuma Manyagala (Kilwa, September 11, 1983); Nyangasi Mohamedi Munga, Kilwa; Abdala Hamani Msede and Ali Omali Kipande (Kwa Dundwa, September 12, 1983); Omali Maligwa Kidiza (Gombero, September 20, 1983); Mwejuma Mbwego and Athumani Mwegango, Kiberashi; Salimu Kisailo, Kwa Maligwa; Mhonda Mission Journal, March 13, 1883; Roger Price, *Private Journal of the Reverend Roger Price*, p. 81.

6. Burton, "The Lakes Regions," p. 57.

7. W. Christopher, "Extract from a Journal by Lt. W. Christopher," pp. 76–103.

of the most important route from the ivory districts."[8] Ultimately, however, the credit offered in the trading camps proved more effective, because
by paying tolls in borrowed currency and cloth caravaneers avoided dissi-
pating their ivory supplies. Thus both the likelihood of strife and the
possibility that caravans would decide to stay away from Uzigua were
reduced.[9]

While the tolls were a nuisance, the Zanzibaris nevertheless supported the chieftains of Uzigua with firearms as well as cash payments,[10]
because overall their regime promoted merchant enterprise. In addition to
cooperating with the commercial agents in Nguu and guaranteeing the
safety of itinerant traders,[11] the Zigua-speaking leaders also instituted markets where caravans found plentiful exports and demand for imports. Indeed, their ability to obtain slaves, ivory, cattle, and foodstuffs from
dependents and furnish them to caravans gave the chieftains pivotal importance in export trade, particularly because they were the link between
coastal merchants and the Maasai and Ndorobo who provided ivory,
cattle, and slaves.[12]

Enterprising chieftains also obtained ivory and slaves by launching
long-distance trading ventures. If they chose not to travel themselves, they
dispatched representatives, such as the chieftain's client from northern
Nguu who bought ivory and slaves in the Lake Tanganyika region and
along the way found his first wife. Another highlander purchased thirty
captives in Singida and thereby transformed himself into the wealthiest
villager in his neighborhood.[13] "The Zigua are inclined to seek wider

8. Quote from G. E. Seward, "Report on the Commerce of Zanzibar . . . 1864–1865,"
in Norman R. Bennett, *A History of the Arab State of Zanzibar*, p. 272 n. 22. Also, *Commercial
Reports Received at the Foreign Office* (1866), p. 282. On trade disruptions: Krapf, *Reisen in
Ostafrika* 2: 310; Burton and Speke, *Source of the Nile*, p. 214; N. R. Bennett and George E.
Brooks, Jr., eds., *New England Merchants in Africa*, pp. 493–494.

9. Paul Reichard, *Deutsch-Ostafrika: Das Land und seine Bewohner*, pp. 438–439.

10. More than 13,000 muskets were imported by a single German firm at Zanzibar in
one year during the late 1850s (Burton, "The Lakes Regions," p. 380).

11. For an example of such a relationship, see Mtoro bin Mwenyi Bakari, "Meine Reise
nach Udoe bis Uzigua."

12. Cado Picarda, "Autour de Mandera," pp. 227, 258–259; Last, "A Visit to the Masai
People Living Beyond the Borders of the Nguru Country," pp. 520–521; Last, "A Journey,"
p. 149; Krapf, *Reisen in Ostafrika* 2: 288; Burton, *Zanzibar* 2: 199; G. A. Fischer, *Das Masai-
Land*, p. 5; Mandera Mission Journal, August 26–27, 1883; Mhonda Mission Journal, Septem-
ber 8, 1878; Pogwa Rashidi, Handeni. On alliances between Zigua-speaking chieftains and
the Maasai: Sir Harry Hamilton Johnston, *The Kilimanjaro Expedition*, p. 112; Alexandre Le
Roy, "Au Kilimandjaro," p. 164; Salimu Kisailo, Kwa Maligwa; Mwejuma Mbwego and
Athumani Mwegango, Kiberashi.

13. Ali S. Sambuguma (Kwediboma, September 10, 1982); Omali Maligwa Kidiza,
Gombero.

horizons," wrote Oscar Baumann, "to compete with Swahili traders and pursue caravan trade in the further interior. . . . They take coastal wares to Irangi, to buy goats and sheep, which are then exchanged with the Maasai for ivory. The latter they take to the coast themselves or trade to a Swahili merchant."[14] These activities hastened the shift of ivory and slaves away from the small trading parties of Uzigua into the hands of the large, well-capitalized caravans. Indeed, as their dependence upon their Zanzibari merchant sponsors for weapons and other imports increased, the chieftains became all the more interested in monopolizing these valuable exports.

The First-Generation Chieftains

Visiting Pangani in 1844, just as the first generation of chieftains were taking power, the missionary Johann Krapf found that Uzigua had only recently become a center of the slave trade. He described its impact in a manner which closely resembles oral and written stories of the chieftains from Handeni District:

> The Arabs from their island of Zanzibar come over here, to promise the Zigua chiefs a quantity of guns with powder and lead for a certain quantity of slaves. When a chief has reached an agreement, he suddenly attacks a hostile village, burns the houses, and drags off the inhabitants, and so fulfills the stipulations of his agreement with the Arab. . . .[15]

During his 1852 journey to the Usambara Mountains, Krapf saw more of the changes brought about by the chieftains. Their raiding, he learned, had caused upheaval in the lower Pangani Valley since 1840. Krapf's hosts in Usambara held three chiefs of Uzigua responsible, including one called "Mabewa," about whom they told tales of capricious cruelty that remain current in modern Uzigua. Krapf wrote that "Mabewa" possessed 600 flintlocks, 200 more than even the great king Kimweri of Usambara could muster. Krapf also observed trade disruptions of the sort that were common before the routinization of toll-collecting. Demands for tribute by chieftains in the Pangani Valley, he noted, forced caravans into circuitous detours and caused the suspension of ivory exports in 1852.[16]

---

14. Oscar Baumann, *Usambara und seine Nachbargebiete*, p. 274.
15. Krapf, *Reisen in Ostafrika* 1: 184–185.
16. Krapf, *Reisen in Ostafrika* 2: 289, 299, 307, 309–310; "Report of E. C. Richards" (September 23, 1925) in Pangani District Book, vol. 3, TNA.

"Feuds," as Richard Burton termed such disturbances, were still hindering trade when he toured the region in 1857. Zigua-speaking chiefs continued to raid the lower Pangani Valley and harass Zanzibari garrisons near Pangani.[17] Like Krapf, Burton blamed the seemingly chaotic situation on the introduction of firearms. Because Uzigua had no "hereditary sultans," wrote Burton,

> this tends practically to cause a perpetual blood-feud, and to raise up a number of petty chiefs, who, aspiring to higher positions, must distinguish themselves by bloodshed, and acquire wealth in weapons, the great title to superiority, by slave dealing. . . . Originally a peaceful tribe, they have been rendered terrible by the possession of firearms; and their chiefs have now collected large stores of gunpowder, used only to kidnap and to capture the weaker wretches within their reach.[18]

"Mabewa," or Mhelamwana as he is remembered in Handeni District, was the most famous of the early chieftains. Around 1840 he took power at Manga, a neighborhood located forty-five miles from the coast on a trade route that provided easy access to Sadani (see Chapter Five). Later he moved closer to his merchant creditors at Sadani by establishing a new base at Palamakaa, a valley that supplied Sadani with grain. Subsequently he extended his authority over a broad area by installing rulers in several villages to the south and west of Manga. His power, nevertheless, reached neither as far south as the Wami Valley, where another major chieftaincy emerged at Miono, nor very far to the north, because his expansion in that direction was checked by rivals who competed for control of the two routes leading inland from Pangani. One of these caravan roads ran northwest along the Pangani Valley towards the Pare Mountains and Kilimanjaro, while the other passed directly westward from Pangani, taking travelers through what is today central Handeni District into southern Maasailand. Along these routes four competing alliances of chieftains arose, each of which tried to situate itself athwart both roads to ensure that Pangani-bound caravans could not evade its tolls.

The growth of the four alliances is traced in several accounts written in Handeni District during the colonial period, of which the most detailed is the anonymous "History of the Zigua." Couched in an idiom of kinship and affinity, these narratives emphasize the chieftains' commercial relationships, their use of armed force and striving for control of dependents, and

17. Burton, *Zanzibar* 2: 145, 148, 159–173.
18. Burton, "Lakes Regions," pp. 100–101.

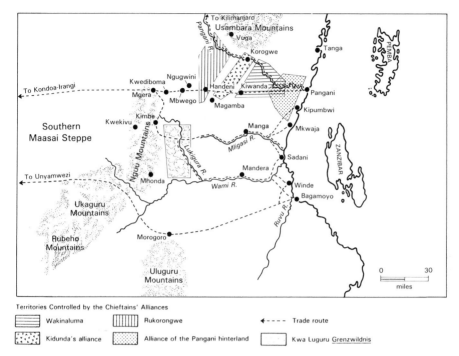

Map 2. Late-precolonial Uzigua.

the importance of group identities associated with small territories called *si*. (The groups which took the name of a particular *si* were the putative descendents of that territory's first settlers. *Si* identities are discussed at length in Chapter Five.) Members of a *si* community called the *Wakinaluma*, states the "History," formed the first alliance.[19] Its founder, Mauya, made marriage alliances in several villages on the Pangani trade routes to ensure that his own children would have legitimate claim to rule those settlements as the nephews and nieces (*wapwa*) of their leaders. "This is why," comments the "History," "there was no trouble in the places where Mauya sent his children. To install someone in a place without making a marriage with its people would create feuds and animosity."[20] Thus *si*

19. "Historia ya Wazigua" ["History of the Zigua"], (anon., n.d.), in Handeni District Book, vol. 1, TNA; also on the *Wakinaluma*: R. S. Kilango, S. M. Mbwana and L. Abdallah, "Historia ya Ufalme" (August 15, 1951), TNA 4/6/5, vol. 2. Similarities in style and content indicate that Kilango, Mbwana and Abdallah were also the authors of the "Historia ya Wazigua."

20. "Historia ya Wazigua," p. 9.

identities and affinal relations aided Mauya, like other chieftains, in forging unity among a number of settlements. Indeed, the rulers of several
villages along the Pangani caravan routes during the 1860s and 1870s would
claim to be Mauya's children and grandchildren.

A second alliance, according to the "History" and other written
accounts, was the creation of Kidunda, who like Mauya built upon commercial as well as affinal relationships, for even after moving from the
Pangani Valley to the central Handeni trade route, Kidunda maintained
contact with coastal merchants. His son and grandson continued the
struggle to control both roads leading inland from Pangani.[21] The immediate hinterland of Pangani, however, was dominated by a third alliance of
chieftains, who probably caused the havoc reported by Krapf and Burton
in the lower Pangani Valley.[22] The center of the fourth alliance among first-
generation chieftains was Handeni Mountain, where the Handeni District
administrative headquarters is now located. Its rulers, who engaged in violent struggles to establish a presence on both Pangani trade routes, are
identified in the "History of the Zigua" as members of the *Rukorongwe si*
community. Members of this alliance held power in central Handeni and
the Pangani Valley until the colonial period.[23]

The Westward Spread of Chieftaincies in the Second Generation

The chieftaincies of the first generation were confined to eastern Uzigua,
so that there were no leaders of regional renown in the Nguu Mountains
during the 1850s.[24] Shortly thereafter, however, chieftains emerged in west-

21. "Historia ya Wazigua"; Mamgaya binti Mgaya and Nassoro bin Thabiti, "Habari
za Uzumbe wa Kwamkoro ambao Uliunganishwa kwenye Uzumbe wa Mgambo na Chanika" in Musa Sefu Abdalahe, "Habari za Wazigua" (a copy was kindly lent to me by
Mwalimu W. Mguhi of Kwa Mkono Primary School); a translation of this appears as "History of the old Kwamkoro Zumbeate now absorbed by Chanika and Mgambo," trans.
J. E. G. Ransome (August 24, 1929) in Tanga Province Book, TNA; Ibrahimu Mohamedi
Mkwayu, Rajabu Sefu Mwenkumba, Ramadhani Maingwa (Kwa Mkono, December 21,
1982).

22. "Historia ya Wazigua"; Zumbe Asumani Mmaka, "Uzumbe wa Mgambo katika
Uzigua," in Musa Sefu Abdalahe, "Habari za Wazigua," translated as "The Mgambo Section
of the Wazigua," by J. E. G. Ransome (August 23, 1929) in Tanga Province Book, TNA; J. G.
Stephenson, "Notes on Mgambo Zumbeate" (July 10, 1956) in Handeni District Book,
vol. 1, TNA.

23. "Historia ya Wazigua"; Zumbe Mohamed Mdoe, "Uzumbe wa Chanika katika
Uzigua," translated as "Mweruwara" by J. E. G. Ransome (July 14, 1929) in Tanga Province
Book, TNA.

24. Krapf, *Reisen in Ostafrika* 2: 299.

ern Uzigua, and by the 1880s they were more powerful than the leaders of the immediate coastal hinterland. Two clients of Mhelamwana, Kisabengo and Mani, were instrumental in the westward spread of the chieftaincies. Kisabengo's career is indicative, in fact, of northeastern Tanzania's cultural unity, for while he began his career in eastern Uzigua, his primary achievement was the foundation of Morogoro, a major caravan depot which, although it became the largest town ruled by a Zigua-speaking leader, was nevertheless located far from the area that would be regarded as the homeland of "the Zigua" in the twentieth century. Accounts from Handeni District say that after a quarrel with Mhelamwana, Kisabengo sought independence by moving to Morogoro and allying himself with the *Mrima* town of Winde. In 1857, Burton learned that Kisabengo, whose slave raiding terrorized the Luguru Mountains, controlled trade between Tabora and the coast.[25]

The other prominent offshoot of Mhelamwana's regime was the chieftaincy founded by Mani at the village of Magamba in central Handeni District. Mani subsequently extended his influence westward by allying himself with Bwana Hamadi, the *Mrima* commercial agent who lived in the Nguu highlands. According to stories from Handeni District, Mani's break with Mhelamwana occurred after a diviner predicted that Mani would one day become a chief. Secretly hoping that Mani would be killed, the suspicious Mhelamwana sent him on an elephant hunting expedition to the *Grenzwildnis* northwest of the upper Wami River. Rather than turning his ivory over to Mhelamwana, however, as a client was expected to do, Mani prepared to seize power by selling it for firearms and slaves. His career, marked by numerous struggles with the *Wakinarukorongwe* alliance and other chieftains, ended with his death in 1884 and the succession of his son Sonyo.[26]

In addition to Kisabengo and Mani, several other chieftains dominated portions of western Uzigua and the Nguu highlands along the trade routes that crossed the region between Maasailand and the *Mrima* ports. One of the western chieftains was Machaku, the ruler of Mbwego, a settlement in northwestern Uzigua which is now part of Mswaki Village. A modern interpreter of Mswaki's history named Yusufu Kaberwa described Machaku as a member of the Mbwego *si* community who, after passing

25. "Historia ya Wazigua," p. 11; Abedi Juma, Manga; Burton, "The Lakes Regions," p. 76.

26. "Historia ya Wazigua"; Elders of Magamba and their "Asili ya Kwa Luguru"; Abedi Juma, Yusufu Selemani and others, Manga; Ernest Mkomwa, Kwa Masaka; "Rapport d'ensemble sur la Mission de Mandera," p. 25.

his youth in the Pangani Valley where he acquired firearms by selling ivory, took control of Mbwego.[27] Thus his account, like many others concerning the chieftains, attests to the importance both of *si* identities—for the basis of Machaku's claim to rule Mbwego was that he descended from the *si*'s founders—and also of commercial connections and armed force. Villagers of modern Mswaki say that Machaku brought scattered hamlets under his rule by providing imports and protection from aggressors. His subjects feared no one, insists Yusufu Kaberwa, and unlike other communities saw no need to construct fortifications.[28]

From Mbwego, Machaku moved westward into the Nguu Mountains, where he installed rulers in tributary settlements.[29] The climax of his career was a struggle for the village of Mgera in northern Nguu. In all likelihood, however, the conflict did not merely pit Machaku against his local antagonist, named Munju, but also set Pangani against Sadani, for Mgera was the point where caravans approaching the coast from the Maasai steppe skirted the northern Nguu Mountains before choosing their *Mrima* destination. Hence at stake in the battle for Mgera was the ability to choke off a rival port's connection with southern Maasailand and regions further west. Machaku procured "shipload after shipload" of firearms and gunpowder from his Pangani merchant allies, while Munju, who lived south of Mgera on the Sadani-Maasailand trade route, probably sought supplies from the merchants of Sadani. After an epic battle of six days, oral accounts relate, Machaku's forces defeated Munju and took possession of Mgera.[30]

Even after his victory at Mgera Machaku did not enjoy unchallenged control of northwestern Uzigua, because an overlapping trade network developed along the Pangani route to Maasailand. At its center was a rival of Machaku named Pogwa Mnowowakala who, say oral accounts, derived his claim to rule a strategic location at Kwediboma Village from inheritance of his mother's *si* name. On a bluff overlooking a steep slope that coastward-bound caravans had to climb, he built a palisaded village, gathered into it the inhabitants of surrounding neighborhoods, and levied tolls

27. "Habari za Wanguu" in Musa Sefu Abdalahe, "Habari za Wazigua," translated as "The Wanguu Tribe: a History" by L. S. Greening (December 12, 1926) in Tanga Province Book, TNA.

28. Yusufu Kaberwa, Mswaki; also, see "Historia ya Wazigua."

29. Yusufu Kaberwa, Mswaki; Omali Gumbo, Kwinji; Abdala Hamani Msede and Ali Omali Kipande, Kwa Dundwa; Rashidi Mwenjuma Manyagala, Kilwa.

30. Yusufu Kaberwa, Mswaki; Elders of Mgera; Ali Mohamedi Masomo, Mgera; Salimu Kisailo, Kwa Maligwa.

while trading in ivory and slaves.[31] Pogwa aligned himself with Kilo Mwanamachau, another trading leader who was fluent in Maa and an ally of Maasai pastoralists.[32] Thus, Pogwa Mnowowakala, Kilo Mwanamachau, and pastoralists living in southern Maasailand formed a competing commercial network along the route which Machaku had fought to dominate. Two other major chieftaincies emerged, moreover, in the central Nguu Mountains south of Mgera, on the caravan route connecting Sadani and Bagamoyo with southern Maasailand. From Kwekivu, the chieftain Kilangola launched slave raids over a wide area.[33] His successors were eclipsed, however, by Mtiga of Kimbe, who exacted tribute from about fifty villages. Mtiga remained an important figure in the early colonial period when both his son and nephew became administrative chiefs under the Germans.[34]

Enslavement, Exclusion and Incorporation

Coupled with Zanzibari demand for slaves, the spread of the chieftaincies placed many inhabitants of Uzigua in great danger of enslavement. The firearms furnished by coastal merchants enabled ambitious, often youthful chieftains to capture slaves for export as well as domestic employment, while their desire to acquire imports and their debts to coastal merchants increased their incentive to do so. Indeed, many residents of modern Uzigua think of the chieftains' era as a time of incessant fighting; women and children, they believe, dared not venture into fields without armed escort.[35] At Mandera in the Wami Valley, wrote the resident missionary Cado Picarda, wars occurred in the early 1880s about four times annually, though disputes were often settled without fighting if one party was intimidated into surrendering captives. Likewise in the southern

31. Pogwa Rashidi, Handeni; Omali Gumbo, Kwinji; Yusufu Kaberwa, Mswaki.
32. Baumann, *Usambara*, p. 276; "Historia ya Wazigua," p. 17; "Einem Berichte des Bezirksamtmanns v. Rode," p. 377.
33. Yusufu Kaberwa, Mswaki; "Habari za Wanguu"; Last, "The Tribes," pp. 662–663; Church Missionary Society Archives, CA6/014, letter of J. T. Last to Rev. H. Wright (January 20, 1879) and Last to Wright (June 2, 1879); Last, "A Journey," p. 151.
34. Franz Stuhlmann, "Bericht über eine Reise durch Usegua und Unguu," pp. 163–167, and "Reise von Bagamoyo"; "Einem Berichte des Bezirksamtmanns v. Rode," pp. 376–377; "The Family Tree of Mahomet Kisome," in Tanga Province Book, TNA; report of J. Wilkie Johnstone, A.D.O. Handeni (September 26, 1925) in Pangani District Book, vol. 3, TNA.
35. For example, Mkomwa and Nkwileh, "Jadi, Mila, Desturi na Historia ya Wazigua," Chapter 10.

Nguu Mountains during the same period, conflicts frequently resulted in enslavement.[36]

The slave trade, the influx of firearms, and the rise of predatory chieftains forced a cruel choice on many powerless farmers: they could risk enslavement or, as the price of protection from slave hunters, subordinate themselves to a powerful leader. Hence at the height of the slave trade chieftains brought dependents, slaves, and kin into large palisaded villages which consisted of as many as three hundred houses and which might be divided into separate quarters for the rulers' kin and dependents.[37] Chieftains—such as one Wami Valley notable whom missionaries saw living in a fortified village with "superb" gardens, goats, and cattle—held the most productive land as well as large herds.[38] The many "sons, slaves, women, children and cattle" of these chieftains, along with "numerous houses and extensive fields," were the "primary distinguishing attributes" of the chieftains' villages observed one European traveler.[39] Prime bottom lands are even today known as the fields of the precolonial chieftains in some villages.

The chieftains also offered limited protection to tribute-paying clients who remained in outlying hamlets, for not everyone lived in large villages. Travelers in Uzigua saw not only the large settlements of chieftains, but also isolated hamlets of about five to a dozen houses whose impoverished, wary inhabitants had few imported goods and no livestock. Usually they wore skins or bark-cloth rather than the imported cloth seen in more affluent communities.[40] Unlike the residents of large settlements, they enjoyed neither the benefits of trade nor a disease environment favorable for cattle keeping.

36. Picarda, "Autour de Mandera," p. 259; Mandera Mission Journal, December 11, 1881, February 12, 1882, September 29 and December 10, 1883, March 27, 1884, September 23 and October 24, 1886, January 30, 1889; Mhonda Mission Journal, November 21–22, 1878, February 2 and June 24, 1881, February 24, 1884, October 3–4, December 13 and December 23–24, 1886, December 5, 1889; "Station Petershöhe," p. 299; Stuhlmann, *Mit Emin Pascha*, p. 24; Stuhlmann, "Bericht," p. 163; Burton and Speke, *Source of the Nile*, p. 210; BC 14 (1887–1888): 641–642.

37. Mhonda Mission Journal, September 8, 1878 and September 23, 1879; Baumann, *Usambara*, p. 271; RKA 217/16; W. H. Kisbey, "A Journey in Zigualand," p. 174. In the Mombasan hinterland, on the other hand, similar developments led to population dispersal: Thomas Spear, *The Kaya Complex*, pp. 108ff.

38. Étienne Baur, "Dans l'Oudoé et l'Ouzigoua," p. 42. Also, Picarda, "Autour de Mandera," p. 197.

39. Ernest Marno, "Bericht über eine Excursion von Zanzibar," p. 364.

40. Picarda, "Autour de Mandera," p. 234; Le Roy, "Au Kilimandjaro," pp. 197–200; Mandera Mission Journal, February 26, 1883; Mhonda Mission Journal, September 23, 1879 and August 8, 1881; Burton, *Zanzibar* 2: 198.

In the view of many modern Handeni residents, the crucial difference between weak and powerful communities was their relationship to the slave trade, a point that one villager made in this way:

> One who was weak was defeated. One who was strong defeated others. A person was able to sell people and take his own slaves. If he was a warrior, he left home and went to fight in another territory and he brought captives home. When the Arabs came, he would sell those captives to them. The people who had to sell their own sisters' sons or daughters were those who were weak. When the Arabs came, they had to sell their own sisters' sons or daughters.[41]

In the period of Zanzibari mercantile ascendancy, therefore, chieftains and their allies prospered by capturing and selling slaves; weaker communities survived scarcity, on the other hand, by pawning or surrendering their own members.[42] Consequently an individual's fate during the years of intense slave trade depended largely on whether she or he entered into or remained outside a chieftain's sphere of influence.

Hierarchy and Alliance Among the Chieftains

A hierarchy of alliances and spheres of interest enabled the chieftains to function effectively within the Zanzibar-centered system of trade despite the disorder caused by slave dealing. The chieftains' regime was two-tiered, with major figures like Mtiga and Machaku claiming as clients the leaders of small settlements, whom one European termed "vassals," within their circles of authority.[43] Witness to the interaction between one of the major chieftains, Kolwa of Miono, and a subordinate village leader, Kingaru of Mandera, were the European missionaries who lived near Kingaru in the 1880s. Kingaru acknowledged the suzerainty of his "uncle" Kolwa, "the great king of the country," whose village was located two and one-half hours' walk from Mandera. He also grudgingly accepted the missionary presence when Kolwa instructed him to make land available to the Europeans. The missionaries found Kolwa to be protective of his prerogative, however, for he resented the gifts which they made to Kingaru and

41. Nyangasi Mohamedi Munga, Kilwa.
42. Dr. Pruen, "Slavery in East Africa," p. 662 and Horner, "L'Oukami (Afrique Orientale) VI," p. 21.
43. Picarda, "Autour de Mandera," pp. 295–296; Baumann, *Usambara*, p. 276.

prohibited negotiations between the Europeans and subordinate village heads in his absence.[44]

Oral accounts rely on the idiom of kinship to depict the political changes that brought lower-tier settlement leaders such as Kingaru to power by contrasting trade-oriented leaders who ruled entire settlements with autonomous household heads of prior generations.[45] Traditions from both Mbwego and Kwediboma contend, for example, that before the time of Machaku and Pogwa Mnowowakala no one stood above the leaders of individual households. The new trading leaders, however, constructed fortified villages, induced the neighbors to relinquish their autonomy, and fulfilled many of the same functions as the major chieftains, though on a smaller scale. They obtained the labor service of subordinates, traded in ivory and slaves, kept livestock, distributed food reserves and imports to their dependents, and enforced the major chieftains' tribute demands.

Both the hierarchical relationship between major chieftains and settlement leaders as well as alliances among the chieftains removed sources of conflict along caravan routes. Because the second-tier village heads dared not demand tolls without the authorization of their superiors, the toll system did not degenerate into the disorganized pattern of numerous and unpredictable levies that would have discouraged caravans from entering Uzigua.[46] The chieftains' alliances also facilitated the movements of traders who, having established favorable relations with one chieftain, could expect hospitality from his allies as they passed through Uzigua.[47] Although Europeans such as Krapf and Burton believed that the chieftains' regime was a confusing, almost anarchic, welter of factions and animosities, in fact patterns of authority, hierarchy, and alliance regulated interaction among chieftains, village leaders and coastal traders. Indeed, the chieftains created a political structure that benefited both themselves and their merchant allies by allowing trade to flourish in spite of the predatory violence which they used to acquire power.

The evidence of the chieftains' relations with each other, with subordinate settlement heads, and with the agents of Zanzibari merchant capital

44. Picarda, "Autour de Mandera," p. 185; Mandera Mission Journal, January 30 and October 30, 1881, February 9 and July 29, 1883, June 9, 1884.

45. Traditions of village leadership were related by Omali Maligwa Kidiza, Gombero; Mdoe Nyange, Kiberashi; Saidi Hatibu (Mkonde, May 29, 1983) and Elders of Kisangasa (Kisangasa, September 17, 1982).

46. A similar pattern of orderly toll collections existed in Ugogo: Carol Jane Sissons, "Economic Prosperity in Ugogo, East Africa, 1860–1890," Chapter 3.

47. The alliances are described in the "Historia ya Wazigua" and the accounts in the collection of Musa Sefu Abdalahe.

demonstrates that they integrated Uzigua into an international commercial system and caused much of the violence that accompanied the slave trade. It reveals relatively little, however, about the political and economic relationships that affected subsistence security and the disease environment. In particular, it explains neither the chieftains' methods of accumulating wealth and dispensing patronage nor the nature of politics within their settlements. The next two chapters use different evidence, therefore, to address these matters. Chapter Four relies on missionary sources to describe relations of production within the chieftaincies. Chapter Five examines the treatment of late-precolonial political life in oral and written accounts from Handeni District.

4. Emulating the Chieftains: Patronage in the Spiritan Missions of Uzigua

At the height of their power in the 1870s and 1880s, the chieftains of Uzigua, who were accustomed to dealing with Swahili mercantile agents and other visitors from the coast, embraced a new foreign element—Catholic missionaries of the Spiritan or Holy Ghost Order. Indeed, because the missionaries were thoroughly assimilated into the political order both as the subordinates of chieftains and as the patrons of their own Zigua-speaking clients, they learned much about the social institutions of Uzigua, not only through observation, but also through their own interaction with patrons and clients. The Spiritans had little alternative to working within prevailing political and economic structures, moreover, because they won almost no Zigua-speaking converts. Hence, even though ethnocentrism and racism shaped the perspective of the Spiritans, in the course of their own affairs the missionaries gained an insider's understanding of patronage, the relationship that governed precolonial accumulation and redistribution.

The Spiritans and Slavery

Long before they entered Uzigua, Spiritan missionaries were predisposed to accommodate themselves to African institutions, for the clerics who founded the Order in 1848 exhorted their evangelists to adapt to non-European culture by "liberat[ing themselves] from Europe, from its customs and spirit," so that they might "perfect [African] practices and habits gradually."[1] In East Africa, shortages of funds and labor strengthened the accommodationist inclination, particularly because the Spiritans believed that Africans would remain unreceptive to their spiritual appeals unless

---

1. Alois Engel, *Die Missionsmethode der Missionare v. Heiligen Geist auf dem Afrikanischen Festland*, p. 41. Most of the Spiritan missionaries in Tanganyika were from Alsace.

they could demonstrate the material advantages of Christianity. They needed resources, therefore, to prove that Christianity offered, "a more advantageous and better life."[2] "Preaching alone," argued the Spiritan Étienne Baur in 1882, "is not sufficient; it cannot penetrate the hard, corrupted hearts [of adult Africans]; they must have the example of young converts, Christian families, Christian villages and missionaries."[3] Thus the Spiritans soon decided that they should establish communities of Christianized African dependents who would provide inexpensive labor for the construction of commodious, self-supporting stations and who would also serve as models of Christian obedience and industry.

Having built their first mainland mission at Bagamoyo in 1868, the Spiritans began seeking workers for a plantation that they hoped would alleviate their financial difficulties and thereby lay the groundwork for expansion into the hinterland. The easiest way to obtain labor, they quickly discovered, was to "redeem" captives at Bagamoyo's busy slave market. Indeed, Spiritan slave purchases and the establishment of a community that looked much like a *Mrima* slave plantation typify missionary adjustment to the economic and social environment, for they abided by the conventions of the slave trade, paid the going price for captives, relied on African creditors, abjured challenges to "justified" claims of slave ownership, and presented captive women to their male dependents.[4] The fine missionary distinction between "redemption" and purchase of slaves confused Africans and Europeans alike, because while the Spiritans regarded themselves as saving chattels from servitude, the individuals settled in the Bagamoyo compound unquestionably remained in a state of dependence, since, as one evangelist remarked, the mission was their only "family."[5] Besides requiring labor the Spiritans restricted the movements of their "redeemed" dependents and made attendance at religious instruction and observances mandatory.[6] The primary difference, in fact, between a Spiritan description of life among the "redeemed" slaves at Bagamoyo and colonial accounts of slavery on *Mrima* plantations is that the mission inmates

2. Alexandre Le Roy, "Lettre," (1884), p. 51.

3. Étienne Baur, "Lettre," (1882), p. 195. In this Baur was echoing an argument advanced by Anton Horner in his "Lettre" (1868), p. 67.

4. Mhonda Mission Journal, October 18, 1888; Theophil Schneider, "Missions-Korrespondenz," p. 54.

5. *BC* 14: 644.

6. At the Mandera mission, African Christians were incarcerated as punishment for attending dances: Mandera Mission Journal, January 6, 1889. Le Roy, "Lettre" (1884), p. 49; Anton Horner, "Lettres," (1865), p. 54 and (1868), p. 383; Mandera Mission Journal, June 28, 1885 and July 4, 1886.

had numerous devotional obligations.[7] Thus, the combination of their evangelistic strategy, poor financial condition and conception of African moral nature persuaded the Spiritans to participate in slave markets and develop relations with African dependents that closely resembled plantation slavery.

The Spiritans as Chieftains

From Bagamoyo the Spiritans moved inland to Uzigua, where they opened missions at Mhonda in the southern Nguu Mountains in 1878 and at Mandera in the lower Wami Valley three years later. Their continuing financial problems, difficulties in finding labor and predisposition to accommodation made the Spiritans receptive to the influence of their Zigua-speaking neighbors, whose attitudes soon convinced them that if they were to make any headway towards conversion, they must, like other leaders who held moral authority, provide a variety of services, including patronage, divination, mediation with ancestors and health care. The issue of moral and political authority led the Spiritans to regard the practitioners of all these activities as rivals, but they were particularly fearful of healers (*waganga*), or the "monsters" as one Spiritan called them, who seemed to inspire hostility to Christian teachings.[8] Although the Spiritans exaggerated the healers' powers (insisting for years that the *waganga* dictated "laws concerning the pettiest details of life from the moment of birth to the instant of death"),[9] their views stemmed from a fairly accurate assessment of the political centrality of healing and divination. *Waganga*, who were often advisors to notables if they were not political leaders themselves, possessed considerable power and frequently used it to resist Christianity.[10] Consequently, the Spiritans determined that they must supplant them if they were to acquire spiritual and political authority (see also Chapter Seven).

7. Compare Le Roy, "Lettre" (1884), p. 53 and RKA 1005/3–112 and 128–151.
8. Cado Picarda, "Autour de Mandera," p. 366.
9. Lugoba Mission Journal, February 20, 1918.
10. Picarda, "Autour de Mandera," pp. 227, 246, 332, 334, 342 and 368; Joseph Karst, "Lettre," (1891), p. 35; Raoul de Courmont, "Lettre," (1885), p. 337; Gommenginger, letter of January 7, 1883 in Hück, *P. Ludwig Karl Gommenginger*, p. 198; Horner, "Lettre," (1874), p. 426 and "De Bagamoyo à l'Oukami," p. 133; James T. Last, "The Tribes on the Road to Mpwapwa," p. 661.

Figure 2. Facets of healing and belief. The inset, framed by red sorghum from which libations were brewed, shows a grave-site where ancestors were venerated. Suspended between the stalks are various medicines, including one intended to ensure fertility. Source: *LMC* 18 (1886): 282.

The Spiritans tried to subvert the *waganga* by proving their superiority as healers and diviners, but in so doing they made another accommodation by competing against the *waganga* within the structure of prevailing practices and beliefs. At Bagamoyo they went so far as to imitate the dress and appearance of *waganga*, and then, having gained permission to visit children and secluded women, administered baptisms while explaining the sacrament as a therapy.[11] In Uzigua, a smallpox epidemic in 1883 provided another opportunity for missionaries to compete with the *waganga*, for after vaccinating the African mission inmates at Mhonda and watching unvaccinated villagers succumb to the epidemic, the Spiritans denounced as frauds the *waganga* who treated the smallpox victims. Although the missionaries believed that their standing improved as the epidemic's progress exposed the ineffectuality of the *waganga*,[12] the healers steadfastly resisted Christian influence, defended their right to determine the fate of witches who were blamed for sickness, and defiantly constructed ancestor shrines near the Mhonda mission.[13]

The Spiritans insisted, nevertheless, that they gained authority and stimulated interest in Christianity by providing medicine.[14] But as the Spiritan François Coulbois remarked, it was not enough merely to dispense medicines: they must also demonstrate their power to influence spiritual forces.[15] To this end, the Spiritans sought to replace not only the *waganga*, but also the *wegazi*, the individuals who, in addition to mediating between the living and the ancestors, were often political leaders who might serve as healers as well (see Chapter Five). The missionaries interfered with ancestor veneration and destroyed shrines where such rituals were performed, although here again the Spiritan position was essentially accommodationist, because their purpose was less to eradicate belief in the powers of ancestor spirits than to defeat the *waganga* and *wegazi* and

11. Courmont, "Lettre" (1885), pp. 322–324 and "Lettre," (1887) p. 101.

12. Mhonda Mission Journal, May 28–29, 1883; T. R. P. Emouet, "Nouvelles de la Mission du Sacré-Coeur de Mhonda," p. 39; Picarda, "Autour de Mandera," pp. 283–284; Baur, "Lettre," (1884), p. 337. Other accounts of Spiritans as healers are in Le Roy, "Lettre" (1884), p. 55; Charles Gommenginger, "Lettre," (1889), p. 347; Karst, "Lettre" (1891), pp. 34–36; Maskati Mission Journal, April 1911 and May 1914.

13. Courmont, "Lettre" (1887), p. 101; Mhonda Mission Journal, September 4, 1893.

14. For example, Baur, "Lettre" (1884), pp. 335–337; Emouet, "Nouvelles," p. 37; "Rapport d'ensemble sur la mission de Mandera," pp. 17 and 26; *BC* 15 (1889–1891): 725; Le Roy, "Au Kilimandjaro," p. 199; Roger Dussercle, *Du Kilima-ndjaro au Cameroun: Monseigneur F.-X. Vogt (1870–1943)*, p. 45. By opposing the methods used to control witchcraft, however, the missionaries created suspicion that they themselves were witches: Mandera Mission Journal, April 21, 1881 and September 12, 1883.

15. François Coulbois, "Une tournée dans le Vicariat Apostolique de Zanguebar, Oct.–Nov. 1884," p. 501.

interpose themselves between the living and ancestors. Accordingly, the Spiritans built their church at Mhonda on the site of an ancestor shrine and incorporated Zigua terms concerning ancestor veneration into their liturgical vocabulary.[16]

While the Spiritans channeled much of their energy into rivalries with *waganga* and *wegazi*, they also staked out spheres of influence within the chieftains' political hierarchy. The palisaded Mhonda station became a formidable political force and a base from which the missionaries launched raids, including the attack that sixty of their supporters mounted on a neighboring village in 1886.[17] Their assault, commented the mission journalist, taught "a lesson, a somewhat rough lesson . . . to the enemy . . . and the prestige of the mission has grown immensely."[18] The Spiritans' power at Mhonda increased dramatically in 1889 after German colonial invaders subdued resistance in the *Mrima* towns. Barely one week after hearing that the principal resistance leader, Bushiri, had been executed by the Germans, many settlement heads descended on the mission with offerings of goats and sheep to request letters stating that they were under mission protection.[19] Steady improvement in the mission's position over the next few years led early German colonial administrators to consider it the "major chiefdom" of southern Nguu.

The place of the Mandera mission in the chieftains' hierarchy was quite different, however, because the Mandera Spiritans were tributaries of an important chieftain, Kolwa of Miono. The mission's founder, Cado Picarda, initiated the relationship by bringing Kolwa gifts of rice, goats, and a coat; thereafter, Picarda's successors rendered annual payments of cloth and currency. Their subordination to Kolwa did not, however, prevent the Mandera missionaries from collecting tribute in surrounding villages. Yet even after the German victory along the *Mrima* in 1889, the Spiritans continued to respect Kolwa, who secured a position in the colonial administration.[20]

While the Spiritans acted as political notables by providing healing,

16. Emouet, "Nouvelles," pp. 39–40; Baur, "Lettre" (1884), p. 337.

17. Mhonda Mission Journal, March 1881, July 17, 1883, February 4, 1884, January 12, 1887. Also, see Horst Grunder, *Christliche Mission und Deutscher Imperialismus, 1884–1914*, pp. 203–204.

18. Mhonda Mission Journal, December 13, 23–24, 1886.

19. Mhonda Mission Journal, December 31, 1889, January 3 and September 18, 1890; RKA 855/114.

20. Mhonda Mission Journal, January 15, February 9 and May 3, 1883. Similarly, the Spiritans at Morogoro became tributaries of the chieftain Simbamwene: Karst, "Lettre," p. 36.

mediation with ancestors, and protection for their allies, they also emulated the chieftains by furnishing the trade connections and patronage that persuaded their neighbors to tolerate the missionary presence.[21] The missionaries bought crops, distributed imports, sent dependents to purchase ivory in Maasailand, and acquired slaves, some of whom they settled at Mhonda and Mandera and others whom they transferred to Bagamoyo.[22] As did their colleagues at Bagamoyo, the missionaries in Uzigua accepted the practices of slave dealers, in one instance reluctantly declining to intervene when a captive who had taken refuge in the Mhonda station was reclaimed by her master and carried bodily out of the mission.[23] The "redeemed" mission inmates were not their only dependents, however, for neighboring farmers and pastoralists also sought mission protection and assistance, particularly in the form of livestock. Numerous individuals pawned themselves or their dependents to the Spiritans, including one leader who compensated the Spiritans for stolen mission property by leaving control of "five or six" settlements in missionary hands. Whenever their patronal authority was challenged, moreover, the Spiritans abided by convention in using force to maintain their status. On one occasion in 1887, for example, they sent forty armed men to seize the female dependents of a client who had absconded with trade goods.[24]

Because their dependents held the missionaries to the same standards of obligation that were incumbent on other patrons and chieftains, they expected them to provide bridewealth and held them liable for restitution when a mission subordinate committed a crime. Thus the Mhonda mission had to pay a sizeable quantity of burial cloth in compensation for an injury inflicted by one client in 1889.[25] Indeed, the extent of the "trust" placed in the Spiritan patrons by their dependents astonished one early colonial official,[26] who appeared unaware that the relationship was grounded less

21. These activities set the Catholic missions apart from the missions of the Church Missionary Society in Ukaguru. Although the CMS adopted some practices which resembled tribute relationships, its missionaries tended to renounce secular concerns, particularly commercial affairs: Thomas O. Beidelman, *Colonial Evangelism*, pp. 116–117 and 145.

22. Mandera Mission Journal, November 11–13, 1883, August 18, 1889.

23. Mhonda Mission Journal, February 1 and 5, 1886. Also on slave purchases: Courmont, "Rapport " (1889), p. 54ff.

24. Picarda, "Autour de Mandera," p. 356; "Rapport d'ensemble sur la mission de Mandera" (1886), p. 24; Mandera Mission Journal, May 30, 1883; Emouet, "Nouvelles," p. 37; Mhonda Mission Journal, February 16–17, 1883, February 19, March 22–24 and 29, and June 7, 1887, July 4, 1888, September 18, 1890 and March 25, 1892; Courmont, "Rapport," (1894), p. 83; Karst, "Lettre," p. 36; RKA 856/113–115.

25. Maskati Mission Journal, October 1914; Mhonda Mission Journal, September 7, 1889 and April 24, 1911.

26. RKA 855/114.

in African faith in the benevolence of European evangelists than in the concepts of reciprocal obligation that governed interaction between all patrons and dependents.

Relations of Agricultural Production

Like Zigua-speaking patrons, the missionaries used the labor of dependents to cultivate large fields, for in addition to employing the mission inmates, they also adopted the practice of neighboring communities by organizing day-long work parties at which they provided food and drink to groups from neighboring villages who performed field work. Their neighbors also entered short term mission employment on an individual basis to earn foodstuffs, cloth, and currency. At Mhonda, the Spiritans engaged many highlanders who, after becoming indebted to the mission during the famine of 1884–1886 (see Chapter Eight), retired their debts by working in mission fields and paying part of their own harvests to the missionaries.[27] Indeed, the readiness of many villagers to work for hire indicates that they were accustomed to agricultural labor outside the household.[28]

Over the years, labor service for the mission and redistribution from the Spiritan granaries acquired a seasonal rhythm. Zigua-speaking clients worked in the mission fields during the hoeing and harvesting seasons, laboring particularly in the pre-harvest months of January, February, and March for grain to carry them until the next harvest. At harvest-time they sold their own maize and sorghum to the Spiritans for cloth.[29] "The Zigua," related a missionary in 1888, "have rendered us valuable service in the cultivation of our fields and vegetable gardens, as well as in a great number of other necessary tasks. . . . They also bring the products of the fields and their poultry which they sell to us at low prices. Likewise they come looking for work at the mission, in order to get something to wear."[30] As the number of farmers who depended upon the Mhonda

27. Mhonda Mission Journal, 1878–1879 and January 19, 1881, March–May 1884, May 14, August 19, 21 and 31, 1886; Mandera Mission Journal, July 21, 1884 and April 1885.
28. For a contrary view, see Deborah Bryceson, *Food Insecurity and the Social Division of Labour in Tanzania, 1919–1985*, p. 39.
29. Mandera Mission Journal, July 4, August 8 and 12, 1887, February 18–20, 1888; Picarda, "Autour de Mandera," p. 249; Coulbois, "Une Tournée," p. 498; Baur, "Lettre" (1884), p. 339.
30. *BC* 14: 640–641.

mission increased throughout the 1890s, some of those who relied on the mission for food and imports became permanently indebted to the Spiritans. In 1893, more than 500 farmers (including at least 200 women) were engaged in construction projects at Mhonda, while at least 100 village heads sent subjects to do agricultural labor under the Spiritans. These patterns of employment and redistribution endured at Mhonda and other Spiritan missions through the German colonial period.[31]

The arrangements between the Spiritans and their short-term employees, as well as the sense of rights and obligations that regulated their relations, evidently derived from similar relationships in the farming villages of Uzigua, for the chieftains, like the missionaries, employed dependents and clients seasonally. During hoeing seasons, when food stocks were low and the need for labor was greatest, chieftains and other patrons engaged workers whom they compensated with grain and root crops. They also distributed food during seasonal shortages with the understanding that it would be repaid at the next harvest, and thus ensured, wrote Father Picarda, that no one would suffer excessively from food shortages.[32] Their dependents replenished grain reserves by performing labor service, making tributary contributions, and repaying part of their own harvests to creditors.

Perhaps the largest community in which these relationships prevailed was Morogoro, the town founded by Kisabengo. A center of trade, rest stop for caravans, and home of slave raiders, Morogoro contained 300 houses. Beyond the town's walls was a broad plain cultivated in maize, sorghum, sugar cane, beans, bananas, and other crops.[33] Spiritan missionaries first visited Morogoro in 1882 during the hoeing season, and one night they saw how field work was organized:

> While we were conversing, a public crier went by, blowing into an antelope horn as he passed through the streets of the village, and shouting at the top of his voice: 'Tomorrow and the day after, all the men from around here must go to Mwanagomera's place to work in his fields and drink his beer.' The next morning, everyone heeded the call.[34]

31. Mandera Mission Journal, September 16–20, 1883, July 21, 25 and 27, 1884, April 1885; Mhonda Mission Journal, September 13 and 27 and October 15–19, 1889, January 1, 1890, December 15, 1891, June 9, 1911, February 16, 1912, November 9, 1914; Maskati Mission Journal, January 1910, May 1914, November 1915; Lugoba Mission Journal, June 9, 1912, June 26, 1914; BC 16: 723; RKA 6467/140.
32. Picarda, "Autour de Mandera," p. 246.
33. Baur, "Dans l'Oudoé et l'Ouzigoua," pp. 86–88; Mandera Mission Journal, February 21, 1882.
34. Baur, "Dans l'Oudoé et l'Ouzigoua," pp. 84–85.

Just as did farmers throughout Uzigua, residents of the village of Mwa-nagomera, the husband of Morogoro's chieftain Simbamwene, joined obligatory work parties to cultivate the fields of their patron.[35] The Spiritans also observed the same practice south of the Wami River, where leaders distributed provisions in return for their subjects' labor and tribute. Food was most abundant, therefore, in the chieftains' villages.[36]

By accumulating food reserves through labor service and tribute, and also, at least in the immediate coastal hinterland, by using *Mrima* connections to import foodstuffs, the chieftains became the principal sources of subsistence during scarcity. Their ability to accumulate food stocks, state some residents of modern Handeni, created both power and servility. "If someone had food," explained one farmer, "he would be the chief and would rule everyone. Many people were kept in servility [*utumwa*] by [the chieftains'] control of food. So when someone achieved mastery of farming ["*ushujaa wa jembe*"], his hoe brought him slaves."[37] The relations between patrons and clients were not only the primary means of accumulation and redistribution in late precolonial Uzigua, however, but also the basis of disease control, for by providing dependents with subsistence they averted widespread migration and permitted farmers to continue management of vegetation despite scarcity. Consequently, the claims of patrons on their dependents' labor, and the counterclaims of dependents on their patrons' wealth were the main sources of late-precolonial political conflict.

35. Mandera Mission Journal, January 16, 1883 and J. Kohler, "Beantwortung des Fragebogens über die Rechte der Eingeborenen in der deutsche Kolonien," Rhodes House, Micr. Afr. 480.

36. Horner, "L'Oukami (Afrique Orientale) IV and VI," (1873), p. 623 and (1874), p. 21.

37. M. A. Mavullah, speaking with Hasani Bakari and others (Balanga, May 23, 1983). Similar comments were made by Mohamedi Mjewe (Kwediboma, September 27, 1982).

5. Ambition and Obligation in Late-Precolonial Politics

Late-precolonial farming communities controlled the disease environment not simply by clearing and burning vegetation, nor even merely by producing foodstuffs and circulating them among patrons and clients, for the politics of patronage played a major role. Political conflicts often determined entitlement to patronage, and thus guaranteed or denied clients the resources needed to continue working the land during droughts and crop failures. The primary sources of information about precolonial politics are accounts from Uzigua which describe the chieftains' lives and the settlement of small territories called *si*. They suggest that political conflicts involved ambitious individuals who tried to overcome the restraint of reciprocal obligations and dependents who tried to check ambition by constraining adherence to the norms of reciprocity. None of these stories are better-known in Handeni District, however, than those which concern the most famous of the first-generation chieftains, Mhelamwana.

Mhelamwana

Residents of Manga, the birthplace of Mhelamwana in southeastern Handeni District, say that when his parents died shortly after his birth, the community concluded that Mhelamwana must be a *kigego* (pl. *vigego*), an individual marked by peculiarities of physical appearance or circumstances surrounding birth as one who will cause death or misfortune to befall those around him. Thus, when the boy's fearful kin urged Kimambulizo, a relative who had taken responsibility for the orphan, to banish the maleficent child, he sent Mhelamwana to live with a man named Kijiamahungwe in the nearby region of Udoe. Years later, when Mhelamwana was an adolescent, he happened to be taunting a playmate one day by boasting,

"Don't you know I am the son of Kijiamahungwe?" when his companion blurted out what everyone else knew, that Mhelamwana was not really Kijiamahungwe's son. After confronting Kijiamahungwe, who told him that his father was Kimambulizo, Mhelamwana set out for Manga to visit him.

Though Doe country is not far from Manga, the oral accounts say that Mhelamwana spent many nights in uninhabited woodland following the old winding footpaths before emerging at Kwangandu, a village only a few miles from Manga. A group of girls preparing to cook were the first to see him, and when they noticed his hair long and garments dirty from many days in the woodland, they laughed and teased Mhelamwana, whereupon, with characteristic impetuosity, he drew his knife and murdered one of them. Immediately he was captured by the men of Kwangandu, who decided that rather than execute him, they would send him into combat with a hostile settlement in the hope that he would slay some of their enemies before being killed. Mhelamwana avoided fighting, however, and upon his return to Kwangandu asked the father of the murdered girl for water. The man was leading him to his homestead when Mhelamwana treacherously shot an arrow into his back, then clubbed him to death. The terrified young men of Kwangandu fled, leaving their elders to try to accommodate Mhelamwana by offering a wife, cattle, goats, and slaves if he would agree to settle among them peacefully. Before consenting to the offer, however, Mhelamwana visited Kimambulizo, who greeted him with consternation, for he was in the midst of preparations for his son's wedding and felt obliged to provide Mhelamwana with a wife before his own sons, all his juniors, married. He was relieved, therefore, to hear of the proposal from the Kwangandu elders, and urged Mhelamwana to accept it.[1]

In this way, relate the Manga accounts, Mhelamwana gained power in the country from which he had been banished as a child. Having terrorized Kwangandu, he consolidated his authority by inducing the villagers to grant him a wife. Later, Mhelamwana's deferential gestures to Kimambulizo won him both recognition as a member of his guardian's *si* group and the right to reside at Manga, where he would control one of

1. Yusufu Selemani, Abedi Juma, Mohamedi Waziri, Mohamedi Nasoro and Idi Sefu, Manga; Ali Bakari Kimonje, Nassoro Ali Kajeze, Saidi Mdoe and Athumani Sevingi Magati (Handeni, April 28, 1983); Ernest Mkomwa, Kwa Masaka; Mohamedi Mjewe (Kwediboma, September 27, 1982); "Historia ya Wazigua," pp. 19–20; R. S. Kilango, S. M. Mbwana and L. Abdallah, "Historia ya Ufalme"; Anthony Mochiwa, *Habari za Wazigua*, pp. 8–9, 37, 47.

the more favorable locations for settlement in the *miombo* woodland of eastern Uzigua.[2] Situated on the seasonally-flowing Mligasi River about forty-five miles from the Indian Ocean, Manga offered water sources, alluvial soils and a location from which Mhelamwana could monitor the caravan traffic of three *Mrima* ports opposite Zanzibar—Sadani, Mkwaja and Kipumbwe. At Manga, moreover, Mhelamwana was close enough to Sadani to trade regularly with coastal merchants.

The Sadani merchants supplied Mhelamwana with firearms, ammunition, cloth and grain in return for ivory and slaves which, in the early years of commercial expansion before the routinization of toll collecting, he seized from coastward-bound caravans.[3] Having thereby armed his dependents, Mhelamwana embarked on the more notorious phase of his career marked by slave raiding and sales of captives to the Zanzibaris. The size of Mhelamwana's arsenal and his profligate use of slave labor are legendary; one story, told in Johann Krapf's time and still related throughout Handeni District, has Mhelamwana ordering slaves to bail water from the Strait of Zanzibar so that he might cross over to the island by foot. Another legend tells of Mhelamwana's attempt to dissipate heavy fog by having his soldiers discharge their guns into the air, while more grisly tales, reminiscent of South African stories associated with Shaka Zulu, depict his cruel treatment of slaves and subjects.

Although their lurid elements fascinate listeners, the deeper attraction of the Mhelamwana stories lies in their ability to encapsulate, and thus inspire reflection and comment upon, the tumultuous developments that brought to power Mhelamwana and the other chieftains of his era. The accounts encourage consideration of different factors and interpretations of these events because, while they make prominent the Zanzibari mercantile connection, they do not attribute Mhelamwana's emergence solely to dealings with traders. Instead, they point out that he entered kinship and affinal relationships which sanctioned his authority, but which also demanded of him, besides a certain degree of deference to elders, the fulfillment of reciprocal obligations. Thus, while in the oral accounts Mhelamwana is a paragon of ambition, his ruthless pursuit of self-interest is constrained by mutual responsibilities.

2. Thomas Beidelman points out that the significance of Mhelamwana's identity as a *kigego* extends to his career as an exploitative political leader, because *vigego* were believed to be capable of sapping the strength of people around them (personal communication). I am also grateful to Allen Roberts for his comparative insights on *vigego*.

3. Abedi Juma, Manga.

Si Traditions, *Si* Identities and Social Tensions

The tension between ambition and obligation is expressed not only in stories of Mhelamwana and other chieftains, but also in accounts which describe the settlement of small territories called *si* in Zigua and *nchi* in Swahili. The settlers, who generally are farmers searching for empty land, usually include a male leader and several women who are considered to be the founders of matrilineages.[4] These cultivating settlers are regarded as honored ancestors by those who inherit the name of their *si* (individuals customarily take the matrilineal *si* names, or *kolwa*, of both parents).[5] The *si* name bearers believe that they belong to a large group, sometimes referred to as "*lukolo*" in Zigua and "*ukoo*" in Swahili, which, they assume, comprises the matrilineages that descend from the female settlers.

Because the social origins of *si* founders are not specified, they appear to be free of entangling relationships that would have complicated efforts to establish autonomous communities. The stories rarely mention the founders' prior membership in a *si* community.[6] Numerous traditions depict them as migrants from distant places, such as the Lake Nyasa region or Uhehe in southern Tanzania.[7] Yet even in the more common stories which recount short movements within Uzigua or between Uzigua and adjacent areas, *si* founders' origins remain obscure. Among the traditions involving short-distance migrations are accounts from the Nguu highlands which ascribe the establishment of *si* to newcomers from Ukaguru, the mountainous region lying not far to the southwest. One of them is told by the "Wanjeja" of Kwa Dundwa Village, a group that, like many others in Nguu, shares its *si* name with inhabitants of Ukaguru.[8] The first part of their story, which describes the lone wanderings of the female founder of their *si* before she reaches Ukaguru, shows that she belonged to no *si*

4. Ernest Mkomwa, Kwa Masaka; Paul Nkanyemka (Muheza-Hedigongo, August 18, 1983); Omali Gumbo, Kwinji; "Historia ya Wazigua"; Anthony Mochiwa, *Habari za Wazigua*, pp. 3–5. *Si* are discussed in Mwalumwambo A. O. M. Muya, "A Political Economy of Zigua Utani," in *Utani Relationships*.

5. Ernest Mkomwa and Godfrey Nkwileh, "Jadi, Mila, Desturi na Historia ya Wazigua," pp. 55–56.

6. "Historia ya Wazigua," Handeni District Book, vol. 1, TNA, p. 6.

7. Omali Gumbo, Kwinji and Rashidi Mwenjuma Manyagala, Kilwa.

8. "Historia ya Wazigua," pp. 5–6; Omali Maligwa Kidiza, Gombero. For similarities between Kaguru and Nguu traditions, see three works by Thomas O. Beidelman: *Moral Imagination in Kaguru Modes of Thought*, p. 70 and Chapters 5 and 10; "Kaguru Oral Literature: Discussion (Tanzania)"; and "Kaguru Descent Groups," pp. 373–396. Professor Beidelman goes far beyond the present study, of course, in drawing complex meaning from these traditions.

community and was unrestricted by obligations that would have impinged upon the independence of her *si*.[9]

Like other *si* founders' stories as well as tales of chieftains, however, the Kwa Dundwa story hinges on a struggle for autonomous control of dependents despite cross-cutting obligations. Indeed, although the narrators of some *si* traditions suppress signs of conflict that mar their image of harmoniously coexisting *si* groups, the elements of tension in the Kwa Dundwa story are typical of *si* accounts. The Kwa Dundwa *si*, relates the oral tradition, was established by Feda, a native of the mountains overlooking Kwa Dundwa Valley who married Chume (the *si*-less female founder) while living temporarily in Ukaguru. After assembling a group of dependents in Ukaguru, he and Chume moved them to Kwa Dundwa where, because they were living far from their kin, he enjoyed unfettered authority over them and used their support to prevail over his brother in a contest for the valley.[10] Thus the plots of this and other *si* traditions, which frequently recount the division of *si* and subsequent foundation of new *si*, intimate not only that rivalries frequently caused the breakup and formation of groups, but also that conflicts over scarce riverine and valley-bottom soils were common, for certainly one purpose of the *si* traditions was to lay claims to land.

Although the *si* founders' accounts describe the creation of what might be thought of as clans composed of several matrilineages, the bearers of a *si* name are not a corporate descent group. Indeed, few people actually live in the neighborhoods where they believe their *si* ancestors settled.[11] Just as is the case now, in fact, the ties of most nineteenth-century Uzigua residents to their *si* were little more than their names and some sketchy, perhaps apocryphal information about *si* locations. The element of uncertainty, however, is what allowed *si* identities to play a part in consolidating loyalties grounded not in kinship, but in politics. Because everyone had an inherited relationship with at least two *si*, and because knowledge of *si* locations, relations among *si*, and membership in *si* groups was imprecise, the possibilities for rediscovering forgotten genealogical relationships were endless. Hence neighbors connected primarily by proximity and subordination to a patron or political notable might well

9. Abdala Hamani Msede and Ali Omali Kipande, Kwa Dundwa.
10. Movements over long distances are often invoked in accounts from Handeni to explain why descent groups lose members, for example, Mkomwa and Nkwileh, "Jadi," p. 40.
11. Alexandre Le Roy, "À la découverte " (1887), p. 309.

discover that they also shared with their leader descent from common *si* founders, and might therefore find reason to participate together in the rituals which the leader conducted to honor ancestors.[12]

Si identities were much less important, however, than political relationships, as the practice of naming settlements after incumbent village leaders, rather than according to *si* designations, indicates. Thus an individual's mental map of Uzigua reflected knowledge of political relations rather than descent.[13] The primacy of politics is acknowledged, moreover, even by those modern residents of Uzigua who conceive of a traditional precolonial society composed of discrete descent groups in autonomous *si*, for they must reconcile this image with their knowledge of political change. The unpublished depiction of precolonial Uzigua written in 1968 by Ernest L. Mkomwa and Godfrey Nkwileh, for example, explains the origin of descent group leadership by invoking the political circumstances surrounding the emergence of Mhelamwana and other chieftains.[14] Mkomwa and Nkwileh contend that during the constant slave raiding of the last turbulent precolonial decades, *si* groups vested authority in leaders (*wegazi*, sing. *mwigazi*) who knew the history of relations between *si*. They did this, say Mkomwa and Nkwileh, because knowledge of past conflicts with other *si* would help them to avoid marriages with old enemies, who were apt to turn wives obtained from former opponents into slaves: "This was the source of the obligation to respect one's mother's brothers (*wajomba*). It was necessary that there be supervision of the *ukoo*, especially for the women." In this way, Mkomwa and Nkwileh situate their idealized image of a kinship-based society in political history by explaining an institution associated with descent groups as a response to changing political conditions.

While political authority and loyalties held together communities, *si*

12. Robert Harms has used the term "clan" in discussing groups which, like the *si* communities of Uzigua, were "grounded in a place and a shrine, not in blood relationships." Robert Harms, *Games Against Nature: An Eco-Cultural History of the Nunu of Equatorial Africa*, p. 150. Similarly, David Lan identifies a close association between "clan," a group which derives "its coherence from an undemonstrable claim to common descent from an unspecified ancestor," and territory. "If you live for a long time in a 'foreign' territory," writes Lan, "gradually you may come to be adopted into the clan of that territory and to be treated as such by other clan members." David Lan, *Guns and Rain: Guerrillas and Spirit Mediums in Zimbabwe*, pp. 22–25. A study of the Uzaramo region south of Uzigua gives a similar impression of "clan": Marja-Liisa Swantz, *Ritual and Symbol in Transitional Zaramo Society with Special Reference to Women*, pp. 112–116.

13. Cado Picarda, "Autour de Mandera," p. 235 and François Coulbois, "Une tournée dans le Vicariat Apostolique de Zanguebar," p. 513.

14. Mkomwa and Nkwileh, "Jadi," Chapter 10.

identities nevertheless played an important role in sanctioning political leadership and facilitating the assimilation of newcomers. Villagers gave captives and their children *si* names, for example, when they entered the settlements of their masters.[15] Communities also altered *si* identities and associated traditions to confirm genealogical links with newcomers or to enhance a leader's legitimacy by showing that he descended not merely from the *si* founders, but from the founder of the *si*'s senior lineage. *Si* traditions continued to be modified for political purposes in the colonial period, especially during the 1920s, 1930s, and 1940s, when accounts recorded in writing placed British-appointed functionaries in the same lines of descent with *si* founders and renowned chieftains of the nineteenth century.[16]

One instance of change in *si* identity involved the son of Mani, the client of Mhelamwana who founded a chieftaincy at Magamba in central Handeni. After the death of Mani in 1884, his son Sonyo was challenged by dissident subjects who, united both by *si* identity and common political interests, asserted that Mani had been a usurper. Sonyo's opponents, the bearers of the Kwa Luguru *si* name, went so far as to repudiate Mani by refusing to permit his burial in what they considered to be their *si* (a form of posthumous condemnation also suffered by other chieftains).[17] They thus forced Sonyo to inter him a considerable distance from Magamba. Some modern residents of Magamba keep alive the views of the chieftains' adversaries in a story which combines an account of the Kwa Luguru *si* founders with a description of Mani's violent conquest of the neighborhood. Indeed, the name "Mani," or literally "uncultivated grass," suggests someone who rises without fostering, just as grass grows without husbandry, and thus connotes appropriation of power by an outsider as opposed to authority achieved through community consent. This interpretation rebuts another version of Mani's career related by the chieftains' self-described descendants, who stress his peaceful assimilation into the settlement.[18]

Sonyo responded to this challenge by forming a new *si* community in

15. Ali Mohamedi Masomo, Mgera; Father Strick, "Organisation of the Tribe-Clan" (1935), Morogoro Province Book, TNA.
16. "Historia ya Wazigua."
17. Mani was buried at Mzimkuru, some distance from Magamba: RKA 217/7. Bungire, a ruler at Kilwa in northern Nguu who was reputed to be a rapacious slave dealer, was also refused burial: Abdala Hamani Msede and Ali Omali Kipande, Kwa Dundwa and Rashidi Mwenjuma Manyagala, Kilwa.
18. "Historia ya Wazigua"; Elders of Magamba and their "Asili ya Kwa Luguru"; Abedi Juma, Manga; Ernest Mkomwa, Kwa Masaka.

order to destroy the unity of the Kwa Luguru group. He began performing ancestor veneration, or *matambiko*, at his father's burial place,[19] knowing that because people think of their own *si* as the place where they prefer to hold such ceremonies and to inter fellow *si* group members, participation by his subjects would hasten their acceptance of the *si* identity which Sonyo claimed through descent from Mani. Although most of his subjects presumably had no relationship with the *si* of Sonyo's father, traditions could be revised to accommodate newly-discovered links with its founders.

Should his subjects become convinced that they shared a *si* identity with Sonyo, they would probably consider him a *mwigazi*, or one of the "chief guardians of the laws and good order of each Zigua *si* group ['*ukoo*']."[20] A community examined *si* names (*kolwa*), say Mkomwa and Nkwileh, when it determined whether someone possessed the "trustworthiness" to be the "keeper of the secrets of the *ukoo*."[21] As *wegazi*, rulers like Sonyo not only gained prestige, since "the *mwigazi* is deeply respected by those under his guardianship ['*uigazi*']," but also occupied a position which required participation in many everyday affairs.[22] For example, in addition to conducting *matambiko*, the *mwigazi* celebrated a newborn's entry into the community by performing the first haircut, gave advice about suitable matrimonial partners and received a portion of bridewealth, presided at marriage ceremonies, collected fines levied against adulterers, supervised burials, and provided food for post-burial feasts.[23] Constant intervention in domestic affairs gave the leaders who served as *wegazi* far-reaching influence and made their exercise of power appear as an essential and commonplace aspect of daily life.[24] At the same time, dependents expected them all the more to safeguard community health and welfare.

As the example of Magamba under Sonyo demonstrates, both rulers and their opponents modified *si* identities and traditions to cement loyal-

---

19. RKA 217/7.

20. Mkomwa and Nkwileh, "Jadi," p. 53.

21. Mkomwa and Nkwileh, "Jadi," pp. 40 and 55.

22. Mkomwa and Nkwileh, "Jadi," p. 4.

23. Mkomwa and Nkwileh, pp. 4, 8–9, 30 and 53–56; Secretary, *Makintano* (Mgera Native Court) to Secretary, *Ufungilo*, Handeni (April 16, 1959), Handeni District File 4/1, "Mgera: Administration"; Dale, "An Account of the Principal Customs and Habits of Natives Inhabiting the Bondei Country," p. 184; Thomas McVicar, "Sibs and Names Among the Wanguru," p. 104 and "Death Rites Among the Waluguru and Wanguru," p. 31.

24. Karen Fields touches upon this aspect of political authority in arguing that "African rulers commanded important nodes of routine—coming of age as a man or woman, marriage and divorce, access to property and livelihood, inheritance, cure, judgement of disputes . . . and religious rites that made collections of individuals into self-conscious units": Fields, *Revival and Rebellion in Colonial Central Africa*, p. 59.

ties, justify exclusion, legitimate power, and challenge authority. The *si* traditions were politically charged, however, not only because they could be changed for political ends, but also because they brought into the open the tension between ambition for power and the restraint of mutual obligations. Any retelling of the *si* stories could become the occasion for reflection upon this theme.[25]

Patronage and the Ideal and Reality of Household Autonomy

Many residents of Uzigua shared with Feda, the Kwa Dundwa *si* founder, the ambition for independent control over dependents. In practice, however, few of them could hope to achieve more than partial authority, because their subordinates were subject to overlapping and cross-cutting obligations. Indeed, the need to balance and resolve conflicting claims on individuals is a central theme in the account of precolonial society written by Mkomwa and Nkwileh. They see such conflicts arising especially between an individual's two *si* communities and emphasize the existence of rivalry by dwelling on the rituals that signified membership in the *father*'s matrilineal *si* community, apparently because they assume that the relationship with the mother's matrilineal *si* group is so well understood as to require only brief treatment. Accordingly, while they comment briefly on the role of a mother's matrilineal *si* group in the rites that follow birth, they devote more attention to the ceremony at which a child is given the father's matrilineal *si* name. Mkomwa and Nkwileh repeatedly advise deference to both *si* groups, noting, for example, that members of a woman's two *si* groups should be kept informed of negotiations leading to marriage because "that's the time to show respect for the givers of each child's names."[26]

Competition for rights in persons, Mkomwa and Nkwileh write, was publicly expressed and symbolically resolved in post-burial rites. They describe ritualized quarrels over inheritance, which ideally involve the deceased's father and the *mwigazi* of the deceased's matrilineal *si* group acting as representatives of two *si* communities:

25. Themes of conflict can be pursued much further through the oral literature of the region, as Steven Feierman's *The Shambaa Kingdom* and Thomas Beidelman's *Moral Imagination*, especially Chapter 11, have demonstrated.

26. Mkomwa and Nkwileh, "Jadi," p. 7.

If they were both there, the father would begin by saying that the deceased child's clothes were his, and not the *mwigazi*'s. The *mwigazi* would respond that the clothes were his and not the father's. It would continue this way for fourteen rounds. Each one would say it seven times. . . . Finally, an elder would stop them, saying that someone ought to bring some juicy meat to the two fireplaces [each *si* group had started its own fire]. . . . Then the father or the *mwigazi* would bring a leg or side of beef or perhaps a whole goat which would be cooked at the two fires and eaten. Thereupon the elder would ask the father, "How many children do you have [with the deceased's mother]?" The father would answer, "two," and he and the *mwigazi* would agree on this point. The elder would then ask how many fireplaces there were, and again they would agree that there were two. In this way they found a solution to the problem of the clothes: the elder child's clothes would go to the father's group, the younger child's to the *mwigazi*'s group. If there was only one child, the clothes would go to someone who belonged to both sides, perhaps a grandchild. This is how they avoided disputes over the way things were divided.[27]

Similar disputes were considered by a colonial-period Native Court in Handeni District, which decided that inheritance should go to the group that had paid the deceased's bridewealth.[28] The court, which tried to apply "the customs of the past [that] deserve to be preserved and written down," thereby affirmed not only the existence of conflicting rights over individuals, but also its belief that in the past wealth allowed a group to prevail in such competition.

Because most persons were subject, therefore, to the authority of matrilineal and patrilineal kin, patrons, and political leaders, an individual rarely attained autonomous control of dependents, even though such authority remained a powerful aspiration, a measure of personal maturity and achievement. Indeed, while residential groups could be sizeable, particularly because they could include dependent non-kin as well as a core group of kin,[29] they were not necessarily the focus of the most enduring loyalties and affections, for their members were tied as firmly to outside social networks as to co-residents. Multiple loyalties led many individuals, such as the young men who moved between the homes of their fathers and their mothers' brothers, to make frequent changes of residence.[30]

27. Mkomwa and Nkwileh, "Jadi," pp. 28–29. Also, McVicar, "Death Rites," pp. 34–35.

28. Secretary, *Makintano* (Mgera Native Court) to Secretary, *Ufungilo*, Handeni (April 16, 1959), Handeni District File 4/1.

29. Cado Picarda, "Autour de Mandera," p. 227 and Burton, "The Lakes Regions," p. 351. Although there are terms in Zigua, such as "*mwango*," which in some contexts are rough equivalents of "household," they are also used to denote larger groups.

30. Picarda, "Autour de Mandera," p. 236. For strategies used to draw new members into households, see Beidelman, *Moral Imagination*, pp. 15–16.

Spouses, moreover, did not establish discrete units of production and consumption; instead, the women of a settlement came together to cook and eat while the men of their households took meals in separate groups. Wives often maintained their own fields, granaries, and homesteads, where they resided with their children apart from their husbands.[31] Sometimes, in fact, women were able to achieve political power as well as economic independence by using wealth obtained through farming, rights in land, and inheritance of livestock to gain control of dependents. Certainly, no Zigua-speaking individual of the 1870s and 1880s was better known to Europeans than Simbamwene, the woman who ruled Morogoro. Other women served as *wegazi*, and at least one prominent caravan leader was a woman.[32]

Both women and men, of course, performed work outside their residential groups, particularly in the fields of their patrons, for patronal authority was probably the most powerful impingement on autonomous control of dependents, as an episode at the Mhonda Mission demonstrated in 1883. A man approached the Spiritans and pledged to become "something like a vassal" if the missionaries would intervene to save his wife and children, who had been sold into captivity by their kin. They were about to be taken to the coast by caravan when the missionaries reclaimed them by asserting their right, as the man's patrons, to override the authority of his wife's and children's kin. This case shows not only that the power of patrons took precedence over kinship in determining control of dependents, but also that overlapping claims concerning dependents could cost a household head his independence. The man had no recourse but to surrender his autonomy because his affines and the matrilineal kin of his children threatened to take away his family.[33] While not all household heads, of course, fell into such perilous circumstances, few of them matched Feda's success in gaining independence from interfering affines and siblings, and fewer still stood free of obligations to patrons.

31. Picarda, "Autour de Mandera," p. 296. For these reasons, comments a recent study of Handeni District, defining modern "households" is very difficult: Suleman Sumra, "Primary Education and Transition to Socialism in Rural Tanzania," pp. 240–241.

32. Mzee Samgome, Kwediboma; Mkomwa and Nkwileh, "Jadi," pp. 39–40; McVicar, "The Position of Woman Among the Wanguru," p. 22; Godfrey Dale, "An Account of the Principal Customs and Habits of the Natives Inhabiting the Bondei Country," pp. 223–224. Aside from Simbamwene, Bibi Mandaro was the most prominent female chieftain; other female leaders are mentioned in RKA 217/5 and Picarda, "Autour de Mandera," p. 271. In Ukami, south of Uzigua, the niece of a chieftain became an important political figure and leader of long-distance caravans: Anton Horner, "L'Oukami (Afrique Orientale) I," p. 585.

33. Mhonda Mission Journal, February 16–17, 1883. For similar cases involving the transfer of dependents, see Mhonda Mission Journal, June 7, 1887 and March 25, 1892; Raoul de Courmont, "Rapport" (1894), p. 83; RKA 856/113–115.

Conclusion

The stories of both the chieftains such as Mhelamwana and the *si* founders reveal a tension between the aspiration for autonomous control of dependents and restraining obligations. These two elements reappear in the dichotomy between the ideal and the reality of the household, and in modern peasant discussions of precolonial society which stress competition between *si* groups. It was, in fact, this very constraint on their authority that mid-nineteenth-century chieftains tried to overcome when, in a period of unprecedented commercial opportunities, they used the trade connections created by Zanzibari mercantile expansion to achieve unchallengeable dominance. Empowered by merchant partners and enriched by trade, leaders such as Mhelamwana placed relations with clients, affines and kin on a less egalitarian, more exploitative, footing. The most conspicuous aspect of Mhelamwana's career in its traditional recounting, his brutality towards subjects, reflects this tendency.

The constraint of reciprocal obligation on individual ambition remained, nonetheless, a crucial element in the maintenance of a favorable disease environment, for although disease control depended upon accumulation by patrons, it also required that the pursuit of individual advantage be tempered by acceptance of the obligation to redistribute wealth. As one modern Handeni resident put it, not only the rich, but also the poor who "push" ["*wanawasukumiza*"] their affluent neighbors to distribute resources, are responsible for prosperity.[34] Communities maintained control of disease when most villagers were able to obtain subsistence reserves from patrons close to home rather than having to migrate in search of food. Ensuring access to reserves, however, was a political struggle conducted by dependents who invoked norms of mutual obligation and pressed patrons to honor their responsibilities.

34. Asumani Nyokka (Kwediboma, May 11, 1983).

Part III

Famine, Disease, and the Decline of Patrons Under German Colonial Rule

6. The Colonial Economy and Its Impact on Patrons and Dependents

Colonial rule, which was imposed on Uzigua by the Germans soon after their conquest of the *Mrima* in 1889, transformed the region's trade, introduced new forms of production, and altered relations between patrons and their dependents, including slaves. While the most obvious immediate effect of the German conquest was to halt the expansion of Zanzibari mercantile activity in Uzigua, the German regime also imposed civil administration, taxation, and labor demands, and thereby changed modes of exchange and accumulation, agronomy and vegetation management, patronage and political institutions. In short, the colonial regime turned the farmers of Uzigua into peasants who would henceforth devote part of their labor to production for colonial markets under conditions established by the colonial state.[1] Confronted with this upheaval in political and economic circumstances, both patrons and their subordinates struggled to protect their interests by modifying relations of agricultural production. However, they could not prevent colonialism from depriving them of subsistence reserves and reducing their ability to maintain a healthy bovine disease environment.

German Intrusion, Commercial Reorientation, and the Decline of the Chieftains

During the two decades preceding the German occupation of the *Mrima* in 1889, the importance of Uzigua in the Zanzibari commercial hinterland increased, both because the island of Pemba became a major clove producer and because the British demanded that the Omani state limit the

1. For definitions of "peasants," see Martin A. Klein, *Peasants in Africa*, pp. 9–14 and Allen Isaacman, "Peasants and Rural Social Protest in Africa," pp. 1–2.

slave trade. Acquiescing to British diplomatic pressure, the Omani Sultan of Zanzibar banned slave exports from the mainland in 1873 and prohibited the entry of slave caravans into coastal towns three years later. Coinciding with these developments was a shift of clove cultivation northward to Pemba after a hurricane devastated plantations at Zanzibar in 1872.[2] For the merchants who wished to evade the restrictions on slave trafficking, these events enhanced the attractiveness of Uzigua and the other mainland regions near Pemba. At the trading camps in the Nguu Mountains, they divided the slaves brought by caravans from western Tanganyika into small groups which, in contravention of the Sultan's 1876 edict, could be slipped unnoticed into *Mrima* towns. From the *Mrima* ports, traders smuggled some captives by small boat past British naval patrols to Pemba and sold others to the plantation sector that expanded rapidly along the coast, particularly in the lower Pangani Valley, after the prohibition of slave exports in 1873. Owners of mainland plantations enjoyed the advantage, of course, of being able to employ slaves in the production of grain for Zanzibar and Pemba, not having to depend on smugglers for their supply of labor.[3] As the demand for slave labor at Pemba and in the coastal regions brought increased caravan traffic to Uzigua, therefore, chieftains found more opportunities to collect tolls and sell captives and provisions.

Hence Zanzibari mercantile activity was at its peak in Uzigua when in the mid-1880s the German East Africa Company [DOAG], basing its demands on treaties obtained in 1884 by Karl Peters, suddenly claimed a monopoly on trade in the *Mrima* hinterland. Peters, during a hasty traversal of Uzigua that avoided all the major chieftains, had won the assent of numerous minor settlement leaders to written agreements ceding territory, even though they usually did not control the areas in question.[4] The DOAG founded trading stations and plantations at Mbusini in the Wami Valley and at Korogwe in the Pangani Valley in 1886, but these ventures failed because hostile neighboring leaders prevented them from recruiting

2. On the developments of the 1870s, see Steven Feierman, *The Shambaa Kingdom*, Chapter 7; Frederick Cooper, *Plantation Slavery on the East Coast of Africa*, Chapter 4; John Iliffe, *A Modern History of Tanganyika*, pp. 49–50 and Marcia Wright, "East Africa, 1870–1905."

3. Oscar Baumann, "Der Unterlauf des Pangani-Flusses," pp. 59–62.

4. J. Wagner, *Deutsch Ostafrika: Geschichte der Gesellschaft für deutsche Kolonisation und der Deutsch-Ostafrikanischen Gesellschaft*, pp. 37–45; Karl Peters, *Gesammelte Schriften* 1: 301–306; Gerhard Rohlfs to Bismarck (Zanzibar, June 29, 1885), RKA 382/16; Franz Stuhlmann, "Bericht über eine Reise," p. 153; Fritz Ferdinand Müller, *Deutschland-Zanzibar-Ostafrika*, pp. 129, 379; *Kolonial-Politische Korrespondenz* 2, 2 (October 16, 1886): 298.

labor.[5] Indeed, DOAG personnel—much less willing than the Spiritans to abide by the region's economic and political conventions—were never integrated into its political hierarchy.

Consequently, despite the DOAG claims, the Germans posed little challenge to Zanzibari mercantile dominance until 1889, when their military crushed the resistance to their intrusion into the *Mrima* towns. The chieftains of Uzigua, wishing a swift end to the German blockade of *Mrima* ports, initially remained neutral.[6] When the principal resistance leader, Bushiri, tried to rally support in Uzigua, however, a village leader in central Handeni handed him over to the Germans. Persuaded, therefore, that he lacked contacts in Uzigua who could help build an administrative structure there, the Germans executed Bushiri immediately, but spared his principal ally, Bwana Heri, because they believed that he controlled the Zigua-speaking communities inland from Sadani where he had taken refuge from colonial forces.[7]

The naval blockade during the *Mrima* war, subsequent anti-slave trade measures, and German customs collecting rapidly reduced trade between Zanzibar and Uzigua. The slave trade was probably the first commercial sector to be affected, for while the trading camps of Nguu were still conducting business in captives in 1891, by mid-decade German surveillance and British naval patrols had made slave dealing extremely dangerous, and after 1900 the remaining trade at the primary slave entrepôt, Bagamoyo, died out rapidly.[8] Tanganyikan exports of ivory, the other highly-valued item in precolonial trade, also declined during this period, from an annual average of 209,292 lb. between 1892 and 1895 to 44,666 lb. between 1906 and 1908. Dwindling slave and ivory exports were part of the wider decline in trade between Zanzibar and its Tanganyikan hinter-

---

5. *Kolonial-Politische Korrespondenz* 2 (1886): 298ff, 3 (1887): 35, 189–190; Ludwig von Höhnel, *Discovery of Lakes Rudolf and Stefanie*, 1: 65–67; Eugen Krenzler, *Ein Jahr in Ostafrika*.

6. German military records of the conflict contain no sign of sympathy in Uzigua for the coastal resistance: Bundesarchiv-Militärarchiv, Freiburg i. B., F. R. Germany, RM 1/v. 2907, 2908, 2909, 2440 and 2441, Band 3.

7. Ernest Mkomwa, Kwa Masaka; Ibrahimu Mohamedi Mkwayu, Salimu Muhando and Selemani Kidanga (Kwa Mkono, December 21 and 23, 1982); Iliffe, *A Modern History of Tanganyika*, pp. 95–97; Müller, *Deutschland-Zanzibar-Ostafrika*, pp. 450–452; Schmidt, pp. 168–182. The depth of support for Bwana Heri in Uzigua, however, was suspect: Lt. Engelhardt (Sadani, March 1, 1894), RKA 284/45–46.

8. *DKb* 2 (1891): 510–511; A. Leue, "Die Sklaverei in Deutsch-Ostafrika," p. 618; Max Schoeller, *Mitteilungen über meine Reise nach Äquatorial-Ost-Afrika und Uganda, 1896–1897*, 1: 38; Gustav Meinecke, "Pangani," p. 155; RKA 1004/70; BC 22 (1903–1904): 108, 24: 55ff.

land that thrust Zanzibari merchant houses into crisis. From 1892 to 1910, the annual value of Tanganyikan exports to Zanzibar fell from £ 208,662 to £ 119,304, while during the same period the annual value of imports from Zanzibar into German East Africa decreased from £ 330,394 to £ 187,675.[9]

The disruption of commercial relations with Zanzibar struck the chieftains of Uzigua especially hard because other forms of long-distance trade also moved away from the region after 1890. Caravan traffic decreased as traders began using the large ports of Tanga and Dar es Salaam, which were served by European steamers. Pangani and Sadani were already losing the competition for caravans in the early 1890s, and Bagamoyo declined soon after as caravans and ships gravitated toward Dar es Salaam's superior harbor.[10] Construction of railroads from Tanga and Dar es Salaam completed the shift away from the smaller *Mrima* ports, for after the Pangani Valley railroad reached Korogwe in 1904 the exports of northern Uzigua flowed via that railhead to Tanga, while southern Nguu diverted its trade toward Mpwapwa and Morogoro along the central railway. The central railroad also provided a connection between Dar es Salaam and Kondoa-Irangi, the destination of many precolonial caravans that had crossed Uzigua from the *Mrima*. Pangani merchants tried to restore their ties with Kondoa-Irangi by opening a caravan route along the upper Pangani Valley, but high costs of porterage made competition with the railroad impossible.[11]

The decline in caravan traffic, which led some communities to move away from the old trade routes in the late 1890s,[12] reduced the commercial role of the chieftains, even though Uzigua by no means abandoned interregional commerce. Many communities found opportunities to send grain toward the railways and the plantations of the Pangani Valley, to take livestock eastward to Korogwe and westward to Iramba, and to sell beeswax and wild rubber from the Nguu highlands and the Pangani Valley to

9. Great Britain, Foreign Office, *Diplomatic and Consular Reports on Trade and Finance*, 1892–1910; RKA 644/1, 6472/203–204, 6478/39, 6565/100.

10. Rochus Schmidt, "Militärische Stützpunkte im Innern Ostafrikas," pp. 51–54; Meinecke, *Aus dem Lande des Suaheli*, p. 115; Schoeller, *Mitteilungen*, 1: 38; E. Werth, *Das Deutsch-Ostafrikanische Küstenland und die Vorgelagerten Inseln*, 2: 34–35; Iliffe, *A Modern History of Tanganyika*, p. 137; BC 24: 513, 25 (1909–1910): 716. Bundesarchiv-Militärarchiv, Grasshof, "Militärpolitische Bericht" (Lindi, April 18, 1914), RM 5/v. 5669, Band 2.

11. RKA 6566/101–102; Hamburgisches Museum für Völkerkunde und Vorgeschichte, A77 Nachlass Fonck, "Jahresbericht: Mpapua" (March 31, 1903).

12. RKA 215/7–12 and 22–24.

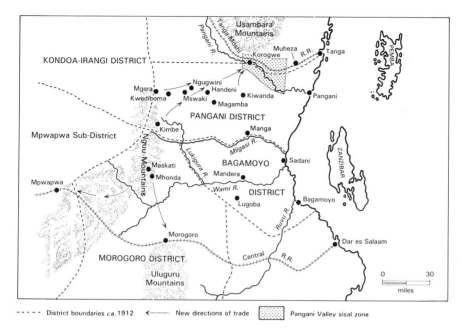

Map 3. Uzigua under German rule, showing new directions of trade toward railroads.

Korogwe.[13] Yet while the colonial economy created new opportunities, it cost the precolonial chieftains their contact with Zanzibari creditors, their chances to sell food, ivory, and slaves to caravans, and their ability to collect tolls. In addition, the chieftains were supplanted by Indian retailers as distributors of imports, for although only one Indian merchant lived in central Uzigua in 1895, after 1900 village stores made their appearance and by 1909 a network of Indian-owned shops, including six stores at Handeni Town alone, were operating along the route between Korogwe and Mgera.[14] Indian businessmen also took control of wild rubber exports from Uzigua, with a single merchant purchasing 250,000 rupees' worth of rubber in one year.[15]

13. *DKb* 13 (1902): 257–259, 15 (1904): 760; *Usambara-Post*, July 17, 1909; *Berichte über Land- und Forstwirtschaft in Deutsch-Ostafrika* (1902), pp. 81–82; *DOAR* 2, 99 (December 15, 1909) and 3, 93 (November 28, 1910); RKA 6472/303 and 238/163. On cattle trading during the German period: Saidi Hatibu, Mkonde.

14. The establishment of rural shops by small traders is described evocatively in M. G. Vassanji's novel *The Gunny Sack.*

15. *Usambara-Post* July 17, 1909; RKA 286/125, 238/163.

Hence, in spite of the new commercial possibilities that developed in the early colonial period, the reorientation of long-distance trade ruined the system of credit on which the precolonial chieftains had depended. Any possibility that they might have recovered and adapted to the new commercial climate was eliminated, moreover, by systematic German destruction of their power (see Chapter Seven).

Colonial Taxation and Patronage

Chieftains and patrons were further weakened by taxation, which the colonial state instituted in 1898 to generate revenue and integrate taxpayers into the colonial economy as peasant producers and wage laborers.[16] Because the first tax collections occurred among a population that not only held little colonial currency, but also was enduring, between 1898 and 1900, the worst famine of the colonial period (see Chapter Eight), the tax collections provoked widespread disorder. Village leaders and patrons, already stricken by commercial dislocation and famine, were required to pay a levy for each house under their control. Many of them reduced their tax burdens by casting off clients, wives, kin, pawns, and slaves. One leader of a settlement near Mhonda, for example, obliged in 1900 to pay one rupee for each of the seventy-two houses in his village, offered all his dependents to the mission as pawns should the Spiritan fathers agree to pay his taxes. The Spiritan evangelist at Mhonda reported in 1899 that so many of his neighbors were willing to pawn themselves to the mission in return for payment of taxes that even the "wealth of the Rothschilds" could not have sufficed to help them all. In June 1900 another village head received a tax bill of 200 rupees, provoking the mission journalist to remark that "The Germans have no sense, are this many rupees to be found in all of Nguu?!"

The mission evangelist saw Mhonda residents fleeing to uninhabited woodland or to Mpwapwa, where revenue collection seemed to be less thorough.[17] To enforce tax demands, a German military patrol entered Mhonda in September 1899 "with the mission of reminding the Africans

16. Iliffe, *A Modern History of Tanganyika*, p. 133.
17. *BC* 19 (1898–1899): 501–502; Mhonda Mission Journal, October 24, 1898, February 9 and May 29, 1899, January 3, June 10, August 9 and December 29, 1900.

about German domination" and immediately pillaged a village, killed a number of its residents, stole cattle, and destroyed grain stocks. "They did not want to pay taxes," complacently remarked the missionary, "but this time they have paid with their losses."[18]

Abandoned by their patrons, many farmers left their homesteads in search of wage labor. Among them were African Christians from Mhonda who, because the mission emulated other patrons by refusing to pay taxes for its dependents, left for six or seven months in 1901, "since here it is very difficult to get money. Unfortunately, most of them returned as poor as they were before."[19] In the same year "several hundred Zigua" earned tax money on European plantations in Pangani.[20]

The alternative to labor migration was sales of livestock, tobacco, ghee, honey, beeswax, and wild rubber, but "to get money was extremely difficult."[21] Occasionally the government permitted cultivators to pay taxes in grain rather than in cash, an option that many villagers found preferable to labor migration, even during the famine of 1898–1900, because it allowed them to continue working their own farms. For this reason, when highlanders learned that sorghum and maize were more frequently accepted in Mpwapwa District than in Pangani District, some of them moved from the portions of Nguu administered by Pangani to areas controlled by Mpwapwa.[22]

Yet while district administrators in Mpwapwa were more inclined than their colleagues in Pangani to allow tax payments in kind, demands in Mpwapwa for taxes in colonial currency nevertheless forced villagers to leave their farms, just as they did elsewhere. In 1902, District Officer August Fonck, proud of his reputation as an efficient tax collector and eager to recruit labor for telegraph construction, pressed ahead with tax collection despite food shortages that by his own admission were causing widespread emaciation and illness. In an effort to prevent further depletion of food supplies, Fonck prohibited both sales of food to the many caravans that crossed his district and the payment of taxes in grain. The

18. Mhonda Mission Journal, September 13 and 16, 1899.

19. *BC* 22: 111.

20. *DKb* 12 (1901): 274.

21. Abdala Hamani Msede and Ali Omali Kipande, Kwa Dundwa; Mohamedi Lusingo, Mafisa; Rajabu Sudi, Manga; Mohamedi Saidi Gota, Ramadhani Mswagala, Mwenjuma Mdachi, Omari Mohamedi Gumbo, Gitu.

22. Mohamedi Lusingo, Mafisa; Abdala Hamani Msede and Ali Omali Kipande, Kwa Dundwa; Mandera Mission Journal, March 23, 1900; *Berichte über Land- und Forstwirtschaft* (1902), p. 82; RKA 1053/105.

effect of these actions, however, was to increase the need for colonial currency just as the primary way of earning money was being outlawed. Consequently, because the telegraph project was virtually the only source of cash in the district, many men left their villages for construction work, even though their after-tax earnings were insufficient for food purchases. Indeed, 70 percent of the 42,000 rupees paid in taxes during 1902 were deducted from telegraph wages. Fonck's tax policies probably caused the unrest that was reported at this time in the Nguu Mountains and in other areas as well.[23]

Cotton, Rubber and Labor in Uzigua

In addition to taxation, compulsory cotton cultivation and conscription of plantation labor also interrupted agriculture and burdened the farmers who were losing patronage. While forced cotton growing did not spark rebellion in Uzigua as it did in southern Tanganyika during the Maji-Maji War of 1905–1907, it nevertheless disrupted farmers' lives and work, as events at Mhonda demonstrate.[24] In 1904 a government-appointed functionary, or "Akida," named Bakari laid out cotton fields early in the year at Mhonda and instructed soldiers under his command to beat village heads who failed to provide laborers. He would not allow the workers time to hoe their own fields, however, during the critical weeks before the long rains. Not until March 12, in fact, when the time for hoeing had nearly passed, did he release them from cotton work, and by then, as the Spiritans noted, farmers who should have been husbanding their energies during the season of pre-harvest scarcity were exhausted and ill: "Finally, Bakari and the people of his village have finished clearing their fields. As for the laborers, they must try to keep from dying of hunger."[25] While

23. Nachlass Fonck, "Jahresbericht: Mpapua" (March 31, 1903), "Notstands- und Steuerverhältnisse in Mpapua, 1902," (Mpwapwa, June 15, 1903), and "Aus Krieg und Frieden in Deutsch Ostafrika: Lose Blätter aus dem Tagebuch eines alten Afrikanere" (Typewritten MSS.), Hamburgisches Museum für Völkerkunde und Vorgeschichte, A77.

24. During the Maji-Maji period the administration reported no signs of rebellion or unrest in Uzigua, and the German military felt sufficiently secure to withdraw most of its troops from northeastern Tanganyika: Bundesarchiv-Militärarchiv, Kapitän Bäck, "Militär-politische Bericht über die Tätigkeit der Majestät Schiff 'Bussard'" (Dar es Salaam, September 26, 1905), RM 5/ v. 6035. Also, RM 121/ v. 443 and 446.

25. Mhonda Mission Journal, March 12, 1904; see also January 8 and 15, 1904 and BC 23 (1905–1906): 370.

Bakari would eventually collect profits from cotton sales, the cultivators forced to perform the work received nothing. If such abuses persisted, warned a missionary in 1905 just before the outbreak of the Maji-Maji uprising further south, a rebellion would certainly result.[26]

In Handeni, the effects of taxation and compulsory cultivation were compounded by rubber plantation production. German settlers responded to high London rubber prices in 1906 and from 1909 to 1910 by purchasing land and planting ceara (*Manihot glaziovii*) rubber trees at several locations in Handeni. By 1911 they were running five plantations, the largest of which expanded from 206 to 1128 hectares between 1910 and 1914, a period of fairly extensive land purchases across the district.[27] Like other rubber planters throughout Tanganyika, once the Handeni settlers had invested in rubber, they ignored troubling portents such as competition from Asian producers and declining world prices after 1910. Their prospects were particularly bad, not only because rainfall in Handeni was much too sparse and unpredictable for ceara, but also because they needed very high rubber prices to compensate for the cost of transporting their goods six or seven days' march to the nearest rail depot.[28]

These factors left the Handeni rubber producers deeply concerned about their constant shortages of workers, for they believed that cheap and abundant labor could offset their competitive disadvantages.[29] While they met part of their demand for labor by engaging migrants from western Tanganyika, planters preferred hiring locally to avoid the costs of recruiting labor in distant regions.[30] Hence the apparent reluctance of "the Zigua" to perform wage labor, which many Europeans in the region attributed to their "tribal" propensity for improvidence and laziness, became an important issue among administrators and plantation managers.[31]

It was the planters themselves, however, who were responsible for the poor wages, oppressive conditions, and long work terms that made rubber

26. *BC* 23: 370.

27. TNA G23/153, G23/156, G23/207, G46/15LR, G55/54−55; RKA 6483.

28. J. Forbes Munro, "British Rubber Companies in East Africa Before the First World War," pp. 369 and 373−374; *Jahresbericht* (1909−1910), p. 24, (1910−1911), p. 23, (1911−1912), pp. 21 and 31.

29. *DOAR* 2, 98 (December 11, 1909).

30. *Jahresbericht* (1912−1913), p. 22.

31. *Jahresbericht* (1896−1897), p. 66.

work unpopular. A laborer's monthly wage in Handeni, depressed partially by child labor,[32] was only 10–12 rupees immediately prior to the First World War, whereas in Tanga and on the Pangani Valley sisal plantations a worker earned 12–15 rupees per thirty days.[33] While it was true that skilled rubber tappers could complete several days' tasks in a single day, less adept workers were relegated to weeding and clearing plots, and thereby lost eligibility for the tapping bonuses that might double the basic plantation wage.[34] The stern discipline of the planters and their African overseers, some of whom are remembered for having killed workers with hippo-hide whips, also discouraged men from seeking rubber work.[35] One settler was known as "Heavy Fist" because "he was able to kill people with only a single blow."[36] Yet rigorous discipline was probably a less powerful deterrent to work on plantations than the inflexibility of managers who, by requiring that employees enlist for at least thirty days, made no allowance for farmers who needed to tend their own fields and provide for dependents. Some administrators, realizing that men resisted leaving their farms and dependents for more than a few days at a time, urged the planters to shorten terms of employment, but the plantation operators insisted on a minimum of thirty days.[37]

Persuaded by the argument of planters and some administrators that only compulsion would break resistance to plantation work, the Handeni administration established separate labor reserves for each estate, permitted the settlers to dominate them as private fiefdoms, and held each village head responsible for furnishing ten workers every month.[38] Households were given collective responsibility for providing plantation labor, an arrangement that created a powerful constraint against flight and desertion

32. USPG, UMCA Archives, Hellier letter of August 19, 1910; Abdala Hamani Msede and Ali Omali Kipande, Kwa Dundwa.

33. RKA 123/130, 6569/51–65.

34. RKA 123/130; Haji Luwambo (Kwediboma, August 27, 1982).

35. Omali Maligwa Kidiza, Gombero; Ali S. Sambuguma, Kwediboma; Mzee Ndege (Mafisa, July 1, 1983); Asumani Mwanamauka and Omali Mwanamauka, Mafisa; Omali Gumbo, Kwinji.

36. Ernest Mkomwa, Kwa Masaka; Mzee Ndege, Mafisa. Other men who described their experiences on German rubber plantations were: Mohamedi Chambo, Kiberashi; Saidi Hatibu, Mkonde; Mohamedi Lusingo, Mafisa and Rajabu Sefu Mwenkumba, Kwa Mkono.

37. RKA 123/131 and 6567/50–51.

38. Karl Kaerger, *Tangaland und die Kolonisation Deutsch Östafrikas*, p. 59. Throughout German East Africa, small plantations depended upon the colonial state to assist them in procuring local labor: Bundesarchiv-Militärarchiv, Grasshof, "Militärpolitische Bericht" (Lindi, April 18, 1914), RM 5/v. 5669, Band 2.

since truants placed co-residents in danger of being punished by planters.[39] Nevertheless, many young men fled to escape the dreaded summons that could take them away from their own plots even during the crucial weeks of hoeing and planting. A more common expedient, however, was for conscripts to arrange with household co-residents to relieve them and complete their one-month labor obligation.[40] The government used the same system to obtain unpaid labor for public works, including construction of the motor road from Korogwe through Mgera that was built after the rubber planters lobbied for a better route to reduce transport costs.[41] Each estate completed a stretch of the road by drawing on its labor reserve to accomplish what is remembered in Handeni as an epic undertaking performed entirely by hand: "Village leaders worked [on the road] even at night, and women were also forced to work."[42]

The minority of officials, however, who believed that labor shortages in Handeni were caused less by "tribal" indolence than by a system which failed to accommodate the farmers' own responsibilities, were eventually vindicated. When the administration of Handeni District relaxed the conscription system in 1912 and allowed workers to choose the time and duration of employment, so many men flocked to the plantations that hundreds had to be turned away. At one plantation, laborers guaranteed themselves jobs by lining up to collect tools as early as 3 a.m.[43]

The End of Slavery and the Decline of Patronage

The circumstances that transformed Uzigua's economy and political structure—reorientation of trade, the outlawing of slave raiding and marketing, taxation, compulsory labor, military attacks (see Chapter Seven), and livestock diseases (see Chapter Eight)—all made the accumulation of wealth and fulfillment of obligations to dependents much more difficult. Many patrons and chieftains reacted by severing ties with all categories of

39. Omali Gumbo, Kwinji; Omali Maligwa Kidiza, Gombero; Iddi Samshehiri (Gombero, September 21, 1983).
40. Omali Gumbo, Kwinji; Omali Maligwa Kidiza, Gombero; Iddi Samshehiri, Gombero; Abdala Hamani Msede and Ali Omali Kipande, Kwa Dundwa; Asumani Mwanamauka and Omali Mwanamauka, Mafisa; Hasani Bakari, Balanga; RKA 123/130–131.
41. *Usambara-Post*, January 29, 1910.
42. Omali Gumbo, Kwinji and Omali Maligwa Kidiza, Gombero.
43. RKA 123/128–131.

dependents, including clients, pawns, and wives. The fate of slaves is the best documented aspect of this process, however, because some slaves received government writs of manumission. Masters, responding less to German abolition of slave trading and judicial mechanisms for slave emancipation than to the tax system that obliged them to pay levies for all dependents, often voluntarily relinquished authority over their slaves. Indeed, although it is true that the Germans sometimes forcibly removed slaves from their owners, they were less interested in eradicating slavery than in reducing the power of political notables.[44]

In exceptional circumstances, a few powerful individuals found opportunities to obtain additional dependents, sometimes by intimidating weaker neighbors into surrendering household members. At least once this stratagem was used by the Spiritans of Mhonda who, claiming that a neighbor had mistreated his dependents, seized two of them.[45] Like others who resorted to these tactics, the missionaries knew that the colonial administration would probably accept their contention that they were simply rescuing slaves.[46] Some wealthy patrons also acquired dependents by loaning slaves the compensatory sum which they were required to pay their owners before receiving a written declaration of emancipation from the German administration.[47]

More characteristic of a period in which patrons and masters withdrew from relations with clients and slaves, however, was the Spiritans' tendency to deny their neighbors patronage, for as colonialism eliminated the chieftains' opportunities to trade and accumulate, formerly powerful patrons were more inclined to cast away subordinates than to accept new dependents. The declining fortunes of slave-owning leaders were typified by those of Sonyo, whose village of Magamba, the largest settlement in early-colonial central Uzigua, contained 183 "large" houses in 1895 and was divided, reported a British missionary in 1900, into separate quarters for slaves, clients, and members of Sonyo's household, including his eighty wives. After German troops sacked it in 1905 and withdrew Sonyo's ap-

44. Salimu Kisailo, Kwa Maligwa; Mohamedi Mjewe (Kwediboma, September 27, 1982); Selemani Kidanga, Kwa Mkono; Shehe Bakari Ruhizo and Sankole Mhandeni (Kwa Mkono, December 28, 1982).

45. RKA 856/116–120.

46. Mohamedi Mjewe (Kwediboma, September 27, 1982) and Haji Luwambo (Kwediboma, September 30, 1982).

47. RKA 1005/13–75. Of the forty-nine declarations of emancipation issued by Pangani District (which included Handeni) in 1898/1899, twenty-one were made in situations of this kind: Bezirksamtmann Sigl, "Bezirksamt Pangani," *Material zur Beurteilung des Standes der Sklavenfrage in den deutschen Schutzgebieten, 1892–1904*, p. 53.

pointment as the local government functionary, however, Magamba lost a considerable proportion of its residents and by 1907 had only one hundred houses. Reports of food shortages and hunger-related illness at Magamba in 1910 indicate, moreover, that Sonyo had difficulty in providing for dependents.[48]

Sonyo's decline was lamented in song: "Sonyo mwana mnyamala kuila kumwa kizungu . . . wakizungu hauna wenyewe . . . aingia mtoto akuhukumu, mwanao aingia mtoto ahukumu." ("Don't cry, Sonyo, about the Europeans . . . [for] Europeans have their own ways . . . [or] about a child who comes in to accuse you, even if it's your own child that accuses you.") According to a modern Handeni resident, Omali Maligwa, the song portrays the sorrowful Sonyo as he watched the departure of his dependents and reflected that European rule had so diminished respect for elders that even their own children now dared bring accusations against them in German courts.[49] Thus political upheaval and the decline of slavery are depicted in the idiom of kinship as the loss of familial loyalty and esteem for elders.

The slaves who left Sonyo and other masters often paid cash compensation, though in Uzigua they rarely received the German writs of manumission to which such payments entitled them. Indeed, in Pangani District (which included Handeni), the government issued an average of only 207 manumission declarations annually from 1892 to 1911, with most of them probably going to town and plantation slaves near the coast, while in Handeni Sub-District officials granted an average of only 160 declarations annually from 1909 through 1912.[50] The sums established by administrators as the standards for compensation were extremely high by comparison with wages and producer prices, and could therefore force slaves who wished to earn compensation money into lengthy terms of wage labor. From district to district, however, the compensatory sums varied widely. At Mhonda, the local administrator decreed in 1901 that 150 rupees were required for manumission, while the norm was between

48. RKA 286/123–129; W. H. Kisbey, "A Journey in Zigualand," p. 174; USPG, UMCA Archives, letter of Hine (1907). On famine and epidemic at Magamba, see Chapter Eight.

49. Omali Maligwa Kidiza, Gombero. The knowledge that the Germans were willing to consider accusations against masters was widespread among slaves: RKA 1005/26–27. The erosion of patrons' authority is discussed at length in Chapter Seven.

50. On compensation payments: Iddi Samshehiri, Gombero; Haji Luwambo (Kwediboma, September 30, 1982); Rajabu Sefu Mwenkumba, Kwa Mkono; Selemani Kidanga, Kwa Mkono. RKA 1005/92, 1007/26, 6475/268, 6476/15, 6477/44, 6478/18, 6480/37, 6565/15, 6569/19, 6570/12; Fritz Weidner, *Die Haussklaverei in Ostafrika*, pp. 141ff.

50 and 100 rupees in Pangani District and 30 rupees in central Uzigua.[51] Because the monthly wage of a plantation hand increased only from six to no more than ten or fifteen rupees between 1892 and 1912, however, even 30 rupees, to say nothing of 150 rupees' compensation, represented savings from many months' wages.[52] Sometimes the compensation was earned by a slave's relative. Abdala Mkomwa of northern Nguu, for example, worked to free his mother's brother, Sada Mgubo, who had been sold into captivity as a child and settled on a plantation near Pangani. Having saved money by working on the rubber plantations, Abdala Mkomwa paid compensation for Sada Mgubo in 1908, only to find that he would not return home and preferred to live out his years in Pangani.[53]

As Sada Mgubo's example shows, paying compensation was not necessarily preparation for a former slave's departure. To the contrary, some slaves who paid compensation were probably trying to guarantee that, at a time when many dependents were being forced out of their villages, they would be allowed to remain in place. Much as men rendered bridewealth, they offered a payment in return for land and the same access to a patron's livestock and subsistence reserves that other dependents enjoyed. By the same token, however, some masters probably refused compensation because they did not wish to make long-term commitments to their former slaves. Women, of course, had less opportunity than men to obtain such rights through compensation payments, because far fewer wage-paying jobs were available to them.

Nor was Sada Mgubo the only slave who decided that the disadvantages of leaving a master outweighed the prospect of autonomy:

> Those slaves who were of a rebellious spirit, when they saw that there was no longer slavery, that the others [the masters] had no way to stop them, they all moved away. Some of them left. But others did not dare to, they said [to those who were leaving] "How can you move away from here?" They were afraid.[54]

51. Mhonda Mission Journal, March 6, 1901; Sigl, "Bezirksamt Pangani," p. 53; Salimu Kisailo, Kwa Maligwa; Ibrahimu Mohamedi Mkwayu, Salimu Muhando and Ramadhani Maingwa (Kwa Mkono, December 21, 1982); Sankole Mhandeni, Kwa Mkono.

52. RKA 123/130, 6569/51–65; Sigl, "Bezirksamt Pangani," p. 53; *Jahresbericht* (1912–1913), p. 20; Haji Luwambo (Kwediboma, August 26, 1982); Omali Maligwa Kidiza, Gombero; Iddi Samshehiri, Gombero.

53. Asumani Abdala Mkomwa (Kwediboma, August 11, 1982).

54. Salimu Kisailo, Kwa Maligwa; also, Iddi Samshehiri, Gombero; Mzee Ndege, Mafisa; Asumani Mwanamauka and Omali Mwanamauka, Mafisa; Haji Luwambo (Kwediboma, September 30, 1982); Ramadhani Maingwa, Kwa Mkono.

One factor that slaves took into consideration was rights in property, as the Spiritans at Mhonda learned in 1900 when they tried to claim a neighbor's slave. Although the woman had been mistreated, she refused to leave her master's homestead without her five goats, two chickens, and the seven sacks of sorghum, one sack of sesame, and one sack of groundnuts which, she declared, "I myself cultivated and harvested."[55] Slaves who wished to establish themselves as independent farmers not only faced grave difficulties in obtaining land, tools, seed, livestock, and food reserves, but also, like this woman, risked losing whatever property they had accumulated. Many slaves who departed their masters' settlements probably did so, in fact, because they were denied access to these resources.

The Increase of Casual Labor

As chieftains and patrons extricated themselves from relations with slaves and other dependents, they had to find substitute labor. Cast-off slaves, clients, and wives, on the other hand, were farmers without resources. They needed seed, food reserves, and other necessities, particularly because the frequent famines, cattle disease, taxation, and forced labor of the early colonial period multiplied the difficulties involved in establishing independent farms. Patrons and dependents modified their old relationships, therefore, in ways that allowed former patrons to employ laborers while avoiding long-term obligations, and former dependents, including freed slaves, to obtain resources while maintaining their autonomy. Although these new labor relations outwardly resembled precolonial arrangements, they nevertheless represented a fundamental change, as the example of the relationship called *kiwiri* shows.

Groups of precolonial farmers had frequently come together on a farm to perform field tasks in return for food and beer, and by participating in these *kiwiri* parties had often laid long-term claims to patronage. In the early colonial situation, however, *kiwiri* became a temporary arrangement involving a one-time payment, a change that the Handeni villager Omali Maligwa attributed to the decline of patrons and the end of slavery:

> As for *kiwiri*, people were seduced by beer. . . . The old ruler did not use *kiwiri*, his people worked for him because he had his authority. . . . *Kiwiri* began when the slaves were sent away. [The old ruler] was powerless now.

55. RKA 856/116–120.

Now he had to use *kiwiri* to entice them [into working for him]. . . . The chiefs who didn't have slaves anymore, they were helped by *kiwiri*.[56]

When slavery ceased and the power of the precolonial notables ebbed, says Omali Maligwa, the former rulers introduced *kiwiri*, fooling or seducing their neighbors with beer and the promise of patronage that in reality they were no longer willing to dispense. Since numerous observations testify to the use of work parties by precolonial patrons, however, he must be taken to mean that modern *kiwiri*, a relationship which involves one payment for work rather than longstanding patronage, emerged as part of the settlement between former patrons, slave-holders, clients, and slaves. A parallel development also took place at the Spiritan missions, where the evangelists continued to make heavy use of seasonal and temporary labor while trying to free themselves from the burdensome obligations of patronage.[57]

Short-term employment was also coupled in the German period with interregional migration. Men from Uzigua went to Bondei and Muheza in the Pangani Valley to work temporarily for the peasants who grew food for the rapidly growing army of sisal plantation workers.[58] Typically, migrants stayed in the Pangani Valley for less than a month before returning home with loads of cassava.[59] Laborers preferred employment under peasants to work on European plantations not only because they avoided the harsh discipline of the European enterprises, but also because the tasks were familiar and, most importantly, because terms of service were short and could be accommodated in the agricultural calendar.[60] Despite the relative familiarity of peasant-migrant relations, however, distances between the homes of employer and employee precluded the formation of longstanding patron-client ties.

Early-colonial labor relations thus became narrower in time and dimension as they lost their permanence and connection to the various long-

56. Omali Maligwa Kidiza, Gombero. Advancing similar interpretations were Hamza Mlingo (Mswaki, May 28, 1983), Asumani Mwanamauka and Omali Mwanamauka, Mafisa; and the Elders of Gitu.

57. Mhonda Mission Journal, January 1894, June 1902, September 1905, November 1906, September 1909; BC 18 (1896–1897), pp. 782–783, 785–786; 19, p. 501; 20 (1899–1900), p. 649; 24, p. 515; François X. Vogt, "Aus dem Gebiete der Hungersnot," p. 111, and "Jahresbericht," (1907–1908), p. 84.

58. From 1904 to 1910, 73 sisal plantations were established in Tanga and the lower Pangani Valley. The plantation labor force grew from about 5000 in 1905 to over 50,000 in 1913: RKA 6476, 6483, 6570/30–31.

59. DOAR, 2, 98 (December 11, 1909) and 2, 99 (December 15, 1909); Abedi Juma, Manga.

60. RKA 6568/76.

term obligations, including the responsibility for providing food reserves, cattle, cloth, and healing, formerly assumed by patrons. This was a gradual process played out over the course of innumerable disputes between former patrons who withheld assistance and dependents who demanded that they respect norms of reciprocity. Such conflicts over the rights of casual employees, the responsibility of employers to provide food and shelter, the amount of work expected in a day, and levels of remuneration, have in fact continued ceaselessly since the early colonial period.[61] The shift away from long-term patronage towards temporary agricultural labor was not a complete break with the past, for just as precolonial farmers employed workers temporarily, patronage has never disappeared altogether. Yet it was a crucial development, because by depriving many villagers of patronage, it left them with no way of surviving subsistence crises except migration, and thus no way of continuing vegetation management during famines.

The importance of this transition is reflected by an analogous change in explanations of spirit possession. During the 1880s, a time when indigent farmers obtained subsistence by accepting servility, the form of possession which the Spiritans learned most about occurred when individuals were offered food by a certain spirit. If they accepted it, they fell in thrall to the spirit, who took them from their homes permanently.[62] In the Ujamaa villages of the 1980s, however, where many residents worked on a day-to-day basis to earn bundles of cassava from more affluent neighbors, the type of possession most talked about was *msekule*, a form of witchcraft that has been prominent at least since the 1950s.[63] The witches who perform *msekule* spirit away their sleeping victims during the night, force them to work in fields concealed on mountain tops or deep in uninhabited woodlands, and return them to their beds before dawn, so that the only evidence of their nocturnal labors is unexpected soreness and exhaustion upon awakening. If late-precolonial explanations of possession, then, expressed fears of being taken from one's home and having to accept servility, in colonial and post-colonial society they appear to have manifested anxieties about being exploited as casual laborers.

61. Examples are in Handeni District File M5/1, "Complaints."
62. Cado Picarda, "Autour de Mandera," pp. 272–273 and 283; Le Roy. "À la découverte," p. 310.
63. For reports of *msekule* in the 1950s, see Thomas O. Beidelman, "Witchcraft in Ukaguru" in *Witchcraft and Sorcery in East Africa*, p. 66 and *Moral Imagination in Kaguru Modes of Thought*, p. 142. *Msekule* is also discussed in M. S. Halfani, "Some Luguru Clan Histories, Utani Relationships, Ancestor Propitiation, and Ownership: A Case Study of Langali Community in Mgeta."

7. Colonialism, Infanticide, and the Destruction of Precolonial Political Authority

Just as the political dynamics of patronage during the period of Zanzibari mercantile dominance are captured by the stories of Mhelamwana, the political impact of colonial conquest is summed up, for many Handeni residents, by the execution of Mtunte, an obscure village head whose elaborately-staged hanging overshadows the decline of famous chieftains. The prominence of his execution owes much to the German officials who used it to dramatize the chieftains' submission to colonial authority, but its importance in oral accounts also stems from its association with the colonial suppression of institutions that maintained health. Indeed, this is where Handeni residents find the connection between the fall of the precolonial patrons under colonial rule and increased vulnerability to illness and hunger.

The Execution of Mtunte

The unforgettably theatric hanging of Mtunte coincided in 1911 with the establishment of a permanent administrative presence in Handeni District. Some Handeni residents say that Mtunte died on the very day the Germans opened the Handeni District headquarters, a building constructed of massive stone blocks, crowned by battlements and furnished with thick wooden doors; others say all this happened on the Kaiser's birthday. Recalling the execution, elderly peasants describe the gallows in the courtyard of the German headquarters and the crowd of villagers from all parts of Uzigua who witnessed the death of Mtunte:

> After Mtunte was imprisoned, the Germans announced, "we want all musical instruments, any instrument at all, even if people only play rattles or do the

selo [a dance with singing done during female puberty rites] they should go to the headquarters, they should go so that everyone will see how Mtunte is hanged." There were very many women there. They were told that when the man was hanged they should make a great noise. All this I saw myself.[1]

All the Wazigua, even those from as far as the Nguu Mountains, were summoned from all parts of Handeni to witness this business of Mtunte.[2]

All the chieftains, the Akidas [appointed administrative functionaries] and the village leaders, all of them were summoned to the German fort . . . so that everyone should see . . . and that day Mtunte was hanged by the Germans at the Handeni headquarters.[3]

Among the spectators were chieftains like Sonyo of Magamba and Mlinde of Mbwego who stood powerless to intercede for Mtunte:

The Germans told Mtunte, "Call for Zumbe [Chieftain] Sonyo, say farewell to him." He called to him, but Sonyo did not answer. "Call for Zumbe Mlinde, make your farewells." He called, but Mlinde did not respond. Then the Germans told Mtunte, "Do you see? Everything is ruined. Your people reject you."[4]

Then the commander of the Handeni station, Adolph Krepp, addressed the crowd to proclaim that the execution was proof of both German might and their leaders' weakness. Krepp drove the point home directly to Sonyo and the other major chieftains:

Then Bwana Krepp made his speech . . . addressing Sonyo he said, "Sir, today you see European rule. You see today what we will do. You people are savages, now you will learn about European power." . . . Then the soldiers were given orders, they hanged Mtunte immediately.[5]

The speech concluded, the trap opened; another man named Dungwe may have perished along with Mtunte, but there is uncertainty on this point. The moment of death, and even the number of the executed, has receded in memory, eclipsed by the indelible impression of Krepp, with gallows and the German fort at his back, lecturing Sonyo and the other chieftains before their subjects.

1. Abdala Hamani Msede, Kwa Dundwa.
2. Ernest Mkomwa, Kwa Masaka.
3. Abedi Juma, Manga.
4. Abdala Hamani Msede, Kwa Dundwa.
5. Ernest Mkomwa, Kwa Masaka.

While the political significance of Mtunte's execution is unmistakable, only the circumstances of his case make clear its full meaning. Mtunte was the head of a settlement in western Uzigua where a child was identified, just as Mhelamwana had been, as a *kigego* (pl. *vigego*) who would probably cause misfortune to befall his kin. Mtunte's offense was to sanction the killing of the *kigego*:

> Mtunte had one wife who was an Mnyamwezi [a native of the western Tanzanian region of Unyamwezi]. Now she gave birth to a child who was a *kigego*. This news was brought to Mtunte who ordered the women [of the settlement] to do what they must, so they killed the child. The mother was so embittered that she decided to go to Handeni, and off she went. There at the German headquarters was a sentry box near the entrance. When the sentry spotted this woman he cursed her. But by chance the German commander happened to be there in the doorway. When he heard the sentry insulting the woman he asked what the problem might be. "Sir, this woman wants to see you." "Well, why have you refused? Come in here, mama." So she explained to him, "Sir, I bore a child but my husband had him killed." The German was writing as he listened. Afterwards he sent his soldiers to apprehend Mtunte. And so he was caught.[6]

Other accounts, however, say that Mtunte killed the child of Mchekumbo, his Maasai dependent:

> [Mtunte] killed the *kigego* of his slave [*mtumwa*]. Then this slave created an uproar, "Why have you strangled my child?" Mtunte replied, "I'd as soon kill even you yourself." So the woman went to the German fort, she accused Mtunte who was arrested.[7]

If the execution of Mtunte dramatized the subordination of the chieftains to colonial authorities, Mchekumbo's defiance demonstrated the erosion of patrons' authority: "All the people who witnessed [Mtunte's hanging] saw that anyone who committed a crime within his own homestead would be treated just as they had seen Mtunte treated."[8] Mchekumbo, a dependent and perhaps servile woman, defied her master knowing that the colonial administration would probably defend her.

6. Ernest Mkomwa, Kwa Masaka.

7. Omali Gumbo, Kwinji and Abdala Hamani Msede, Kwa Dundwa. Others who provided accounts of the Mtunte episode were Haji Luwambo (Kwediboma, August 18, 1982), Omali Maligwa Kidiza, Gombero and Rashidi Mwenjuma Manyagala, Kilwa. In addition to Mtunte, other persons were executed or imprisoned for infanticide: Sankole Mhandeni and Leonard Kilua (Kwa Mkono, December 28 and 30, 1982) and Abedi Juma and others, Manga.

8. Abedi Juma, Manga.

The Issue of Infanticide

Both the significance of the infanticide issue and the impact of colonialism are better appreciated, however, when the Mtunte case is compared with a confrontation in 1883 between Zigua-speaking leaders and the Mandera Mission which stemmed from the belief of the Spiritan pastor at Mandera, Father Cado Picarda, that surrounding communities were killing children in great numbers. Though he lacked real evidence of infanticide, Picarda began pleading with chieftains in early 1883 to proscribe the killing of *vigego* and have them sent to the mission. When he heard that child-killing was continuing despite his protests, however, Picarda decided to press the issue at a meeting of local notables. Thus on July 29, 1883, Picarda greeted an assembly of thirty settlement heads, representatives of major chieftains, and healers (*waganga*) at the Mandera mission. Speaking in Swahili, he opened the discussion by promising rewards of cash or gunpowder to settlement leaders and cloth to parents and midwives who would bring *vigego* to the mission.

The response of some of his listeners was to try to intimidate Picarda by raising the question of payment for the land occupied by the mission. Their threat was deflected by others who reminded the assembly that the matter of land had been settled by Kolwa, the dominant chieftain of the area, but Picarda's opponents had made their point: interference with treatment of *vigego* would mean trouble. Members of the assembly then explained that the kin of *vigego* would suffer if nothing was done about them (although they never stated that *vigego* must be killed).[9] Their argument, however, carried little weight with Picarda. Believing that their objections were rooted in a suspicion that the mission intended to traffic in captive children, Picarda tried to clarify his position by saying that while he wished to reward those who left *vigego* at the mission, he was not attempting to purchase slaves.

Realizing that his audience was not persuaded, Picarda decided to advance his own explanation of illness by arguing that it was caused not by *vigego* but by infanticide. But when he warned that God would use smallpox to strike down the murders of *vigego*, members of the assembly defended their position vigorously, saying that everyone would die if *vigego* were handed over to the mission. Perhaps the secret missionary

9. Mandera Mission Journal, July 29–30, 1883. Picarda's account of the meeting, it must be stressed, did not quote anyone as saying that *vigego* were killed; his opponents maintained that *vigego* should not be sent to the mission, but did not defend their right to slay *vigego*.

intention, contended one man, was to cause the deaths of all the villagers around Mandera by interfering with their methods of handling *vigego* so that the missionaries would be left in possession of the land. Picarda's final argument was that children must be allowed to survive so that villages would be bigger and better able to defend themselves, but this convinced no one.[10]

Had his audience unanimously rejected his views, Picarda probably would not have encountered open expressions of hostility, for unity would have made counter-argument unnecessary. Some of his listeners appeared ready, however, to accept both the proposal that *vigego* be placed with the missionaries and the suggestion that the causes of illness be rethought. As one participant remarked, since *vigego* might be banished or sold to slave dealers, why not sell them to the mission rather than to coastal traders? Apparently sensing danger in such comments, several audience members, particularly one speaker who declared that *vigego* were never killed, tried to halt the discussion by saying that nothing could be done in the absence of Kolwa and other major leaders. More diplomatic members of the assembly were careful to allow Picarda some satisfaction at the meeting's conclusion, by agreeing that they would not prevent anyone from bringing *vigego* to the mission. His initiative, nevertheless, was a failure; by April 1885 the mission had received only two *vigego,* and ten more years would elapse before attempts to rescue *vigego* would again be mentioned in the journal of the Mandera Mission.

Like other Spiritans, Picarda tried to conform to the conceptions of proper authority that prevailed in Zigua-speaking communities. By intervening in matters of health, however, he became a threat to their leaders, for he presented himself both as a superior healer, offering an alternative method of dealing with *vigego* and proclaiming his ability to protect against smallpox, and also as a patron who might decide to withdraw his trade connections and protection. Indeed, some members of his audience, including one leader who reminded his fellows that they had grown accustomed to "getting cloth and selling crops at the mission," felt that to obtain missionary patronage they must accept Picarda's proposals. Others in the assembly perceived Picarda more as a rival than as benefactor because his bargain—patronage in return for recognition as a superior healer—

10. Mandera Mission Journal, July 29–30, 1883. Picarda published several accounts of the 1883 meeting taken almost verbatim from the Mandera Mission Journal: "Autour de Mandera," p. 285; "Rapport"; "Compte-Rendu de la réunion des chefs du Miono et du Loupoungwi (Zanzibar)," pp. 400–413; and *L'Echo des Missions d'Afrique de la Congrégation du Saint-Esprit et du Saint Coeur de Marie,* pp. 171–183.

brought into question the preeminence of their healing powers and ultimately the legitimacy of their leadership. The majority of notables decided, therefore, that the missionaries would be permitted to serve only as patrons, not as healers. Hence after 1883 they frustrated persistent Spiritan efforts to use healing to win Christian converts, yet because they wished to retain missionary patronage they never ostracized the Spiritans. For their part, the Spiritans thought that their evangelical efforts would eventually succeed and assumed that neighboring villagers, who sometimes sought their medicines, respected them as *waganga*. Nevertheless, Picarda's neighbors had demarcated the limits of their interaction with the mission, for they would not allow the Europeans to meddle with the authority of political leaders and healers.

Thus the outcome of the Mandera meeting provides a measure of the change in political and patronal authority that took place between 1883 and Mtunte's execution in 1911. In 1883, a year before Karl Peters staked the first German claim to Uzigua, the Spiritan challenge to local authority failed utterly. To be sure, unanimity did not reign at the Mandera gathering, but the majority of the assembled leaders succeeded in restraining minority opinion and containing disquieting influences. Three decades later, however, even a subordinate woman such as Mchekumbo could defy her patron and cause his execution.[11]

A more obvious connection between the 1883 meeting and the Mtunte execution is the role of the Spiritans in the matter of infanticide. It was they who made it a political issue by convincing German officials that child-murder was common in Uzigua.[12] Although Picarda and other Spir-

---

11. German administrators acted on other charges brought by dependents against patrons, particularly in cases of infanticide: Mzee Ndege, Mafisa and Omali Gumbo, Kwinji.

12. The question here is not whether infanticide occurred, but rather its incidence. Infanticide is reported from many societies and many historical periods, and presumably occurred in precolonial Uzigua as well. Yet Europeans, and this point cannot be stressed too strongly, had no basis on which to estimate the incidence of infanticide. The Spiritans never reported seeing child-killing first-hand. In all likelihood the Uzigua situation was analogous to that of western Europe, where abandonment of children was much more common than infanticide. Indeed, the most famous *vigego* in oral traditions, including Mhelamwana and Mbegha, the founder of the Kilindi dynasty in the Usambara Mountains, suffered banishment rather than death: Steven Feierman, *The Shambaa Kingdom*, Chapters 2 and 3. On the European evidence: John Boswell, *The Kindness of Strangers: The Abandonment of Children in Western Europe from Late Antiquity to the Renaissance*, esp. pp. 44–45; Susan C. M. Scrimshaw, "Infanticide in Human Populations: Societal and Individual Concerns"; Martin Daly and Margo Wilson, "A Sociobiological Analysis of Human Infanticide," in *Infanticide: Comparative and Evolutionary Perspectives*, pp. 439–462, 487–502; William L. Langer, "Infanticide: A Historical Survey," pp. 353–365; Michael Tooley, *Abortion and Infanticide*, p. 315. Beliefs and practices such as those associated with *vigego* are found throughout Africa: S. Lagercrantz, *A Contribution to the Study of Anomalous Dentition and Its Ritual Significance in Africa*.

itans lacked first-hand evidence of infanticide, they frequently presented pictorial and written images of strangled as well as abandoned *vigego* in missionary publications as proof of the need for philanthropic contributions.[13] Donations in their support, wrote the missionaries, would enable them to shelter banished *vigego* and eradicate the state of primitive paganism in which infanticide flourished.[14] Not only were the charges of infanticide wholly unsubstantiated, however, but they also shifted from region to region as the missionaries moved inland. As long as they remained in Bagamoyo, they leveled their accusations principally against communities along the *Mrima,* but after building stations in Uzigua they showed no further interest in child-killing near the coast.[15] The longer they stayed in Uzigua, moreover, the more wildly exaggerated their estimates of child-murder became, for some of the Spiritans contended that infanticide was a more important cause of population decline than famine, disease, and slave hunting, and also predicted that the inhabitants of Uzigua would exterminate themselves.[16] German colonial officials accepted the Spiritan notion of a child-murdering "Zigua tribe" just as readily as they adopted the Spiritan belief that the Doe-speakers near Bagamoyo were cannibals. Indeed, the stereotypes of "the Zigua" as child-killers and "the Doe" as people-eaters would long remain current

13. A similar comment on Spiritan publications is made by Edward A. Alpers, "The Story of Swema: Female Vulnerability in Nineteenth-Century East Africa," in *Women and Slavery in Africa*, p. 189.

14. Étienne Baur, "Lettre" (1884), p. 337, and Raoul de Courmont, "Lettre" (1885), pp. 316–339. Spiritan accounts of group participation in child-killing may have been particularly shocking for their nineteenth-century French readers who assumed that the knowledge of birth by a number of persons would naturally protect the infant. Thus under French law, infanticide was distinguished from murder (and punished more harshly) as an act which occurred immediately following birth, before the child gained that protection: Paul Camille Hippolyte Brouardel, *L'Infanticide*, pp. 10–11.

15. The development of Spiritan ideas about infanticide can be traced in Anton Horner, "Lettre" (1870), p. 52; Baur, "Lettre" (1873), p. 62 and (1875), p. 522; Anton Horner, "Lettre" (1880), p. 39; Baur, "Lettre" (1883), p. 109; Alexandre Le Roy, "Lettre" (1884), pp. 46–47; "Mission de l'Immaculée-Conception, à Morogoro (Ouzigoua)," p. 119; Picarda, "Rapport" (1884), pp. 505–509; Baur, "Lettre" (1884), p. 337; Picarda, "Les Wazigoua," p. 156; Le Roy, "Rapport" (1886), pp. 195–196; Picarda, "Autour de Mandera," pp. 284–285; "Rapport d'ensemble sur la mission de Mandera," p. 20; Courmont, "Rapport" (1889), p. 58; Charles Gommenginger, "Lettre" (1889), p. 347.

16. Picarda estimated that two-thirds of all infants were killed: "Autour de Mandera," p. 284. Another report from Mandera (probably written by Picarda) increased the estimate to 70%: "Rapport d'ensemble sur la mission de Mandera," p. 20. Also, Le Roy, "Lettre," (1883), p. 321; Gommenginger, letter of September 1883 in Th. Hück, *P. Ludwig Karl Gommenginger*, p. 233; Le Roy, "Lettre" (1884), pp. 46–47; "Mission de l'Immaculée-Conception, à Morogoro," p. 119; Gommenginger, "Lettre" (1889), p. 347; Courmont, "Rapport" (1889), pp. 58–59; Le Roy, "Au Kilimandjaro," pp. 198ff; Le Roy, *Sur terre et sur l'eau*, p. 47; François X. Vogt, "Jahresbericht," (1908–1909), p. 84; Vogt, "Bericht," p. 84.

as first German, then British colonialists defined "tribal" identities and characteristics.[17]

Primarily responsible for the crime of infanticide, believed the Spiritans, were the *waganga,* whom one evangelist described unrestrainedly as, "the most detestable, nauseating, bloodthirsty creatures on the face of the earth." They blamed healers for making midwives and parents accomplices by playing upon their "state of crude superstition" to fill them with "empty fears."[18] Indeed, it was the Mandera confrontation that convinced the Spiritans that the *waganga* were their archenemies, for they felt that several village leaders had been prepared to accept Picarda's proposals, only to be dissuaded by the healers. "But what is the authority of a chief," despaired Picarda's colleague Raoul de Courmont, "or even of the Sultan [of Zanzibar] himself, against that of the sorcerers (*waganga*) and the tyranny of superstitious custom!"[19] "Never would an African dare to contravene custom," declared the Spiritan Ludwig Karl Gommenginger shortly after the 1883 meeting, "so long as the infernal band of sorcerers, who are the true holders of power in Africa, are present."[20]

After the German invasion of the *Mrima* in 1889, the Spiritans insistently conveyed their concerns about *waganga,* infanticide, and cannibalism to the German civil and military personnel who relied on them for information about Uzigua.[21] The missionaries informed German officials about suspected malefactors, especially the *waganga* who dealt with *vigego* and witchcraft, and sent individuals accused of infanticide to German courts.[22] When German forces patrolled near the missions, moreover, the evangelists settled old scores by encouraging the colonial military to punish their prime adversaries, the *waganga.* In 1890 and 1891, for example, missionaries and colonial officials cooperated in suppressing *waganga* and

17. Dr. K.Ganzenmüller, "Usegura und Usaramo, Ukhutu, Usagara und Ugogo," p. 117; A. Bloyet, "À la Station de Kondoa," p. 363; Kohler, "Beantwortung des Fragebogens" and Dr. Alfred Reuss,"Wazeguha," Rhodes House, Micr. Afr. 480; "Kindermord unter den Wadoe- u. Wasegua Stammen," p. 23; Lorenz, "Sitten und Gebräuche unserer Wanguru," p. 103; RKA 6479 [where the Spiritan attribution of low population density to infanticide gains official credence], 217/14, 6569/25; Charles Dundas, "Native Laws of Some Bantu Tribes of East Africa," p. 235.

18. Quotes from Gommenginger, letter of January 7, 1883, in Hück, *Gommenginger.* On *waganga* treating women during and after childbirth: Vogt, "Missions Korrespondenz," p. 177.

19. Courmont, "Lettre" (1885), pp. 319–321; Gommenginger, "Lettre" (1889), p. 347; Le Roy, "Au Kilimandjaro," p. 199 and "Lettre" (1883), p. 319; RKA 6476/192–193.

20. Gommenginger, letter of September, 1883 in Hück, *Gommenginger.*

21. Lugoba Mission Journal, August 23 and 29, 1912; RKA 6476/192–193.

22. Mandera Mission Journal, February 7, 1895; Lugoba Mission Journal, August 27 and 29, 1912, June 12, 1914.

ZANGUEBAR. — *Autour de Mondéra.* — La sorcière et l'enfant : d'après un dessin du R. P. Le Roy.
(Voir page 284)

Figure 3. Spiritan depiction of one of the healers whom missionaries blamed for infanticide, holding an apparently fearful child. Source: *LMC* 18 (1886): 283.

other leaders of southern Nguu. When a German military column reached Mhonda in January 1890, the Spiritans told its commanders that accusations of witchcraft, involving the *waganga* who helped determine the treatment of witches, were the chief cause of violence in the area. Over the following weeks, German forces and African Christian residents of the mission seized on allegations of witchcraft-related disputes to attack numerous settlements.[23] A year later the Spiritans and German officials renewed the campaign after the head of the mission brought several individuals to the attention of a German officer, whose soldiers then plundered their villages. At a public meeting conducted subsequently in the mission compound, the German official prohibited both warfare and infanticide.[24]

On other occasions the Spiritans took matters into their own hands. At their Lugoba station near the Wami River, they waged a struggle against *waganga* for several years, administering beatings and confiscating medicines before finally declaring victory in 1914. Because they had driven the *waganga* underground, reported the missionaries triumphantly, the healers could now practice only in secret.[25] The German government also remained attentive to the purportedly common practice of infanticide, particularly after Governor Eduard von Liebert declared that the resolution of this "problem" was to be the primary aim of his tour through Uzigua in 1898.[26] Administrators accused some chieftains, such as Bibi Mandaro at Mgera, of condoning or committing infanticide and, when little evidence of child-murder surfaced, concluded that their efforts had been successful, never realizing that the notion of widespread infanticide in Uzigua was a missionary invention.[27]

Colonial Pacification in Uzigua

Accusations of infanticide were thus a pretext for military aggression against Zigua-speaking leaders, for by attacking their villages and confiscating crops, livestock, and dependents, German officials denied chieftains

23. Mhonda Mission Journal, January 3, 11–13 and 25–27, 1890.
24. Mhonda Mission Journal, January 5–8, 1891. For a similar meeting at Mandera: Mandera Mission Journal, March 9, 1893.
25. Lugoba Mission Journal, April 13, November 6 and 8, 1913, January 1, 1914, January 15, 1915.
26. RKA 217/14, 237/1/70, 6472/328, 6469/308, 6569/25.
27. RKA 217/14, 6469/306–308, 6472/238.

and settlement heads the ability to employ armed force, maintain village fortifications, adjudicate disputes, provide patronage, and protect their subjects' health, particularly by controlling witchcraft. Having used force and terror to destroy their independent political authority, colonial administrators then attempted to transform some of them into compliant administrative functionaries. The violence of colonial pacification was epitomized by the military operations at Mhonda, which began in January 1890 when German attacks on *waganga* and other enemies of the Mhonda mission caused "many" deaths.[28] A year later, ninety African soldiers and six German officers, after pausing at Mandera to capture accused "thieves" and burn "several" villages, returned to Mhonda to destroy at least seventeen settlements in eight days, capture or kill numerous villagers, and leave others "horribly" wounded. Turmoil continued following the withdrawal of the soldiers, reported the Spiritans, because patrons burned the homesteads of dependents who had failed to rally to their defense.[29]

In 1893, another military detachment, consisting of several high-ranking military and civil officials, five German non-commissioned officers, and 150 African soldiers, began a series of attacks throughout Uzigua by making retaliatory raids on villages near the coast that had mustered resistance during the *Mrima* war of 1889.[30] At Mandera it destroyed the settlement of a leader whom the Spiritans identified as a thief and kidnapper. (Shortly afterwards, the Spiritans themselves led a force of mission inmates that burned another village.)[31] At Mhonda the Germans held court to settle several cases which, according to the missionaries, stemmed from witchcraft accusations.[32] "The purpose [of the German expedition]," commented a missionary, "was to show the German flag in the area and judge serious disputes. Chiefs and others who wished to present grievances came in large numbers; but when it was seen that the first complainant, who seemed to be in the wrong, received fifty strokes of the hippo-hide whip, everyone else kept his mouth shut."[33]

As the column continued its tour of Uzigua, many settlements,

28. Mhonda Mission Journal, January 3, 11–13, 25 and 27, 1890.

29. Mandera Mission Journal, December 15, 1890; Mhonda Mission Journal, January 1891; *BC* 16: 727.

30. *Koloniales Jahrbuch* (1893), p. 211; "Einem Berichte des Bezirksamtmanns v. Rode," p. 375.

31. Mandera Mission Journal, March 9, 11, 13 and 24, 1893; "Bericht des Kompagnieführers Leue über die Expedition nach Mhonda," *DKb* 4 (1893): 247.

32. RKA 283/31; "Bericht des Kompagnieführers Leue," p. 249 and "Einem Berichte des Bezirksamtmanns v. Rode," p. 376; Mhonda Mission Journal, March 19, 1893; A. Leue, "Nguru," p. 362.

33. *BC* 17 (1893–1896): 687.

having heard of the punishments meted out to village heads, emptied as the Germans approached.[34] At Magamba, however, the detachment met Sonyo, decided (partly because he was one of the few leaders who did not flee the advancing Germans) that he must be "certainly the most powerful chief in all Uzigua," and recognized him as the primary government appointee in central Uzigua. Sonyo took advantage of the column's visit to have the Germans apprehend three old rivals whom he accused of cattle stealing. Soon after leaving Magamba the expedition returned to the coast, where one of its satisfied commanders wrote that the operation had succeeded in spreading "salutary terror." Prior to 1893, he remarked, leaders of the region scarcely recognized colonial suzerainty, but now they could be expected to heed administrators.[35]

Over the next ten years, the colonial military patrolled regularly in Uzigua to grant letters of appointment to some leaders and destroy the villages of others.[36] In mid-1895, for instance, a German force chased "robbers" through Uzigua, deposed a chieftain at Kiwanda, attacked two settlements at Mgambo, imprisoned the head of Kwa Konde, destroyed the villages of Sonyo's rivals at Handeni, and took hundreds of cattle, sheep, and goats.[37] The operation, which according to the Mandera missionaries had a "happy effect" on the residents of Uzigua, "again re-established respect for the administration."[38] The colonial state employed "salutary terror" once more in 1896 when a large force, equipped with a maxim gun and led by ten German officers, "made war," as a Spiritan put it, "on some robbing and murdering chiefs." The expedition attacked villages, offered bounties for leaders who fled, and took cattle and captives. In November 1896 another German column burned a village in the Nguu Mountains and expropriated its livestock.[39]

Numerous village leaders became as adept as Sonyo and the Spiritans, however, at turning the colonial military against their enemies, often by playing on German concerns with *waganga*, infanticide, and witchcraft.[40] One appointed village head in northern Nguu named Nkumuwlwa Pogwa,

34. RKA 283/31–32.

35. "Einem Berichte des Bezirksamtmanns v. Rode," pp. 377–380.

36. RKA 215/7–12, 217/8–10, 282/137–142, 1034/33–43.

37. RKA 286/123–129.

38. Mandera Mission Journal, July 22, 1895; *Jahresbericht* (1894–1895), p. 89.

39. RKA 6467/298–301; Mandera Mission Journal, July 16, 1896; Mhonda Mission Journal, November 1, 1896; *BC* 18: 784.

40. An example of Spiritan use of this tactic was the attack on Mweruguru of Kwa Manda. For the background, see: "Bericht des Kompagnie-führers Leue," p. 247; "Aus dem Bezirk Pangani," *DKb* 13 (1902): 257; "Notes on the History and Customs of the Wazigua," Morogoro Province Book, v. 2, TNA.

for example, drew the Germans into a dispute with the neighboring settlement of Kwa Deleza, from which the wife of his mother's brother had come. The quarrel developed after the woman's death, when Nkumuwlwa Pogwa charged that her kin at Kwa Deleza had killed her in the belief that she was a witch. In precolonial society the murder of a witch would have been no crime, but under the new colonial dispensation it was likely to provoke a punitive government response. Nkumuwlwa Pogwa informed the Germans, who predictably sent troops from Pangani to burn Kwa Deleza and imprison a number of its residents.[41]

Taxation and the Installation of Akidas

The structure of local administration that rested on the authority of appointees such as Sonyo and Nkumuwlwa Pogwa failed to survive the introduction of monetary taxation in 1898, for when the German government required that local functionaries become tax collectors, the appointees lost all ability to protect their subjects and thus their precolonial legitimacy as well. Taxation placed the appointees under pressure from both administrators, who wanted thorough revenue gathering, and their taxpaying subjects, who wanted protection from colonial impositions. Their dilemma was shared, in fact, by the Spiritans, who until administrators threatened to charge them with sedition, encouraged their clients to refuse to pay taxes.[42] As the ineffectiveness of local appointees became apparent, not only in Uzigua but throughout German East Africa, the government replaced them with new functionaries called Akidas, most of whom were educated men from *Mrima* towns whose literacy in Swahili enabled them to maintain contact with superiors through written reports and directives. Although some Akidas encountered opposition from entrenched notables, in most areas literate Swahili men supplanted the Zigua-speaking chieftains.[43] "Those chieftains who cooperated with German rule," commented the "History of the Zigua," "were made Akidas, while others were removed and replaced by men from the coast."[44]

Administrators hoped that the Akidas would follow bureaucratic

41. Ali S. Sambuguma, Kwediboma and Pogwa Rashidi, Handeni and Kwediboma.
42. RKA 856/110–112, 125–128 and 157, and 1053/198.
43. RKA 6469/298 and 305–306. For opposition to the Akida at Mhonda, see Mhonda Mission Journal, May 11, 1900 and *Jahresbericht* (1898–1899), p. 244.
44. "Historia ya Wazigua."

procedures more faithfully than the locally-appointed chiefs who were sus-
ceptible to pressures from kin, neighbors, and dependents, but partly because soldiers were at their disposal, they often proved to be despots who
had scant regard either for bureaucratic niceties or for their subjects' welfare. The actions of Akida Salim Said, for example, provoked the residents
of Mhonda to complain that he had virtually enslaved them.[45] Indeed,
although the Akidas increased tax revenue in Uzigua, they did so by making demands which often exceeded official tax rates.[46] "It's stupid," remarked a Spiritan at Mandera about their methods of collecting taxes,
"people have nothing." When cattle owners were unable to pay cash, he
continued, the Akida took their livestock, "and as for those who have no
livestock, he takes their women."[47] Towards the end of the devastating
1898–1900 famine (see Chapter Eight), Mhonda's new Akida expropriated
livestock and other goods, not only from ratepayers with outstanding tax
bills but also from those who had already paid taxes. Residents fled
Mhonda as the irregular levies continued, particularly in February 1901
when the Akida announced that he would collect all unpaid taxes within
twenty days. Frightened taxpayers tried to sell maize, rice, chickens, goats,
and firearms at the mission, while many farmers began wearing bark cloth
and hides, the Spiritans noted, because taxes and famine prevented purchases of cloth. Eventually the district administrator from Bagamoyo visited Mhonda to investigate grievances against the Akida.[48]

Although the Akidas had power, they possessed little of the legitimacy that precolonial leaders had derived from kinship, marriage alliances,
and service as patrons, healers, and ritual leaders. Perhaps for that reason,
Swahili Akidas tried to counter the influence of *waganga* and *wegazi* by
serving as Islamic teachers and prayer leaders. Akidas not only prohibited
attendance at Christian schools but also required that children be enrolled
in Qur'anic classes or the government primary schools that were generally
staffed by Muslim teachers.[49] They also tried to develop patronage networks by sponsoring the construction of mosques and Qur'anic schools
and by distributing food during Islamic celebrations. Indeed, with the

45. Rajabu Sudi, Manga; Mhonda Mission Journal, May 11, 1900.
46. *DKb* 12 (1901): 274 and Mhonda Mission Journal, January 15–17, 1901.
47. Mandera Mission Journal, March 10, 23, April 2–5, May 22 and August 28, 1900.
48. Mhonda Mission Journal, November 19, 1900, January 15–17, February 10, 22, 25
and March 6, 1901, February 2 and June 23, 1902.
49. *BC* 24: 515, 25: 711–712; Mandera Mission Journal, March 10, 1900, October 4 and
7, 1910, April 2, 1914; *Jahresbericht* (1912–1913), p. 19; M. Klamroth, *Der Islam in Deutsch
Ostafrika*, p. 11.

Akidas' encouragement the generation that were young adults between 1900 and 1915 became the first in Uzigua to profess Islam in large numbers.[50] Yet Islamic observance—perfunctory in the opinion of European missionaries—was probably as much a sign that converts accepted the authority of Akidas as an indication of transformed religious and intellectual outlook.[51] Food prohibitions, for example, which in precolonial society had connoted political loyalties as tokens of *si* community membership, continued to have political significance as marks of allegiance to the Akida.[52]

The Crisis of Authority and Environmental Control

The pacification campaigns and installation of the Akidas, combined with taxation and reorientation of trade, pushed the chieftains inexorably into decline. Among the first to fall was Sedenga, a formerly powerful figure in the Pangani Valley who by 1896, according to German traveler Max Schoeller, was only a minor settlement head:

> Nine years earlier, when Graf Telecki and Von Höhnel travelled through the same district, political conditions were much different. German authority in the area was not yet established and Sedenga reigned all-powerful. Nine years before he was a vigorous man; now he is old and blind, and whereas he had returned numerous gifts of Graf Telecki, now he thankfully accepted from me a handful of rupees. . . . Under the power of the [German] protectorate, where no warfare among petty sultans is allowed, their power, energy and importance soon declines.[53]

While in Sedenga's case age and infirmity may have contributed to his downfall, many chieftains shared his fate. Unable to accumulate wealth and satisfy the obligations of patronage, they could no longer exercise authority over wide circles of clients and subjects.

The modern Handeni resident Yusufu Kaberwa contends that the

50. Remarking upon the small number of Muslims in precolonial Uzigua, particularly outside major trade centers and chieftains' villages, were James T. Last, "The Tribes on the Road to Mpwapwa," p. 662, and Le Roy, "Au Kilimandjaro," pp. 197–198. On the role of Akidas in Islamic proselytization: C. H. Becker, "Materialien zur Kenntnis des Islam in Deutsch-Östafrika," pp. 15–16; *BC* 25, pp. 711–712 and 27 (1918–1920), p. 276; Klamroth, *Der Islam*, p. 23; G. T. Manley, "Mohammedan Advance in Africa," p. 22. On conversion under the Akidas: Elders of Magamba and Haji Luwambo (Kwediboma, September 30, 1982).

51. W. H. Kisbey, "A Tour in the Zigua Country," p. 205, and "The Work at Korogwe," p. 35; untitled note in *Central Africa* 31 (April 1913): 108.

52. Mhonda Mission Journal, June 12, 1900, February 2 and July 20, 1902; *BC* 20, p. 653.

53. Schoeller 1: 59 and 63.

inability to provide patronage brought chieftain Kilo Mwanamachau not only political ruin, but also betrayal and death. Although Kilo Mwanamachau was a prominent trader with many Maasai clients, when the Germans began selecting administrative chiefs in the early 1890s, says Yusufu Kaberwa, they rejected his application for an appointment. Returning home from an unsuccessful meeting with colonial officials, Kilo found that the great rinderpest panzootic of 1891 (see Chapter Eight) had impoverished his Maasai allies. Unable to respond to their pleas for assistance, he fell victim to the treachery of old friends when a bribe offered by Kilo's rival Sonyo (who in contrast to Kilo had received a German appointment) induced one of his Maasai confidants to murder Kilo. Thus, in Yusufu Kaberwa's account, Kilo died because he could not retain the loyalty of clients.[54]

Like Kilo Mwanamachau's pastoralist clients, most residents of Uzigua suffered deprivation during and after the German colonial period. In modern Handeni District, farmers who seek an explanation of twentieth-century famine and scarcity often speak about the worsening of environmental conditions, particularly the increase of crop-destroying bush pigs and birds, the spread of tsetse flies, declining rainfall, and reduced soil fertility, which they attribute to weakened ties with the dead.[55] Asumani Nyokka of Kwediboma Village says, for instance, that "the land is tired" because settlements and neighborhoods have ceased performing the community rituals which renewed relations with ancestors, particularly *si* founders.[56] Mohamedi Mjewe of Kwediboma believes that "people have stopped getting blessings [*baraka*] since they abandoned the indigenous customs [*mila za kienyeji*]."[57] The *matambiko* [sing. *tambiko*], the rituals which once ensured the blessings of ancestors, are no longer observed, these elders assert, because they have been discouraged by Islam and Christianity. Consequently, no one knows how to perform them.[58]

The disappearance of ritual leaders was in fact accompanied by the narrowing of the groups that perform *matambiko*. In late precolonial society, several settlements cooperated in the performance of the most important *matambiko*, particularly those intended to bring rain, and in

54. Yusufu Kaberwa, Mswaki and Ernest Mkomwa, Kwa Masaka.
55. One example of such a discussion was with Mohamedi Lusingo, Mohamedi Mkande, Ibrahim Kigobwa and others, Mafisa.
56. Asumani Nyokka (Kwediboma, August 30, 1982 and March 29, 1983); also, Mohamedi Mjewe (Kwediboma, February 8, 1983).
57. Mohamedi Mjewe (Kwediboma, September 27, 1982).
58. In similar circumstances, peasants in Mozambique have also disavowed knowledge of rituals: Sherilynn Young, "What Have They Done With the Rain."

Figure 4. Mohamedi Mjewe, a healer and expert on local history, with his wife, at Kwediboma Village in Handeni District in 1982. Author's photograph.

addition, individual villages held their own *matambiko* at public shrines built in central courtyards or near village entrances.[59] During the colonial period, however, ancestor shrines disappeared and the performance of *matambiko* became increasingly subterranean. Hence, rather than reflecting political loyalties and modes of cooperation that extended across whole settlements and neighborhoods, modern *matambiko* have fallen into the attenuated sphere of shallow descent groups and single households. Their purposes have changed correspondingly, for now they are performed to protect individual health and fecundity rather than to benefit the community as a whole.[60]

59. Descriptions of ancestor shrines were given by Mohamedi Mjewe (Kwediboma, September 27, 1982) and Mzee Samgome, Kwediboma. Also, Gommenginger, letter of September 1883, in Hück, *Gommenginger*.

60. This process has been noted in Uzigua by Elisabeth Grohs, *Kisazi: Reiferiten der Mädchen bei den Zigua und Ngulu Ost-Tanzanias*, pp. 40–42, and in the Uzaramo hinterland

One reason for the disappearance of ritual leaders and the major *matambiko* is that few individuals, knowing that they would face the disapprobation of Islamic teachers and Christian administrators and missionaries, wish to assert their qualifications to conduct public *matambiko*. Another reason is that the *si* identities that defined the groups participating in the rituals lost their political significance when the colonial state deprived local leaders of power. The *matambiko* which both reaffirmed *si* group identities and sanctioned political authority fell into disuse as the decline of precolonial authority erased the political relevance of the *si* identities themselves.

Among the Handeni residents who link diminished ritual life to environmental difficulties and political change was Nyangasi Mohamedi Munga of Kilwa Village. He begins his argument with a simple example of environmental control, saying that farmers formerly cultivated contiguous plots where they coordinated planting and harvesting to make guarding crops from birds and bush pigs easier. They did this rather than work independently, said Munga, because they were under the authority of settlement heads:

> The head person could compel others to do things. Now a person was not able to go off and cultivate by himself some place. He might be killed by people from there. That's why people cultivated together. It was because of the threat of war and violence, because at that time there was no central government. The only government was of the head person who rules others. He was the ruler who protected people. That's why people cultivated together, not because they wanted to.[61]

With this last point Munga goes to the heart of his argument: farmers obtained the benefits of a healthy, productive environment only when they submitted to the authority of patrons who dominated entire neighborhoods and coordinated the labor of their dependents. Group cohesion was lost, however, in the colonial period: "When colonial government was introduced, people dispersed . . . in other words, that form of government destroyed the old forms of unity."

of Dar es Salaam by Marja-Liisa Swantz, *Ritual and Symbol in Transitional Zaramo Society*, pp. 173–179. Swantz links the "change away from community rites toward group and individual rites" with the decline of communal agricultural practices and the disappearance of "traditional leadership." The distinction between *matambiko* conducted by *si* communities and those performed by individual lineages and households is made by Thomas McVicar in "Wanguru Religion," pp. 17–21.

61. Nyangasi Mohamedi Munga, Kilwa. This last point is emphasized by others as well, for example Mzee Samgome, Kwediboma.

Then Munga connects political change to another, more subtle influence over the environment, saying that formerly the head of a neighborhood organized the *matambiko* which brought together households and settlements when they needed rain or protection from pestilence.[62] This kind of *tambiko* has disappeared, he says, though today minor rituals, such as the first shaving of an infant by an influential elder, are still practiced in small groups.[63] "The *matambiko* are dead," declares Munga, "but the shaving ritual has not died." Whereas in the past *matambiko* united settlements and neighborhoods, now "*matambiko* and the shaving rituals stay within a single household." Uzigua suffers adversity, peasants like Nyangasi Mohamedi Munga believe, because there no longer exists the political authority that formerly combined control of entire villages and neighborhoods with the power to obtain the blessings of ancestors.

62. In this he echoes Mohamedi Semsambia, Kilwa, who said that one would identify the organizer of a *tambiko* by asking, "Who is the head person [*mkubwa*] in a certain *si*? If the *mkubwa* is so-and-so, then that's who is the leader of the *tambiko*."

63. This rite is described by Mkomwa and Nkwileh, "Jadi, Mila, Desturi na Historia za Wazigua."

8. Colonialism, Famine, and Epizootic, 1884–1914

Peasants such as Nyangasi Mohamedi Munga say that environmental conditions became worse and relations with the ancestors more distant because colonial conquest changed the nature of political authority. Their view can be tested by comparing the worst subsistence crisis sustained by the precolonial chieftains, the famine of 1884–1886, with subsequent famines under German colonial rule. During the crisis of the mid-1880s, relatively few farmers fled long distances, but during famines of the German period, flight from the region and many deaths reduced the farming population, allowed the spread of vegetation, wildlife, and disease-bearing insects, and resulted in epizootics of trypanosomiasis and theileriosis. Because diseases heightened scarcity by destroying wealth in livestock, they helped set in motion a cycle of subsequent famines, continued depopulation, and further deterioration of the bovine disease environment. These reversals produced a prolonged period of chronic hunger whose duration, from the mid-1890s through the mid-1940s, had no nineteenth-century precedent.

The "Lugala" Famine of 1884–1886

Residents of early-colonial Uzigua could remember no episode in at least the preceding fifty years comparable to the famine that, because it coincided in 1884–1886 with the appearance of a comet, became known as "*lugala*," or "star."[1] *Lugala* was a tragedy, and in Handeni continues to be regarded as such because for the destitute, the cost of survival was servility

---

1. Mandera Mission Journal, July 24, 1898. A survey of East African travel literature reached the same conclusion: Eduard Kremer, *Die Unperiodischen Schwankungen der Niederschläge und die Hungersnöte in Deutsch-Ost-Afrika*, pp. 29–39.

or dependence upon the chieftains whose powers and commercial involvement were at their height. Yet it is important, even so, to distinguish between its tragic social impact and its demographic and environmental consequences, for by comparison with famines of the colonial period, the effects of *lugala* were limited: most farmers found food reserves, remained in their homes or moved only short distances, and continued to manage vegetation.

Lugala followed a drought that lasted from late 1883 through the long-rains season of 1884, but scarcity became severe only after the failure of the farmers' second line of defense, the pumpkins (*Cucurbita spp.*) that were interplanted with sorghum and maize as a famine reserve.[2] Yet, despite widespread shortages, relatively little population movement occurred. At Mandera, for example, cultivators generally stayed in their homes throughout the famine and relied on Zigua-speaking and Spiritan patrons who, like chieftains and patrons throughout Uzigua, were prepared to claim new dependents because they had accumulated currency, food reserves, and livestock during the commercial boom of the 1870s and 1880s.[3] Indeed, relations with chieftains and other patrons determined the fate of many farmers, for while the clients, kin, and affines in the chieftains' closer circles of dependents received stored and imported foods, politically peripheral communities not only had no claim on the resources of chieftains, but might well find their grain reserves drained away as tribute. This in fact was the situation in much of the Nguu Mountains, where leaders such as Mtiga, having obtained grain from tributary farmers, distributed some of it to their core constituencies and sold the rest to caravans, merchant camps, and the lowlands residents who sought food in Nguu during the famine. Consequently, although food was available in the chieftains' settlements, hunger became so widespread in outlying areas that even after an early harvest in May 1884 increased maize supplies, reduced prices by sixty percent, and attracted food purchasers from the lowlands, many highland farmers still lacked staples.[4]

Some tribute-paying highlanders survived *lugala* by leaving their homes for the chieftains' core territories, but their departure emptied villages in politically peripheral areas such as the portions of northern Nguu that were

2. Omali Maligwa Kidiza, Gombero.
3. Mandera Mission Journal, February, May, July (especially July 28), 1884.
4. Mhonda Mission Journal, 1884.

to a great extent depopulated by a famine two years ago, which drove away
the people into Uzeguha, and they have not yet returned. Where there used
to be villages and shambas [cultivated plots] there is now nothing but jungle.[5]

The refugees of northern Nguu moved no more than fifteen or twenty
miles eastward, however, where they entered the domain of the Mbwego
chieftains and settled in attractive locations such as the valley beneath
Kilindi Mountain that welcomed the German visitor Franz Stuhlmann
in 1888:

> The enchantingly fertile valley has a nearly flat bottom with dark soils,
> through which flows the small Msiri creek. . . . Numerous villages have been
> established at slight elevations in the valley and on the surrounding mountain
> slopes. From a single vantage point one can see six villages, which is a rare
> occurrence in Africa. . . . The people appear to be fairly prosperous, for I saw
> very good cattle and many firearms. Often people from the coast stop here to
> buy food, tobacco, etc.[6]

The newcomers, drawn to these areas by trading opportunities and a
healthy cattle environment as well as by patronage, made this and other
valleys east of Nguu some of the most densely-settled localities in Uzigua
after *lugala*.[7]

The price of refuge in these favored environments, however, was the
status of client, pawn, or slave. For this reason, residents of modern Handeni associate *lugala*, much more than subsequent famines, with loss of
autonomy by the powerless and predatory behavior by the powerful:

> If you went travelling on the road with your wife and your possessions you
> could be robbed of everything. . . . If you were weak you would be
> robbed . . . that's the way the *lugala* famine was . . . The locust famine [of
> 1894–1896] did not cause this same type of chaos . . . the number of slaves
> increased [during 1884–1886].[8]

Yet while *lugala* not only meant upheaval in personal fortunes, but also
environmental reversals in the areas that lost farmers, management of

---

5. Bishop Parker, "Letter," p. 693.
6. Mohamedi Lusingo, Mafisa, born during *lugala*, was taken as an infant to Kilindi;
also, Omali Maligwa Kidiza, Gombero; Franz Stuhlmann, "Bericht über eine Reise durch
Usegua und Unguu," pp. 167–168; and "Reise von Bagamoyo." 2.
7. Other centers of political power also attracted migrants during 1884–1886: Carol Jane
Sissons, "Economic Prosperity in Ugogo, East Africa, 1860–1890," p. 144.
8. Mzee Ndege, Mafisa.

vegetation continued in many places and probably improved in the neighborhoods where the chieftains attracted refugees, for the newcomers expanded the cleared, cultivated, and vector-free areas where much of the region's livestock lived. Indeed, the movement of many farmers into the chieftaincies during *lugala* confirms Nyangasi Mohamedi Munga's belief that submission to political authority—the concession made by the newcomers to populous, more secure settlements—was the foundation of late precolonial environmental control.

Establishing the Pattern of Colonial Famine: The Crises of 1894–1896 and 1898–1900

The patronage that saved many farmers during *lugala* had already disappeared, however, when from 1894 to 1896 the first major famine of the colonial period caused the dispersal of farming communities, not only in the politically peripheral regions that had lost farmers ten years earlier, but throughout Uzigua. Among the first villages to be stricken by shortages were the communities of southern Nguu that had endured repeated German attacks during the early 1890s, for scarcity developed there even before locust plagues destroyed successive crops from early 1894 through August 1896.[9] Although numerous famine-related deaths occurred in 1894, considerably worse conditions in the following year forced many villagers to flee the highlands. Nevertheless, lowlanders continued searching for provisions in southern Nguu, for like the fleeing highlanders they were discovering that patronage was much harder to find than it had been in the mid-1880s.[10] Even the Mandera Spiritans were refused assistance by their patron, the formerly formidable chieftain Kolwa.[11] Farmers without patronage abandoned villages and disrupted agriculture throughout the region as they streamed towards *Mrima* towns.[12]

   The destitute besieged missions and government installations, including the district headquarters at Mpwapwa where former slaves established

9. On the causes of periodic locust plagues, see Chapter Ten.
   10. Mhonda Mission Journal, 1894–1896 and *BC* 17: 686–687; Hamburgisches Museum für Völkerkunde und Vorgeschichte, A77; Nachlass Fonck, "Aus Krieg und Frieden," pp. 107, 118–120.
   11. Mandera Mission Journal, 1894–1896 and *BC* 17: 724.
   12. Mandera Mission Journal, September and December 15, 1894 and June 1895; Nachlass Fonck, "Aus Krieg und Frieden," pp. 107–108, 118–120; *BC* 17: 724 and 18: 785; Raoul de Courmont, "Lettre" (1896), p. 68; *Koloniales Jahrbuch* (1895), p. 114.

a squatters' camp.[13] But rather than providing patronage with all of its long-term obligations, government officials and missionaries offered only short-term loans. While the Spiritans, for instance, furnished food on credit, their terms placed great pressure on debtors, forcing some to leave children at the mission as pawns and others to bring missionary creditors their first grain harvest in more than two years during May and July 1896 despite continuing scarcity.[14] Yet the indigent could not refuse short-term credit, because the ties between patrons and dependents that had formerly persisted through seasonal cycles of indebtedness, labor service, and post-harvest repayments were breaking. However, these forms of credit did not stem the flow of migrants, and as a result Uzigua's post-famine population was noticeably smaller and more scattered. In the Wami Valley and the southern Nguu Mountains, only a few households inhabited formerly size-able settlements, while Pangani Valley villages likewise contained fewer residents and were less numerous than before the crisis.[15]

The pattern of depopulation and disruption of environmental man-agement that developed in 1894–1896 reappeared during the famine of 1898–1900, though this time on a vaster scale, for Uzigua's worst modern famine was but a microcosm of the disaster that swept East Africa.[16] Con-tributing to the catastrophe was a new factor which, like demographic and environmental reversals, would also become characteristic of colonial fam-ine—sales of food reserves to pay taxes. The famine began in lowland Uzigua when locusts destroyed short rains maize in January 1898, and be-came much worse after drought ruined subsequent long rains plantings. At Mandera, many villagers had already taken flight by July, including five-sixths of the African Christians who during *lugala* had served as patrons themselves.[17] The enormity of the disaster understandably blinded most observers to the uneven impact made by drought and locusts, although one missionary in the Uzaramo hinterland of Dar es Salaam nevertheless described, in much greater detail than any report from Uzigua, the variety of conditions that undoubtedly existed throughout northeastern Tanza-nia.[18] While drought and locusts, he noted, left some districts and house-

13. Fonck, "Aus Krieg und Frieden," pp. 107–108, 118–120.

14. Courmont, "Lettre" (1896), p. 68; *BC* 18: 785–786; Mandera Mission Journal, June 1895, May 20 and July 6, 1896.

15. *BC* 18: 783–785; RKA 237/1/79; Oscar Baumann, *Usambara und seine Nachbargebiete*, p. 276; Max Schoeller, *Mitteilungen über meine Reise*, 1: 59, 61, 75.

16. Reports of famine in German East Africa are in RKA 771.

17. Mandera Mission Journal, 1898–1899; *BC* 19: 501 and 649.

18. RKA 771/19–24.

holds entirely without subsistence, others had sufficient food stocks and replenished them with abundant harvests in 1900.[19] Indeed, many farmers lost access to food reserves not merely because of crop failure and locust plagues, but also because grain sales to raise tax money drained away food supplies that formerly would have circulated within the region along patronage and trade networks. For this reason, Uzigua exported grain to southern Tanganyika between 1901 and 1903, and the Spiritans at both Mandera and Mhonda were able to make substantial crop purchases in the midst of famine. "Great quantities of maize," wrote the Mandera journalist in 1900, "have been brought here to pay taxes."[20]

Crop marketing continued throughout the famine both because taxpayers needed tax money and because a few relatively fortunate villagers were able to make regular food purchases. For while coastal merchants raised grain prices by 100 percent and thus pushed marketed food beyond the means of many individuals, particularly the women and children who were abandoned by husbands and fathers, a minority of Uzigua residents nevertheless managed to buy grain, sometimes by traveling to Pangani for supplies of "*karachi*," the sorghum imported from India.[21] Eventually, however, merchants suspended imports into Uzigua as declining purchasing power depressed market demand, partly because seasonally fluctuating grain prices prevented the farmers who raised tax money through postharvest crop sales from earning enough cash for subsequent food purchases.[22] Cultivators at Mandera, for example, sold grain to the missionaries for 7 *pesa* per *pishi* after the 1898 harvest, only to find that the missionaries offered them the same grain for 16 *pesa* per *pishi* during the following pre-harvest season.[23] A similiar situation developed at the Mpwapwa administrative headquarters, where many farmers indebted to the wives of African soldiers disposed of crops at one-third to one-half of their market value.[24]

Because many famine victims could neither purchase food nor obtain patronage, they fled to coastal towns, the more favored portions of the highlands, the missions, and administrative centers, just as the destitute

19. RKA 6472/299–303; *Berichte über Land- und Forstwirtschaft* (1902), p. 82.
20. Mandera Mission Journal, March 23, 1900; also, RKA 6469/294–308. For food exports: RKA 771; *Berichte über Land- und Forstwirtschaft* (1903), p. 232.
21. Mhonda Mission Journal, July 6, 1896 and March 26, 1899; Mohamedi Lusingo, Mafisa; Abdala Hamani Msede and Ali Omali Kipande, Kwa Dundwa.
22. RKA 6472/299–303; *Berichte über Land- und Forstwirtschaft* (1902), p. 82.
23. A *pishi* equals one-half gallon or six pounds.
24. Hamburgisches Museum für Völkerkunde und Vorgeschichte, A77; Nachlass Fonck, "Notstands- und Steuerverhältnisse in Mpapua, 1902" (Mpwapwa, June 15, 1903) and "Jahresbericht: Mpapua" (March 31, 1903).

had done in the mid-1890s. Should the rains fail only once, commented a Spiritan at Mandera in 1899, many families would have to migrate long distances,[25] but some would fail to reach safety: "Alas! Not all have arrived: utterly exhausted and without any strength, many have died *en route* and their corpses line the roads." In congested centers of refuge smallpox epidemics developed and contributed heavily to the mortality which, reported the Spiritans, claimed half of Mandera's residents.[26]

Thus the population of Uzigua became ever smaller and more scattered in the wake of the 1898−1900 disaster, not only because famine increased mortality and migration, but also because dependents, even those who were not expelled outright by patrons trying to reduce tax bills, found less reason to live in large villages as leaders abdicated responsibility for wives, slaves, clients, and kin, sometimes by accusing them of witchcraft.[27] Increasingly, village leaders could not exert sufficient authority, and patrons either could or would not provide sufficient benefits, to outweigh the attraction of autonomy.[28] Consequently, whereas even after the 1894−1896 famine villages had usually consisted of twenty to forty houses, a decade later most settlements contained only eight to twelve houses, while many cultivators inhabited hamlets of only three or four dwellings.[29] Bush pigs, monkeys, and birds ravaged isolated farms, while lions attacked scattered farmers.[30] Environmental control was disappearing along with patronage and precolonial leadership.

Scarcity and Illness, 1900−1914

After 1900 food deficits in Uzigua were, as one Spiritan commented, "an habitual scourge" associated with widespread emaciation, low birth rates,

25. *DKb* 10 (1899): 285; *Jahresbericht* (1898–1899), p. 242; Mhonda Mission Journal, February 1899 and January 1900; RKA 6467/140, 6469/294−308 and 311, 6473/6, 6476/ 189−190.

26. Quote from *BC* 20: 649−650; also, *BC* 19: 503; Mandera Mission Journal, 1899–1900; Mhonda Mission Journal, 1898−1904; RKA 6473/6; *Jahresbericht* (1898–1899), p. 242.

27. Pogwa Rashidi, Handeni.

28. A similar process in early-colonial western Kenya, set in motion by farmers who broke away from centralized settlements to live in small, autonomous homesteads, and who thereby disrupted precolonial land use patterns, is described by David William Cohen and E. S. Atieno Odhiambo, *Siaya: The Historical Anthropology of an African Landscape*, p. 10.

29. *BC* 23: 369; 24: 515; 25: 735.

30. RKA 771, 5750/46−62, 6468/172, 6469/294−311, 6472/299−303, 332, 6473/6, 33; *Jahresbericht* (1897−1898), p. 71, (1898−1899), p. 242; *BC* 20: 651, 653; W. H. Kisbey, "A Tour in the Zigua Country," p. 206.

and heavy infant mortality.[31] Acute famines developed again in 1907–1908 and 1910–1912, though they were not catastrophes on the scale of 1894–1896 and 1898–1900. At Mandera, the now familiar symptoms of colonial famine reappeared in 1908: food was available, but many villagers were "walking skeletons" who could not purchase it. Hundreds of the Spiritans' neighbors, including many women and children, worked at the mission for daily rations. In northern Nguu similar conditions induced highlanders to leave their homes in search of subsistence.[32]

Famine redeveloped in 1910–1912, despite adequate rains and the availability of foodstuffs which in some places were bought up by traders for shipment outside the region.[33] Such purchases pushed up local pre-harvest prices and made impoverished farmers reliant on seed distributed free by the German administration.[34] It was not food marketing in itself, however, but rather the combination of taxes, debt, the absence of patronage, and the depletion of livestock holdings that, by forcing farmers to sell at prices too low to permit savings for later food purchases, caused hunger. Another cause of scarcity in these years was heavy labor conscription, for this was the period when Handeni rubber plantations expanded rapidly. Government labor demands probably helped induce farmers, in fact, to substitute maize for sorghum, even though they sacrificed sorghum's drought resistance for a shorter growing season.[35]

Throughout Uzigua, the indigent survived by gathering fruits, seeds of grasses, leafy plants, and undomesticated roots, including *mdudu*, the tuber root of the shrub *Thylachium africanum* which is toxic unless thoroughly boiled.[36] Poisonings occurred regularly, perhaps because the poorest villagers lacked the energy to gather firewood for prolonged boiling. In 1911, German physicians diagnosed an epidemic of *mdudu* poisoning in Handeni District, with the primary outbreak at Magamba, where at least forty cases of illness and five deaths testified to Sonyo's declining ability to

31. *BC* 24: 515; Mandera Mission Journal, 1902; *BC* 23: 368; Nachlass Fonck, "Notstands- und Steuerverhältnisse," and "Jahresbericht: Mpapua" (see note 24).
32. François X. Vogt, "Jahresbericht," (1907–1908), pp. 80, 84; and (1908–1909), pp. 83–86; "Aus dem Gebiete der Hungersnot," pp. 111–112; RKA 6564/89.
33. RKA 5750/46–62; Maskati Mission Journal, January 1910; Mhonda Mission Journal, February 13, 1911 and October 14, 1912; François X. Vogt, "Reisebericht," (1910), p. 50. Rainfall records from Pangani, Kwa Mkoro, Sadani, Mhonda, Kwediboma and Mandera are in RKA 6565/20, 6566 and 6570/179.
34. "Der Bezirk Pangani in Jahre 1909," *DOAR* 3,93 (November 28, 1910); RKA 6566/21.
35. *Die Deutsche Schutzgebiete in Afrika und der Südsee* (1912–1913), p. 25; Nachlass Fonck, "Jahresbericht: Mpapua."
36. Nachlass Fonck, "Notstands- und Steuerverhältnisse," and "Jahresbericht: Mpapua."

provide patronage.[37] In addition to *mdudu* poisonings, smallpox repeatedly spread across Uzigua from 1909 through 1912 in epidemics that, according to colonial medical authorities, caused the deaths of about half of the infected.[38]

Epizootic in Uzigua, 1891–1914

The deterioration of the bovine disease environment began in 1891 with the rinderpest panzootic. Accounts of the panzootic conventionally state that it "wiped out" cattle or killed at least ninety percent of livestock,[39] an impression supported by the recollections of Handeni residents such as the elder who said that, "every morning my father awoke to find more cattle dead."[40] While the extent of rinderpest losses in Uzigua is nevertheless unknown, the apparent severity of the panzootic might well suggest that it was responsible not merely for worsening bovine health but more broadly for the collapse of patronage and depopulation during the 1890s famines. At least three circumstances, however, indicate that rinderpest was only a contributing factor. First, with the possible exception of leaders such as Kilo Mwanamachau who relied especially heavily upon pastoralist allies, the chieftains did not lose power immediately in 1891, but only after a series of bloody German military campaigns in the 1890s. Second, there are no signs of depopulation during the panzootic. Instead, some villages gained inhabitants with the arrival of impoverished Maasai who had to take up "work with a hoe."[41] Third, and most importantly, cattle owners were able to restock through trade soon after the panzootic (hence the impressive herds seen in the Pangani Valley in 1896[42]) and once again after

37. Germany, *Medizinal-Berichte über die Deutschen Schutzgebiete* (1910–1911), pp. 166–167.

38. Mhonda Mission Journal, July and August, 1909; Mandera Mission Journal, October 26, 1910; *Die Deutsche Schutzgebiete* (1911–1912), p. 7; "Der Bezirk Pangani"; *Medizinal-Berichte* (1910–1911), pp. 116, 156–157, 163; *Usambara-Post* 9,46 (November 19, 1910), 10,2 (January 14, 1911).

39. John Iliffe, *A Modern History of Tanganyika*, p. 124; Meredeth Turshen, *The Political Ecology of Disease in Tanzania*, p. 113; Andrew Coulson, *Tanzania: A Political Economy*, p. 28, and Charles Ambler, *Kenya Communities in the Age of Imperialism*, p. 96, who notes that these estimates are "highly impressionistic."

40. Salimu Kisailo, Kwa Maligwa.

41. Quote from Mzee Ndege, Mafisa; Omali Maligwa Kidiza, Gombero; Iddi Samshehiri and Msulwa Mbega, Gombero; Mohamedi Semsambia, Kilwa; Salimu Kisailo, Kwa Maligwa; Schoeller *Mitteilungen*, 1: 59.

42. Schoeller, *Mitteilungen*, 1: 59.

a recrudescence in 1901, only to lose their livestock to trypanosomiasis and theileriosis a few years after each occurrence of rinderpest. Rinderpest, in fact, created conditions that for a brief time were actually conducive to rebuilding herds, because even though it eradicated much of the region's invaluable stock of trypanosomiasis- and theileriosis-resistant cattle, it also caused the temporary disappearance of tsetse and ticks by killing off their wildlife hosts.[43]

Had farming communities remained stable and continued to manage vegetation, recovering herds would have reacquired resistance to trypanosomiasis and theileriosis by contracting occasional infections. Small and dispersed post-famine settlements could not, however, prevent the encroachment of vegetation and the spread of wildlife and insects that transmitted intolerably frequent infections. Post-rinderpest herds were in particularly acute danger because they were composed of non-resistant cattle, some of which had lost immunological defenses with the post-panzootic cessation of infections and others which had been imported into Uzigua from vector-free regions. Thus, when wildlife and insects occupied formerly cleared land close to villages and cattle, they transmitted trypanosomal and theilerial infections that, rather than reestablishing immunological resistance, killed non-resistant herds. Testimony to the spread of insect vectors in this period is the widely held belief in Handeni District that tsetse appeared for the first time during the German era.[44]

Unfortunately, post-panzootic developments in Uzigua were not recorded in detail, but Spiritan accounts from Mandera following a recrudescence of rinderpest in 1901 permit reconstruction of the events that occurred after the panzootic. In 1901, rinderpest killed most livestock in the mission's vicinity (for cattle in Mandera had made limited recovery from the panzootic) as well as wild animals such as bush pig, bushbuck, and buffalo.[45] Because, in the absence of their hosts, tsetse seemed to have disappeared as well (the missionaries did not notice the tiny *Rhipicephalus appendiculatus* tick vectors of theileriosis), the Spiritans decided to raise cattle for export in what were now tsetse-free pastures near the mission.[46] They restocked with non-resistant cattle, however, just as livestock owners

43. Other sources on rinderpest in the region are John Berntsen, "Pastoralism, Raiding and Prophets," p. 281; *DKb* 4 (1893): 205; Schoeller, *Mitteilungen*, 1: 60ff; RKA 855/III and 283/28–31; Mohamedi Lusingo, Mafisa.

44. Abdala Hamani Msede and Ali Omali Kipande, Kwa Dundwa.

45. Heavy mortality among wildlife is recognized as a sign of rinderpest: Mohamedi Lusingo, Mafisa; Salimu Kisailo, Kwa Maligwa; Msulwa Mbega, Gombero.

46. Mandera Mission Journal, February 1901; *BC* 22 : 110.

had done a decade earlier, for once again traders brought cattle from the Maasai steppe, where the climate was unsuitable for tsetse and *R. appendiculatus*.[47] But about five years after tsetse appeared to have vanished, cattle deaths increased dramatically, probably due to a combination of trypanosomiasis and theileriosis. In 1907 the missionaries reported that while returning tsetse had infected African-owned herds near the mission, their own livestock were as yet unaffected. But by August 1908 a tsetse-borne "cattle plague" was killing mission cattle. Although the Spiritans tried to save their livestock by placing them in several communities outside Mandera, they lost cattle to trypanosomiasis during succeeding rainy seasons when tsetse and their wildlife hosts moved beyond riverside vegetation into freshly-leafed bush and wood.[48]

Heavy bovine mortality occurred in 1907–1908 because contacts between vectors and livestock, which had been interrupted by rinderpest, resumed among non-resistant livestock. Once again the demographic factor was decisive, just as it had been during the 1890s, for the continuing decline of the farming population around Mandera (in 1900 missionaries said it had fallen from precolonial levels by one-half) meant less clearing and burning of vegetation. In 1905, a Spiritan at Mandera noted, "the great dispersal of the Zigua. . . . They rarely gather together in villages: each of them prefers to build his house apart, to live as he wishes." Five years later settlements were still dwindling because some inhabitants left the region and others chose to establish homesteads near their fields. As thicket, grasses, and trees reclaimed formerly cleared areas, the habitat of vectors and wildlife hosts continued to expand.[49]

The sequence of rinderpest, a lull in cattle infections, and subsequent epizootics was not chronicled elsewhere in as much detail as at Mandera, but it undoubtedly occurred throughout Uzigua between 1901 and 1908.[50] In 1902, colonial officials noted the absence of cattle disease in Uzigua. Almost everywhere, however, vegetation was colonizing formerly cleared land, wildlife were lurking near settlements, and lion attacks were increas-

47. On cattle trade and restocking: *DKb* 13 (1902): 257–259, 15 (1904): 760; *Usambara-Post*, July 17, 1909; *Berichte über Land- und Forstwirtschaft* (1902), pp. 81–82; *DOAR* 2,99 (December 15, 1909) and 3,93 (November 28, 1910); Saidi Hatibu, Mkonde and Leiluli Namania, Tangano Orleerewi and Kari Orleerewi, Gitu. On tick distribution: G. H. Yeoman and Jane B. Walker, *The Ixodid Ticks of Tanzania*, pp. 107–108.

48. *BC* 24: 515; 25: 735; 27: 285; Mandera Mission Journal, August 12, 1908; Vogt, "Jahresbericht" (1908–1909), p. 84.

49. Quote from *BC* 23: 369; also, 25: 725; Vogt, "Jahresbericht" (1908–1909), p. 84.

50. *BC* 20: 654; *Berichte über Land- und Forstwirtschaft* (1902), p. 82; Omali Maligwa Kidiza, Gombero.

ing. In 1904–1905 administrators began to report outbreaks of cattle infection and became particularly concerned about theileriosis, which researchers in Tanganyika and South Africa were just beginning to understand. Government veterinarians uncovered evidence that cattle no longer resisted theileriosis, for only about one-eighth of the cattle examined in Uzigua carried *Theileria*, whereas nearly all would have been infected had theileriosis been enzootic. Indeed, the veterinary reports that show increased incidence of East Coast fever between 1906 and 1908 corroborate the modern Handeni residents who recall 1907 as the year when "*ndigano*," as they refer to lethal theileriosis, began to exact heavy mortality.[51] Bovine trypanosomiasis also caused heavy mortality in 1907–1908, particularly along roads used by cattle traders. More evidence of deadly cattle disease was produced by Anglican Bishop John Hine, who during a tour of central Handeni in 1907 saw that a recent epizootic had destroyed the once "vast" herds of cattle in Uzigua. Hine learned that some livestock keepers, particularly former chieftains, had lost as many as forty or fifty head in a short time.[52]

The epizootics deprived farmers of an important food source, a critical store of wealth, and a vital element in the political, patronage, and kinship relations that had provided security from precolonial scarcity. Immediate causes of the epizootics were the decline and dispersal of population during famines and the disruption of vegetation management. A more fundamental cause, however, was the downfall of precolonial leaders whose patronage had maintained demographic stability.

51. RKA 6070/98–102, 6468/176, 6472/37, 6475/130, 6564/128; *Jahresbericht* (1897–1898), p. 72; *Berichte über Land- und Forstwirtschaft* (1904), p. 47; *Medizinal-Berichte* (1910–1911), p. 288; G. Lichtenheld, "Ergebnisse der von R. Koch Ausgeführten und Vorgezeichneten Forschungen über das Küstenfieber der Rinder in Deutsch-Ostafrika," pp. 261–272; Rajabu Sefu Mwenkumba, Kwa Mkono; Mohamedi Mjewe (Kwedikoma, September 19, 1982); Rashidi Mwenjuma Manyagala, Kilwa; Abdala Hamani Msede and Ali Omali Kipande, Kwa Dundwa and Mohamedi Lusingo, Mafisa.

52. Gustav Meinecke, "Pangani"; *Medizinal-Berichte* (1908–1909), p. 86; Dr. Franz Stuhlmann, "Beiträge zur Kenntnis der Tsetse-fliege," p. 303; *Usambara-Post* 10,32 (August 12, 1911); USPG, UMCA Archives, letter of Hine (also quoted in Iliffe, p. 164).

Part IV

British Administration,
Obstacles to Peasant
Production, and Ecological
Crisis

9. Indirect Rule and Peasant Production in Uzigua

German rule in Uzigua ended with the conquest of northeastern Tanganyika in 1916 by British and South African forces, but several years would elapse before the British reestablished effective administration in the region. From the mid-1920s until the Second World War, however, they governed in accordance with the principles of Indirect Rule, dividing their subjects by introducing what they considered to be "traditional" or "tribal" political structures, and appointing chiefs whom they presumed to be the heirs of precolonial authority. Yet far from enjoying "traditional" legitimacy, the appointees derived their authority almost entirely from the colonial state and rarely assumed the responsibilities for patronage and environmental management that had been incumbent upon precolonial leaders. Thus, while Indirect Rule did not revive or preserve precolonial authority, it did provide room for opposition to appointed chiefs on the "traditionalist" grounds that they were not the true heirs of hereditary leadership. The chiefs' opponents were as untraditional, however, as the chiefs themselves, for they often wished to rid themselves of appointees who failed to fend off the hindrances to exchange and accumulation introduced under Indirect Rule so that they could take advantage of commercial opportunities.

Indeed, aside from the appointment of chiefs, obstacles to trade and market production were the aspect of Indirect Rule that made the greatest impact on Uzigua. In Handeni District these obstacles are associated with E. Pienaar, an agricultural extension officer. Pienaar enforced compulsory cultivation of cotton and cassava, a practice which many peasants hold at least partially responsible for interwar scarcity, by unexpectedly appearing in villages aboard his motorcycle to bully administrative chiefs and whip negligent farmers. On occasion, however, "Bwana" Pienaar was himself beaten by villagers whom he had treated with brutality and disrespect.[1]

1. Mohamedi Mjewe (Kwediboma, September 20, 1982); Nyangasi Mohamedi Munga, Kilwa; Mzee Sekiteke, Kwediboma and Asumani Kilule (Kiberashi, May 17, 1983). A beating

Pienaar served in a bureaucracy that insisted on preserving what administrators considered to be "traditional" social and political structures, but he and other officials showed little regard for the precedents of precolonial agronomy and trade. Preoccupied with maintaining political stability and ensuring that the region made some contribution to the export-oriented colonial economy, they overlooked precolonial safeguards against environmental adversity and famine, obstructed accumulation—the prerequisite of precolonial patronage—and reduced the diversity of food sources by restricting trade and requiring cultivators to concentrate on a narrow combination of crops. Hence the bitterness that colors memories of Bwana Pienaar throughout Handeni reflects not only his rough and insensitive behavior but also farmers' resentment of government initiatives that frustrated their efforts to recover subsistence security and environmental control.

Local Political Authority Under Indirect Rule

The governor who portrayed himself as the architect of Indirect Rule in Tanganyika, Sir Donald Cameron,[2] wrote that colonial administration must be based upon "the people's own traditions,"[3] but the only traditions in which his government was interested were those which supported the premise that precolonial Tanganyikan societies had been organized into "tribes" ruled by one or several chiefs. Cameron urged administrators in Uzigua and elsewhere to collect traditions that would reveal precolonial tribal organization, but at the same time he tacitly encouraged them to suppress knowledge that did not support his "tribal" model. Indeed, soon after becoming governor in 1925 he criticized one administrator in Handeni for reporting that, "there has never been a paramount chief of the whole [Zigua] tribe, in fact in the past adjacent villages [in Uzigua] were

administered to Pienaar at Kwa Chagga Village has been described in a school reading primer: *Tujifunze Lugha Yetu!:6*, pp. 10–14.

2. On Cameron's role, see Sir Donald Cameron, *My Tanganyika Service and Some Nigeria*, pp. 31–32; John Iliffe, *A Modern History of Tanganyika*, pp. 318ff; Margaret L. Bates, "Tanganyika Under British Administration, 1920–1955," pp. 58–59; and Ralph Austen, "The Official Mind of Indirect Rule," pp. 577–606.

3. Governor's Circular Letter no. 1733/16/4 (May 18, 1925), quoted in Pangani District, Annual Report (1924), TNA Early Secretariat File 1733/16:98. For accounts of Indirect Rule in southern Tanzania which show close parallels with Uzigua, see James D. Graham, "Indirect Rule: The Establishment of 'Chiefs' and 'Tribes' in Cameron's Tanganyika" and Terence Ranger, "European Attitudes and African Realities: The Rise and Fall of the Matola Chiefs of South-East Tanzania."

often hostile to each other."[4] In dismissing this reasonably accurate assessment of late precolonial Uzigua with the comment that it showed insufficient research into "tribal" history and organization, Cameron in effect authorized the invention of interpretations that would support his characterization of the chiefs appointed under Indirect Rule as the heirs of precolonial "tribal" authority.

The "chiefdoms" which Cameron's government created in Handeni replicated not the precolonial regime, however, but rather the Akidates that had been demarcated by the Germans. Initially, British officials divided the counterparts of the Akidas, the *mazumbe* [sing. *zumbe*], into two "tribal councils," one for the "Zigua tribe" of the lowlands and the other for the Nguu highlands "tribe," although eventually, when they realized that the distinction was meaningless, they combined the two bodies.[5] Knowing that Cameron wanted historical precedents for chiefs' councils as well as other institutions of Indirect Rule, officials in Uzigua looked to the *si* founders' accounts they collected in the 1920s for the forerunners of "tribal" councils and *mazumbe*. There they found evidence that, "from the original patriarchal state, [Zigua-speakers] developed a clan system and even on occasion, in times of great danger, had achieved a temporary federation of clans. . . . In the clan leader one can see some semblance of personality worthy to be called ruler." Thus, officials discovered earlier versions of councils and chiefs, but because they were still unable to identify the elusive "Zigua" paramount, they devised an ingenious solution by arguing that German conquest had cut short a nascent movement towards "tribal" unification: ". . . given time . . . the Wazigua might have achieved complete and final union under one chief. . . . But . . . European occupation came too swiftly." Hence, despite their failure to find wholly satisfactory precedents for Indirect Rule, administrators were able to contend that they were bringing to fruition a suspended course of indigenous development.[6]

Mazumbe as well as the village heads called *majumbe* [sing. *jumbe*] were appointed following elections which, though they appeared to give voters the opportunity to judge the "traditional" qualifications of competing claimants, often were orchestrated by British officials, for administrators influenced both the selection of candidates, particularly for the more

4. Governor's Circular Letter no. 1733/16/4.
5. Tanga Province, Annual Reports (1927–1928), TNA; TNA Native Affairs File 11412, "Native Administration: Pangani District."
6. "Tribal Government" (n.d.), pp. 17ff, Tanga Province Book, TNA.

important office of *zumbe*, and the voting itself. A typical instance of government interference occurred at Mgera in 1931, when Handeni's District Officer nominated a candidate to be the *zumbe*. Many villagers supported another contestant, citing their right to elect a *zumbe* who was both a descendant of precolonial leaders and a native of Mgera. Their candidate later described how the District Officer intervened: "The District Officer and his clerk who knew how to speak English arrived and the people were asked who they wanted, at once the majority of them said that they wanted me, but the D.O. and his clerk talked in English and told the people that they need not choose this man because he will be of no use, but the people did not hear them."[7] Although the District Officer could not persuade the voters, the government eventually prevailed when his superior, the Commissioner of Tanga Province, journeyed to Mgera and summarily installed the government's candidate.[8] From its standpoint, the new *zumbe*, Sefu Massomo, was a wise choice, for "he was able to hasten the payment of various fees and the colonial tax, and overall revenue increased greatly."[9] Although the administration overrode election results in numerous such instances, elections were fiercely contested nevertheless, particularly at the village level where district officers were less likely to intervene.[10] If village factions could find candidates to whom administrators had no objection, elections provided them with the opportunity to thwart particularly unpopular office-seekers or install men (for women never held administrative office under Indirect Rule) known to be too weak to execute administrative directives effectively.[11]

Even the weaker administrative chiefs became less responsive to their

7. Mambosasa bin Msunga to Governor of Tanganyika Territory (November 17, 1931) in TNA 4/6/5, v. 1.

8. TNA 4/6/5, v. 1; letter of S. E. Mohamed (Mgera) in *Muli* (Handeni), no. 10, 1952; Mohamedi Mjewe (Kwediboma, September 16, 1982); Salehe Mlinde (Mswaki) to D.O. (Handeni), March 30, 1931, TNA 4/6/5, v. 1. Another account showing that hereditary claims were fabricated to justify the selection of a *jumbe* is in the Mandera Mission Journal, March 27, 1933.

9. Musa Sefu Abdalahe, "Habari za Wazigua," Chapter 4, "Habari za Uzumbe wa Mgera." An English translation appears in the Tanga Province Book, TNA.

10. Report by J. W. Johnstone (September 15, 1925) in Pangani District, Annual Report (1925), TNA; Pangani District Book, v. 3, TNA; D.O. (Handeni) to P.C. (Tanga), September 23, 1930, TNA 4/6/5, v. 1; D.O. (Handeni) to P.C. (Tanga), October 26, 1936, TNA 4/6/5, v. 1; ARPC, 1929. One highly unpopular *zumbe* remained in office for twenty-four years despite ceaseless challenges from local opponents: "Life of Zumbe Majugwe" (1949), TNA 4/6/5, v. 2; Handeni District, Annual Report (1956), TNA; "Chiefs' Barazas: Zumbe Majugwe of Mazingara, Summary of Proceedings" (1926), Tanga Province Book, TNA.

11. Report by Johnstone (1925); Pangani District Book, v. 3, TNA; D.O. (Handeni) to P.C. (Tanga), September 23, 1930, TNA 4/6/5, v. 1. An administrator working in Uzaramo in 1931 commented that communities selected "the weakest and most characterless persons" as village headmen: Bates, "Tanganyika," p. 258.

subjects, however, after modification of the tax system in the mid-1920s gave them incentive to enforce tax demands rigorously, for the British reintroduced an arrangement used by the German administration which allowed chiefs to keep a proportion of tax revenue.[12] While it did not make office-holders rich, the system provided tax-collecting functionaries with a rare opportunity to obtain lump sums large enough for major purchases or trading ventures. The village *majumbe*, who administered an average of 150 taxpayers in 1928, earned Shs. 30 for each one hundred ratepayers and thus on average collected Shs. 45 yearly.[13] While this sum equaled only two months' plantation wages in the late 1920s, it was a considerable amount nonetheless, for most laborers, who paid daily living expenses or had the cost of rations deducted from their wages, actually had to work many months to save Shs. 45.

Although the tax system thus gave *mazumbe* and *majumbe* a strong interest in maximizing revenue, they walked a fine line in collecting taxes because aggressiveness could instigate their subjects to challenge their "traditional" legitimacy.[14] Indeed, their position as intermediaries between the state and their subjects constantly tested the chiefs' political acumen, for they had to persuade subjects that they were able to delay or avert tax collections and labor conscription, while simultaneously convincing administrative superiors that they were honest and as efficient as anyone could be in their circumstances. Consequently, even though they risked gaining a reputation at administrative headquarters for "lethargy," administrative chiefs might occasionally choose to conceal tax defaulters, perhaps by overlooking a ratepayer who had gone into hiding, even if he had fled no further than the rafters of his own house.[15] Nevertheless, while the delicate position of the administrative chiefs in the "double articulation" of Indirect Rule required that they be perceived by subjects as having some ability to shield them from government demands, appointees usually provided neither patronage nor the other services expected of precolonial leadership.[16]

12. Bates, "Tanganyika," pp. 58–59; Cameron, *My Tanganyika Service*, pp. 31–32; Alexander Bursian, *Die Häuser- und Hüttensteuer in Deutsch-Ostafrika*.

13. "Census of Handeni" (1929), Tanga Province Book, TNA; Tanga Province, Annual Report (1928), TNA; Pangani District Book, v. 3, TNA; TNA 4/8/6, v. 1.

14. For cases of rejection of administrative chiefs' legitimacy, see Mhonda Mission Journal, September 28 and October 18, 1925, February 12, 1928; Pangani District Book, v. 3, TNA; "Life of Zumbe Majugwe" (1949), TNA 4/6/5, v. 2; Handeni District, Annual Report (1956), TNA; "Chiefs' Barazas: Zumbe Majugwe of Mazingara, Summary of Proceedings" (1926), Tanga Province Book, TNA.

15. Pogwa Rashidi, Handeni.

16. The term is from Karen Fields, *Revival and Rebellion in Colonial Central Africa*, pp. 51 and 59. In Handeni District, however, it would not be possible to apply her argument

Among the obligations abdicated by most *mazumbe* and *majumbe* were those related to public health and environmental control, including supervision of ancestor veneration. Unlike precolonial settlement heads, the administrative chiefs could not take an active role in organizing the burning of vegetation, for example, because their British superiors expected them to enforce conservationist bans on bush fires. Office-holders did not entirely ignore health-related concerns (some permitted witch detection, for instance, even though it violated colonial law).[17] But missionary and government opposition to healing and ritual activities which Europeans associated with witchcraft and infanticide persuaded many chiefs to avoid public *matambiko*, fearing that if opponents reported these activities to administrative superiors, participation in ancestor veneration, divination, spirit exorcism and control of witchcraft would cost them their offices and stipends. Some appointees chose instead to become leaders of the Islamic congregations that were growing throughout Uzigua. There was no risk in active Islamic observance because the government did not interfere with Muslim devotions and teaching. But Islamic practices brought administrative chiefs into closer association with the proselytizers who, declaring that, "the traditional customs are forbidden" ["*mila ni haramu*"], discouraged public ancestor veneration.[18]

The distance between appointed chiefs and environmental control increased, moreover, when administrators involved the appointees in Pienaar's cotton-and-cassava campaign by placing demonstration plots in their fields and requiring that they oversee compulsory cultivation. Perhaps acting under pressure from the District Officer, the chiefs' council at Handeni took a leading role in the cotton-and-cassava campaign when it passed ordinances in 1932 and 1934 making cassava cultivation mandatory for all adults.[19] Another of the council's ordinances was an even more telling measure of the widening gulf between the chiefs and concern with

that political authority under Indirect Rule "grew upon its roots in the precolonial collectivity of African peoples" (p. 57).

17. On witch detection: Mhonda Mission Journal, March 9, 1926 and March 9, 1931; Lugoba Mission Journal, February 25 and September 9, 1923. Missionaries and administrators tried through the early 1920s to suppress witchcraft eradication practices and activities of *waganga*: Lugoba Mission Journal, 1920–1924. Their activities were sanctioned by Tanganyika's Witchcraft Ordinances of 1922 and 1928: G. St. J. Orde-Browne, "Witchcraft and British Colonial Law." On tax evasion: D.O. (Handeni) to P.C. (Tanga), April 2, 1932, TNA 4/1161/1, v. 4; ARPC (1932), p. 55; Mandera Mission Journal, February 15, 1932.

18. Mohamedi Mjewe (Kwediboma, September 27, 1982).

19. Mohamedi Mjewe (Kwediboma, September 20, 1982); Handeni District Book, vol. 1, TNA.

public health, however: during the mid-1930s famine, the council, perhaps acting again at the direction of district administrators, declared that all men must work on sisal plantations of the chiefs' choosing for at least three months. The edict held a potential benefit for the chiefs by placing them in a position to collect fees from plantation managers for recruiting labor. It was a dire threat to the women, children, elderly, and infirm, however, since they depended on conscripted men. Had the measure been enforced, most labor conscripts would have been unable to provide any support for their dependents because the council stipulated that overdue taxes and bills for government famine relief be deducted from wages.[20] The chief's declaration was quickly rescinded by the Commissioner of Tanga Province for that reason, but it nonetheless demonstrated that the council members were unwilling or unable to defend the interests of their famine-stricken subjects.

The Imposition of Self-Sufficiency

Implicit in the "tribal" premises of Indirect Rule were the assumptions that each precolonial "tribe" had been a discrete economic entity and that "inter-tribal" economic interrelations were best avoided in the interest of political stability.[21] These views led the interwar administration to discourage trade and other interaction between different occupational groups and across environmental frontiers, as its treatment of the Parakuyu Maasai pastoralists in western Handeni shows. In 1926, the government, acting in utter ignorance of social and economic realities along the steppe-woodland border, decided to expel all Parakuyu from Handeni and settle them in a distant Maasai reserve. The expulsion order threatened not only to deprive pastoralists of woodlands water sources and dry-season browsing in farmers' fields, but also to end the exchange of goods and labor between farmers and pastoralists. The British abandoned their attempt to relocate at least one thousand pastoralists, however, after fighting between Parakuyu men and colonial police culminated in scores of imprisonments. Cameron himself rescinded the expulsions and censured responsible ad-

20. Ag. P.C. (Tanga) to Chief Secretary (Dar es Salaam), July 17, 1933, TNA 13079, vol. 1.

21. This view is accepted in at least one recent study of Tanzania, Deborah Bryceson's *Food Insecurity and the Social Division of Labour in Tanzania, 1919–1985*, which states that "Before colonial rule . . . Tanzania was a collection of local tribal agrarian economies" (p. 38).

ministrators, though in truth they were only acting in accordance with the premises of Indirect Rule by trying to separate different "tribes."[22]

Underlying government prohibitions on trade between farmers and pastoralists, as well as the more general administrative uneasiness with "inter-tribal" economic relationships, was the supposition that the "tribe"'s constituent settlements and households ought to be self-sufficient. Administrators felt that economic relations outside the bounds of the "tribe" should be confined to supervised colonial markets that would serve as vents for surplus labor and products. Restricting unsupervised trade, they believed, would improve the productivity of farmers who would have to spend their time tilling the ground rather than pursuing commercial opportunities and would also prevent improvident cultivators from selling off food reserves. Accordingly, they imposed constraints on trade by limiting access to credit, taxing itinerant traders, and forcing them to purchase licenses.[23] Additional regulations promulgated in the early 1920s required households to produce enough food for their own needs and authorized embargoes on food shipments between and within districts.[24] While the government could not prevent all forms of exchange, particularly short-distance movements of goods in small quantities, these measures did permit administrators and police to interdict trade.

The goal of officials in suppressing trade was to maintain the self-sufficiency of "tribe," village, and household so that the colonial government would not have to bear the cost of famine relief. As cultivators well knew, however, their policies suppressed forms of exchange which, a generation or two earlier, had been a crucial source of security. Given the impossibility of self-sufficiency in the Uzigua climate, particularly with the decline of patronage and cattle-keeping in the colonial period, restrictions on trade inevitably meant heightened risk of famine.

Taxation and Wage Labor

While they believed that "tribes," settlements, and households should be self-sufficient, British officials also wanted all regions to contribute to export production by supplying either cash crops or wage labor. In that respect, Uzigua was a disappointment to administrators in the early 1920s

22. All material on the 1926 expulsions is from TNA Early Secretariat File 7834.
23. D. M. P. McCarthy, *Colonial Bureaucracy and Creating Underdevelopment: Tanganyika, 1919–1940*, pp. 24ff., 27ff., 40ff.
24. McCarthy, *Colonial Bureaucracy*, pp. 77–78.

because its residents seemed little interested in either wage labor or export crops. Among the circumstances that dissuaded farmers from engaging in these unrewarding activities were the insistence of Pangani Valley sisal estates on long work terms, the low wages offered by the few European employers remaining in Uzigua, fluctuating crop prices, and, perhaps most importantly, ineffective tax collection in the pre-Indirect Rule period. Indeed, British tardiness in reestablishing administration following the German withdrawal was a crucial factor, because in the absence of pressure to pay taxes, farmers had freedom to refuse unattractive, poorly-paid wage labor, to bargain with employers, and to disregard administrative preferences when determining which crops they would grow. Consequently, Indirect Rule in Handeni District was largely an attempt to force the "Zigua tribe" into wage labor and export production, on terms which provided neither immediate security nor the prospect of future prosperity, by using "traditional" chiefly authority to improve tax gathering and adherence to crop quotas.

Although in other regions of Tanganyika postwar labor shortages may have been caused by expansion of plantation production, in Uzigua, where the plantation sector never recovered from the repatriation of German settlers, ineffectual tax collection and workers' refusal to accept low wages were the decisive factors.[25] In the early 1920s, only four of the thirteen plantations established in Handeni District under German rule were still operating.[26] Yet despite the scarcity of jobs and the strong preference among farmers for employment close to home, the region's few remaining European employers, including the Spiritans, had great difficulty in obtaining labor. The comments of a Spiritan at Mandera who complained in 1924 that "lazy" Africans did not "wish to work for the Europeans because, since the armistice, they have no [tax] obligation to the government," was typical of missionaries who blamed government laxity in enforcing tax and labor obligations for their inability to retain workers.[27]

The Spiritans not only found many of their neighbors unwilling to enter unremunerative wage labor, but also discovered that their remaining employees were increasingly aggressive in bargaining over wages and work

25. Kenneth Ingham, "Tanganyika: The Mandate and Cameron, 1919–1931," in *History of East Africa*, p. 556.
26. *Dar es Salaam Times*, April 30 and July 2, 1921, April 1 and May 13, 1922, October 10, 1923 and August 2, 1924; Mhonda Mission Journal, June 15, 1921 and September 12, 1925; Pangani District, Annual Reports (1921 and 1925), TNA 1733/5; Handeni Sub-District, Annual Report (1925), TNA; Tour reports of J. E. G. Ransome of January 26, 1929 and August 17, 1929, Tanga Province Book, TNA.
27. *BC* 28 (1923–1924): 284; Lugoba Mission Journal, November 15, 1920, June 19–21, August 5 and December 20, 1922, January 12 and October 17, 1924.

terms. A brief strike by field laborers at Mandera in April 1919 over the work required to earn one rupee forced the missionaries to reduce the standard task, and a year later renewed threats of a strike extracted a 50 percent wage increase, which did not, however, prevent many of the mission's employees from quitting over low pay in 1925.[28]

The Spiritans were not the only European employers who failed to maintain a stable work force during the early 1920s. Throughout the region Europeans found that employees refused month-long terms of employment, generally wanted work for no more than three days per week, and were prone to quit unexpectedly.[29] Hence the few plantations that were still open in Handeni could not respond to temporary improvement in rubber prices in 1925, and the recruiters who sought workers in Handeni for the Pangani Valley sisal fields had little success.[30] Eventually employers granted pay increases to attract labor. Even the Mhonda Mission, which in 1920 had reported a surplus of laborers willing to work for 16 cents per day, had to raise the daily wage of an agricultural laborer in 1925 to 26 cents and the weekly pay of a carpenter from ten to thirteen shillings.[31] Sisal plantations also offered wage increases in response to labor shortages, a trend that in 1922 prompted the Chamber of Commerce at Tanga to propose setting a maximum plantation wage. The sisal producers could not halt wage inflation, however, and after further increases in 1925 the Tanga District administration lamented that "the labour situation during the past year has been the worst in the history of the local Sisal Industry." To force peasants into plantation labor, sisal interests began calling on the government to curtail the production of cotton and other cash crops.[32]

It was in this context of labor shortages and rising wages that Cameron's administration implemented Indirect Rule, installed administrative chiefs, and reformed the tax system. Both tax revenue and labor recruitment improved immediately. In Handeni District, where only 8600 of 19,543 registered ratepayers had paid taxes in 1924/1925, more than 15,600 individuals paid hut or poll tax in 1927/1928, despite an increase in the

28. Mandera Mission Journal, April 7–10, 1919; June 8, 1920; February 7, September 19 and 26, 1921; October 20, 1925.

29. Mandera Mission Journal, April 7–10, 1919; June 8, 1920; September 19 and 26, 1921; October 20 and November 14, 1925.

30. *BC* 28: 285; Pangani District, Annual Reports (1923–1925), TNA; Handeni Sub-District, Annual Report (1925), TNA 1733/16.

31. Mhonda Mission Journal, May 17 and November 27–30, 1920; August 1924; May 24, 1925.

32. *Dar es Salaam Times*, February 4, 1922 and April 18, 1925; Tanga District and Pangani District, Annual Reports (1925), TNA.

personal tax rate from six to ten shillings.[33] Village *majumbe* pursued rate-payers energetically, sometimes by menacing the wives and children of taxpayers who went into hiding.[34] By late 1925, therefore, many villagers were seeking jobs at the Mandera mission, and in the following year farmers sold much of their maize because "a real terror of taxation has spread through the country."[35]

The plantation sector also benefited from administrative reforms, for increasing labor migration from Handeni to the Pangani Valley contributed to the unprecedentedly large number of workers seeking sisal labor. Labor costs stabilized as the flow of workers improved, with sisal wages leveling off at Shs. 24 per thirty days in 1928 before beginning their Depression decline of 50 percent from 1929 to 1933.[36] Yet thinly-populated Handeni District still remained a relatively minor source of labor for the Pangani Valley sisal estates, even though its taxpayers regarded the sisal plantations as their primary source of cash, there being virtually no wage-paying jobs in the district.[37] Migration to the sisal estates was inconvenient, even in the post-harvest "off season" when it interfered with dry-season burning of bush and grasses, but many taxpayers had no alternative since Handeni's three operating plantations employed only about seventy-five workers in 1932 and paid only half the wages offered in the Pangani Valley sisal fields.[38]

The difficulties which doomed plantation production in Handeni District were exemplified by the problems of the most active of the interwar operations in Handeni, the Tamota Estate, whose owner, A. W. Hoffmann, was beleaguered during the early 1930s by labor shortages, lack of demand for crops suited to Handeni's environment, and 125 miles of miserable motor road between his plantation and the nearest rail depot. After he became indebted to the Indian business community at Handeni while experimenting unsuccessfully with coffee, rice and bananas, Hoffmann tried to recover by employing tax defaulters and cheating his workers. As

33. Pangani District, Annual Reports (1920–1925), TNA; Handeni Sub-District, Annual Report (1925), TNA; "Hut or Poll Tax Comparative Statement: Handeni District," Tanga Province Book, TNA; Tanga Province, Annual Report (1933), TNA.

34. Pogwa Rashidi, Handeni.

35. Mandera Mission Journal, July 1, 1926; also, November 14, 1925.

36. Report of Provincial Commissioner (Tanga), May 2, 1927 and A.D.O. (Handeni) to D.O. (Pangani), January 20, 1927 in TNA 4/1161/1, v. 1; Tanga Province, Native Affairs Annual Report (1927), TNA 11682, v. 1; Pangani District Book, v. 3; TNA 4/8/6, v. 1, and Grace Bridges Lee, "Famine in Zigualand," p. 247.

37. "Labour Inspection Reports—Tanga Province (1932)," TNA 21192; F. Longland, "Report on Labour Matters in Sisal Areas," no. 1 (March 29, 1936), TNA 23544.

38. "Labour Inspection Reports—Tanga Province (1932)."

was customary under Tanganyika's *kipande* system, he contracted to pay wages upon completion of thirty daily tasks, but after men had worked 28 or 29 days, he refused either to allow them to finish their terms or to pay them any wages. In 1932, one laborer charged that Hoffmann, falsely claiming that the employee had lost the card recording the number of days he had worked, declared that he owed him nothing. Hoffmann "told me," related the complainant, "'Your *kipande* card has been lost and I know nothing about it. If I give you your *kipande* and you lose it, that's your problem.' I argued with him until he threw me out, saying if I continued to argue he would hit me. It is certain that he never gave me that *kipande* and he still has it today." This was one of many instances in which appointed chiefs interceded with the district administration on behalf of workers, and prompted increasingly exasperated officials to scold Hoffmann. Nevertheless, administrators continued to instruct *mazumbe* and *majumbe* to send Hoffmann tax defaulters whose thirty-day wage, which Hoffmann deposited directly into the district treasury, usually equaled the amount they owed in taxes. Unwilling to work without pay, however, many defaulters fled before completing their service, often within a day or two after arriving at Tamota. When 27 of 44 men sent to Tamota by one *zumbe* deserted in February 1932, Hoffmann informed the District Officer that the men "said they do not fear the government."

Their boldness reveals a good deal about how district-level administrators balanced political and economic interests under Indirect Rule. Realizing that Hoffmann's prospects were hopeless, the Handeni administration chose neither to pursue deserters nor to press appointed chiefs to meet Hoffmann's demands for labor, because it preferred to allow *mazumbe* and *majumbe* the opportunity to enhance their legitimacy by mediating successfully over labor disputes. The chiefs, on the other hand, recognizing that Hoffmann was no favorite of British officials, tried to demonstrate their ability to protect their subjects by ignoring escaped labor conscripts, procrastinating before sending defaulters to Tamota, and lodging grievances against Hoffmann on the workers' behalf. Because he received only half-hearted government support, therefore, Hoffmann went bankrupt in 1933 and was swiftly repatriated, leaving behind many claims for unpaid wages. His circumstances typified the fate of a plantation sector ruined by falling commodity prices, scarcity of labor, insufficient rainfall, a poor transportation infrastructure, and an uncooperative government obsessed with the maintenance of "traditional" political stability.[39]

39. All material on the Tamota Estate is in Handeni District File no. 11/8. On Hoffmann's land purchases, see Tanga Province, Annual Report (1927), TNA 11682, v. 1.

Figure 5. A Handeni plantation in ruins: the house built at Kwediboma about 1910 by a rubber planter. Abandoned and overgrown for several decades, the Kwediboma estate was occupied in the 1950s by several entrepreneurial farmers, one of whom still resided in the house when it was photographed in 1983. Author's photograph.

Cotton and Cassava

The failure of Handeni's plantations and the reluctance of its farmers to enter long-term sisal labor in the Pangani Valley persuaded British administrators that cotton production should be the district's primary source of cash income.[40] Their efforts to increase cotton cultivation in Uzigua began immediately after the First World War, when the government announced that all households had to have cotton plots, and continued sporadically thereafter as the administration stipulated that cultivators must work parcels of 50 × 50 yards which were to be laid out contiguously in large village

40. Suleman Sumra, "An Analysis of Environmental and Social Problems Affecting Agricultural Development in Handeni District," p. 71.

cotton fields.[41] Government cotton campaigns continued through the 1920s and 1930s, but were hampered by Uzigua's erratic rainfall and uncooperative growers who, because they considered cotton earnings wholly inadequate compensation for the time diverted from grain crops, boiled seed or simply neglected cotton plantings to free their energies for sorghum and maize.[42] Those harmed most by cotton quotas were the villagers, particularly women, who were unable either to hire labor during hoeing and harvest seasons or to shift the burden onto spouses. Because earnings were instantly collected by tax gatherers at government buying stations, moreover, farmers had good reason to regard cotton work as nothing more than compulsory unremunerated labor.

Fluctuating prices also discouraged growers, for although high prices stimulated planting during 1920 and 1921, farmers reduced output when producer prices fell by 50 percent from 1921 to 1924, and once again reduced the cotton harvest in Pangani District (which then included Handeni), this time from 210 to 57 tons, when prices declined by one half in 1926/1927. Farmers simply let cotton rot in fields and refused free government seed. Output was influenced not only by producer prices but also by the difference between cotton prices and wages, for ratepayers chose between cotton and plantation work as a way to earn tax money.[43] When sisal wages were relatively high, farmers withdrew from cotton for short-term plantation labor, as happened after the reform of the tax system and the fall of cotton prices in 1926/1927. But during the Depression, when plantation wages hit rock bottom and jobs were scarce, cotton production increased regardless of price. Indeed, Handeni's cotton crop was almost ten times larger in 1932 than in 1925 despite a two-thirds decline in the producer price. Yet many growers, reported Handeni's District Officer, cultivated "just sufficient cotton to return the price of their taxes."[44]

41. *BC* 28: 280; Mandera Mission Journal, February 7, 1921 and January 31, 1926; Mhonda Mission Journal, February 9, 1922 and January 27, 1925; Pangani District, Annual Reports (1923 and 1924), TNA. See also Bryceson, "'The Tepid Backwater': Bagamoyo District and Its Marginal Commodity Production Within the Tanganyikan Colonial Economy, 1919–1961," pp. 3–4.

42. Lugoba Mission Journal, February 1 and 19, March 8, May 12, July 17 and 29 and August 8, 1921; February 23, 1922.

43. The Spiritans noted the relationship between the thoroughness of tax collections and cotton output: Lugoba Mission Journal, 1921–1922.

44. Quotation is from D.O. (Handeni) to Treasurer (Dar es Salaam), November 5, 1932, TNA 4/1161/1, v. 4. Also, Mhonda Mission Journal, May 16, 1921; Mandera Mission Journal, October 16–17, 1924; A.D.O. (Handeni) to D.O. (Pangani), September 19, 1924, Handeni District Book, v. 1, TNA; A.D.O. (Handeni) to D.O. (Pangani), January 20, 1927 and Report of P.C. (Tanga), May 2, 1927, TNA 4/1161/1, v. 1; Handeni Sub-District, Annual Report (1925), TNA. On administrative efforts to stimulate cotton growing: H. H. Allsop (D.O. Pangani), "History of Cotton" (September 17, 1927) in Handeni District Book, v. 1,

While the British tried to increase export production in Handeni District, they also sought to guarantee self-sufficiency in food through compulsory cultivation of cassava.[45] Administrators viewed drought-resistant cassava, whose tubers are invulnerable to birds and locusts, as the perfect food source for farmers concentrating on cotton. When the government initiated compulsory cassava growing in 1933, rigorous enforcement by Pienaar and other officials resulted in hundreds of convictions.[46] Even so, compulsion did not lead to wide adoption of cassava in the 1930s, as Pienaar himself acknowledged in reporting that only 10 percent of Handeni District farmers grew it in 1942. The lack of interest in cassava may have been partly attributable to the relatively poor nutritive value of cassava tubers, which are primarily carbohydrates and fiber, but a much more important factor, given Handeni's depleted population and extensive unmanaged vegetation following the 1932–1935 famine (see Chapter Ten), was the need to protect maturing cassava day and night from bush pigs and baboons for at least a year. When farmers interplanted cassava and maize, observed Pienaar, cassava left unguarded after the maize harvest was invariably consumed by pests.[47]

Probably the decisive consideration for many cultivators, however, was the one mentioned often by peasants in the 1980s—their reluctance to spend time on a crop which, unlike maize and sorghum, could not be sold for cash.[48] The tax burden was heavy and indebtedness widespread among cultivators after the 1932–1935 famine, but creditors refused to take cassava, for which there was no market, instead of maize and sorghum. Farmers

TNA. Also on cotton prices and production: Pangani District, Annual Reports (1924, 1925), TNA: Tanganyika Territory, Department of Agriculture, Annual Reports (1925–1932), TNA; ARPC (1932, 1935, 1937, 1939, 1940); Korogwe District, Annual Reports (1937, 1938), TNA; Sumra, "An Analysis of Environmental and Social Problems," pp. 74–75. Accounts of compulsory cotton cultivation were given by Rajabu Sefu Mwenkumba, Kwa Mkono; Mwalimu James Kibwana (Kwa Mkono, December 30, 1982), Mohamedi Mjewe (Kwediboma, September 20, 1982) and Asumani Kilule, Kiberashi; also, Mandera Mission Journal, March 12, 1938.

45. Bryceson, "'The Tepid Backwater,'" pp. 12–13.
46. Letter of Simon Mgaza (Handeni), *Muli* (Handeni), no. 25 (August 1953); Tanga Province, Annual Report (1934), TNA 11682, v. 1; Korogwe District, Annual Report (1938), TNA 72/62/6; Tanganyika Territory, Department of Agriculture, "Agriculture in Tanganyika," p. 4. For government compulsion to grow cassava, Mandera Mission Journal, February 4, 1937, and for resistance to cassava quotas, D.O. (Handeni) to P.C. (Tanga), June 3, 1937, TNA 4/6/5, v. 2.
47. Report of E. Pienaar (February 1944), TNA 4/8/40, v. 2. The problem of guarding cassava is discussed by Sumra, "An Analysis of Environmental and Social Problems," pp. 76–77.
48. Maize did not supplant sorghum as the staple grain in Uzigua until the late 1940s, when a market in maize developed: "Agriculture in Tanganyika," p. 2. For the prevalence of sorghum during the 1930s: Director, Department of Agriculture to Chief Secretary (Dar es Salaam), April 30, 1935, TNA 11747, v. 1.

who needed money, therefore—whether to retire debts, pay taxes and bridewealth, or purchase cloth and other necessities—concentrated on a combination of staple grains, a cash earner such as cotton or tobacco and the legume varieties which brought the best market prices. (Hence kidney beans [*Phaseolus vulgaris*] replaced velvet beans [*Mucuna utilis*].) "We tried in every way possible," remembered one Handeni farmer, "to get money quickly."[49]

Thus until the late 1940s, when government encouragement of crop marketing transformed Handeni's economy, cassava was grown primarily by farmers who were either exempt from taxes or able to hire labor which could be used to expand cultivation and protect crops from pests. Employers of casual labor such as the Spiritans grew cassava, which they distributed to laborers during pre-harvest seasons, in addition to marketable maize and sorghum.[50] This pattern was revealed by the government official who, in a report written in 1944 on the cultivation of cassava and other tubers such as arrowroot, noted that, "In every area that I visited . . . certain people were to be found, generally old men exempted from taxation or Wanyamwezi, who . . . had large areas of native cassava, in most areas sufficient to last them another nine months or a year."[51] Like other administrators, he applied the term "Wanyamwezi" to men who, regardless of whether they had actually come from the western Tanganyikan region of Unyamwezi, had migrated to the sisal estates from outside Tanga Region and accumulated enough savings to marry locally and hire labor. Indeed, they were among the relatively few Handeni residents who had enough money to employ labor regularly. Ironically, however, while the colonial administration tried to ensure, by restricting trade in foodstuffs, that farmers would have sufficient food, and, by making cotton cultivation mandatory, that they would have a cash income, most Handeni residents were suffering scarcity for lack of a medium of exchange.

Obstacles to Accumulation Under Indirect Rule

Integral to Indirect Rule was the presumption that colonial administration must preserve the fragile cohesion of "tribes," which officials thought

49. Msulwa Mbega, Gombero.
50. Mandera Mission Journal, November 8, 1930; Bryceson, "'The Tepid Backwater,'" p. 17.
51. Agricultural Officer (Tanga) to D.O. (Korogwe), February 25, 1944, TNA 4/8/40, v. 2.

would be destroyed by increased social differentiation.[52] The economic corollary was that accumulation, the cause of differentiation, had to be avoided. Throughout the interwar period, therefore, administrators tried to prevent rural accumulation. For example, Governor Cameron refused to compensate chiefs for the abolition of their tributary powers in 1925 by making cash payments that might have enabled them to hire labor and enter market production.[53] The administration squandered opportunities to assist potential rural accumulators at least twice more, once in 1929, when a proposal to make credit available to chiefs failed to overcome bureaucratic resistance, and again in 1933, when chiefs were prohibited from holding trading licenses. As D. M. P. McCarthy has shown, the administration intended to ensure that the chiefs remained mere government functionaries dependent solely on their salaries, but these policies were also part of a wider effort to prevent rural differentiation.[54]

Entrepreneurial Handeni residents, including Indian traders as well as Zigua-speaking farmers, were victims of this tendency. Even though the district administration was striving to increase cotton output, it denied Indian merchants—the only individuals in Handeni prepared to invest significantly in agriculture—permission to acquire land for cotton production. Most of the merchants were emigrants from Gujarat who had prospered during the 1920s and early 1930s by opening shops, employing a few laborers in maize production, making small crop purchases, and extending credit during the 1932–1935 famine.[55] Although they were now poised to begin relatively large-scale cultivation, the British blocked their plans.[56] The few Zigua-speakers able to undertake commercial ventures were also frustrated by administrative obstacles and inaction. While many farmers traded a variety of products in small quantities (some villagers, for example, occasionally sold headloads of cattle- and goat-hides in Korogwe[57]), only the handful of chiefs, teachers, and other government and mission employees earning a steady cash income could trade regularly, and licensing requirements and lack of credit restricted their activities. Antoni

52. This view was criticized by Charlotte Leubuscher, *Tanganyika Territory: A Study of Economic Policy Under Mandate*, p. 50.

53. Cameron, *My Tanganyika Service*, pp. 31–32.

54. McCarthy, *Colonial Bureaucracy*, pp. 42–43.

55. Athumani Abdalla Mkomwa (Kwediboma, August 24, 1982); Mohamedi Saidi Nyange (Kwediboma, September 5, 1982).

56. Director, Department of Agriculture (Morogoro) to Senior Agricultural Officer (Moshi), December 11, 1934, D.O. (Same) to P.C. (Tanga), May 21, 1935 and P.C. (Tanga) to D.O. (Same), May 25, 1935 in TNA 4/8/6, v. 1.

57. Mohamedi Saidi Nyange, Kwediboma.

Mhina, for example, who was educated at an Anglican school in Korogwe and taught at mission stations in Handeni, traded throughout eastern and central Handeni District after the First World War. With his brother, he purchased salt in coastal towns and hired porters to carry it back to Handeni, where they exchanged it for tobacco and chickens that they subsequently resold.[58] Another entrepreneur was Saidi Hatibu, who began cattle trading after serving as a government clerk and *jumbe*. During the 1920s and 1930s he made frequent trips to Kondoa, where he bought one or two dozen cattle at a time for sale in the Pangani Valley and the coastal towns, and eventually used the profits to open a shop.[59] Commercial ambitions were common, but very few residents of Handeni could overcome government discrimination and restrictions, the absence of opportunities to accumulate savings, and the administration's refusal to provide credit.

The concerns with self-sufficiency and egalitarianism, derived from the British conception of "tribal" societies, thus worked against government efforts to ensure that Uzigua would secure itself from famine and contribute to export production. Likewise, these concerns prevented farmers from exploiting opportunities for trade and peasant production in order to replace precolonial patronage with new forms of accumulation and redistribution. The farmers of Uzigua remained, therefore, in a state of imposed self-sufficiency that, rather than providing security from hunger, brought successive famines and steady deterioration of environmental conditions between the world wars.

58. Antoni Mhina (Kwa Mkono, December 29, 1982).
59. Saidi Hatibu, Mkonde.

10. Famine, Depopulation and Epizootic, 1916–1940

By restricting trade, obstructing accumulation, and appointing chiefs who collected taxes but failed to provide patronage, Indirect Rule helped perpetuate the cycle of famine, depopulation, and epizootic that had begun in the 1890s. The major famines of the period occurred, in fact, at the moments when lack of market opportunities made state impositions most burdensome: in 1925, as the government introduced more effective tax collecting, and in 1932–1935, when the fall of commodity prices and wages during the Depression left farmers without cash for tax payments. As the ecological and subsistence crisis deepened in Handeni, government officials became aware of the connection between famine and lethal cattle disease, but they never absorbed the insight of Handeni's farmers, who understood that these afflictions were also related to the transformation of political authority under colonial rule.

Famine, War, and Monopsony, 1915–1930

The crises of the British colonial period began with a famine that was caused by labor conscription, crop requisitions, and military operations during the First World War. Before retreating from Tanga Region in 1916, the German military not only expropriated grain and livestock but also drafted women to prepare soldiers' food and as many as 8000 men to carry provisions across Uzigua from the Central Railway to the Tanga-Moshi Railroad. Throughout Uzigua, German officials amassed stores of grain (they obliged each Akida to provide hundreds of headloads of sorghum and maize) in camps where women pounded it "until their hands split."[1]

---

1. Mohamedi Mjewe (Kwediboma, September 21, 1982). Also, Mwalimu James Kibwana, Kwa Mkono; Salimu Machaku and Mohamedi Rashidi (Kwediboma, August 18, 1982) and W. O. Henderson, "German East Africa, 1884–1918," in *History of East Africa*, p. 160.

Severe food shortages developed immediately after the commencement of conscription and requisitions.[2]

The military campaign that led to German withdrawal from northeastern Tanganyika in 1916 inflicted enormous hardship, for in retreat the Germans burned crops and food stores. Fearful of hungry soldiers on both sides (British-South African troops and their porters were described as being near starvation in June 1916), villagers fled into uninhabited woodland with their livestock.[3] Some refugees spent months in hiding, quieting children and cooking in pits to conceal their whereabouts, as first German, then British-South African forces swept through their settlements.[4] New rounds of conscription and expropriations began when the British occupied the region. At Mandera, they repeatedly collected foodstuffs and enlisted almost all the men except the very elderly for forced labor. The British were aware of widespread food deficits, but responded only by "insanely" compelling farmers, as a missionary at Mandera put it, to plant beans and rice after the long rains had ended.

Similar events occurred throughout Uzigua. "One fine day," recalled a Spiritan at Maskati in southern Nguu in 1916, "while our workers were cultivating a field, two soldiers captured them and tied them, all by one cord, in my presence. The schoolchildren who witnessed this scene burst into tears when they saw their fathers and brothers leaving." A month later the British impressed another fifty men at Maskati. By May 1917 there was "no money, no clothes, no food" because "no one cultivates sufficiently, since all men are absent or, following their return, they hide." At Mhonda, meanwhile, the British took "craftsmen, schoolboys, old men, any men fit to go, women who the soldiers want to sleep with." Particularly disturbing to the Spiritans was the violation of the Sabbath peace one Sunday in 1918

2. Mhonda Mission Journal, August 23, 1914; Maskati Mission Journal, February–December 1915, January–February 1916; Lugoba Mission Journal, December 29, 1914; January 15, May 21 and June 24, 1915; March 16, 1916.

3. Charles Hordern, comp., *Military Operations: East Africa*, 1: 299–307; Geoffrey Hodges, *The Carrier Corps: Military Labor in the East African Campaign, 1914–1918*, pp. 52–53, 127, 171–172.

4. Accounts of the First World War in Uzigua were contributed by Msulwa Mbega, Gombero; Rajabu Sefu Mwenkumba, Kwa Mkono; Saidi Mohamedi Mwakilinga (Kwa Mkono, December 23, 1982); Leonard Kilua, Kwa Mkono; Asumani Mwanamauka, Mafisa; Hamza Mlingo, Mswaki; Antoni Mhina, Kwa Mkono; Asumani Abdala Mkomwa (Kwediboma, August 12, 1982); Salimu Machaku and Mohamedi Rashidi, Kwediboma; Mohamedi Mjewe (Kwediboma, September 21, 1982) and Mrisho Kizenga (Kwediboma, September 22, 1982). The Spiritan accounts are from the mission journals of Mandera, Mhonda, Lugoba and Maskati, 1914–1918, and BC 26 (1913–1914): 96–100; 28: 275–286.

when British soldiers captured churchgoers as they emerged from Mass at Mhonda.[5]

Between war's end and the onset of famine in 1925, Uzigua experienced the influenza pandemic as well as constant food shortages. Convinced that the disease was spread by howitzers' smoke or malevolent spirits brought home with conscripted porters, many Handeni residents blamed the war for the swift, widespread mortality caused by influenza.[6] Having suffered the prewar collapse of redistribution networks, wartime disruption of agriculture, and the loss of much of their livestock, moreover, few farmers held sufficient reserves after the war to carry them through pre-harvest seasons. Now farmers' survival depended heavily upon the short-rains planting of November and December, which earlier generations had expected to produce no more than a supplementary harvest. When the short rains failed, as happened at Mhonda and Mandera in 1919 and 1923, they faced serious shortages.[7]

In 1925, a severe famine developed during a drought when ratepayers, under recently intensified pressure to pay taxes, sold food reserves and livestock despite deepening scarcity. Conditions had become so desperate, the Mandera mission reported, that by late 1925 farmers tried to plant maize and beans a month or more before the short rains were likely to begin. Although many destitute farmers subsisted on undomesticated foods such as the root *mdudu*, if they did not flee the region altogether (the administration estimated that at least 5000 of perhaps 55,000 to 60,000 Handeni residents left the district during the famine), some of their neighbors were able to purchase the staples that were sold throughout the crisis to missionaries, shopkeepers, and relatively affluent villagers

5. Maskati Mission Journal, December 1916; January 3 and May 1917; July 1918; Mhonda Mission Journal, January 23, 1917; July 14 and December 8, 1918; Lugoba Mission Journal, February 21 and December 28, 1918.

6. Salimu Machaku and Mohamedi Rashidi, Kwediboma; Athumani Nyokka (Kwediboma, August 30, 1982); Mohamedi Mjewe (Kwediboma, September 21, 1982); Mhonda Mission Journal, December 15, 1918; Maskati Mission Journal, December 3, 25 and 31, 1920; January 1, 1921; and Lugoba Mission Journal, December 24, 25 and 29, 1918; January 2 and 15 and February 6, 1921.

7. Mhonda Mission Journal, January 22 and February 16, 1919; Mandera Mission Journal, March 20, 1919 and February 11, 1923; Pangani District, Annual Report (1923), TNA; Maskati Mission Journal, January 1, 1921 and May 24, 1921; Lugoba Mission Journal, January 18, March 15, 18 and 23, April 2 and 5 and May 26, 1919; April 27 and 28, 1920; February 26, April 14, May 27 and 29, June 5 and 9, 1922; March 7, July 5 and November 14, 1923; January 12–13 and 27, 1924. Seasonal food shortages were also commonplace in the Uluguru Mountains after the war: E. E. Hutchins, "The Waluguru," Rhodes House MSS. Afr. s. 1059.

by farmers who needed cash to pay taxes and retire debts. For just this purpose, an "immense multitude" of cultivators descended on the Mandera mission, despite persistent shortages, to sell maize in June 1926.[8]

After 1925, neither favorable weather nor bountiful harvests erased food shortages, as Handeni's District Officer learned in 1929.[9] Touring the central Nguu highlands, where carefully tended plots surrounded settlements, covered depressions, and crowded along watercourses, he was bewildered to find widespread hunger only two or three months after the year's principal harvest. "Natives state they are short of food," he reported, "obviously through no fault of their own, as they have cultivated intensively."[10] The cause of these post-harvest deficits was sales of crops at low prices despite chronic scarcity.[11] "So many people have come to sell maize," wrote a Spiritan at Mandera in 1931, "that [we have] much more than is needed."[12]

Together with increasingly thorough tax collecting, it was mainly the disappearance of patronage that induced food sales, because it left many farmers, particularly those who lost livestock to diseases, with no choice but to take short-term loans during deficit seasons. Although some credit was provided by the Spiritans and a few Zigua-speaking wage-earners and office-holders, the primary lenders in interwar Handeni were the Gujarati business community. Through their network of village shops, they advanced foods and other goods in return for post-harvest repayments in grains and beans. Hence farmers who took loans to pay taxes, obtain food, meet burial costs, and make other expenditures had to surrender portions of their crops to creditors or sell them at low post-harvest prices.

8. Mhonda Mission Journal, January 21, 1925; Mandera Mission Journal, February 19, May 11 and 25, July 1, September 7, October 2–3, and 20, 1925; April 17, June 7, 25 and 28, July 19, 1926; Maddocks, Report from Kwa Mkono, p. 200; Pangani District, Annual Report (1925), TNA; Handeni Sub-District, Annual Report (1925), TNA; *Dar es Salaam Times*, June 13, July 4, 1925; Grace B. Lee, "Famine in Zigualand," pp. 245–248.

9. Rev. G. W. Douglas, "The Archdeaconry of Zigualand," Tanga Province, Annual Report (1929), TNA; Tanganyika Territory, Department of Agriculture, Annual Reports (1928–1929, pt. 1 and 1930), TNA; A. K. Mhina, "Agricultural Change in Korogwe District-Bungu Division," p. 27; J. E. G. Ransome, tour report of January 26, 1929, Tanga Province Book, TNA.

10. ARPC, 1930; quote from J. E. G. Ransome, tour report of October 1929, Tanga Province Book, TNA.

11. This had also been true during the early 1920s: Lugoba Mission Journal, September 7, 1924.

12. Mandera Mission Journal, July 30, 1928, August 23, 1930, June 13 and 23, August 31, 1931; February 18, July 11, 1932. Similar comments on crop sales in the Uluguru Mountains are found in Hutchins.

Farmers were all the more likely to become dependent on creditors because tightly regulated markets that allowed them to sell crops in only small amounts and at low prices prevented them from saving for future seasons of scarcity. Older residents of Handeni sum up these circumstances by saying that sorghum and maize "had no price" during the 1920s and 1930s. Nevertheless, some wage-earners, office-holders, and farmers struggled to carry on trade and petitioned the district administration for crop buying posts and permission to establish weekly markets. The government was blind, however, to the possibility that food crop sales might benefit farmers.[13] Although one Handeni official, for example, was perceptive enough to see that hunger was being caused by "the sale of crops by natives to pay Hut and Poll taxes," he remained convinced that only "economic crops" such as cotton, and not foods, ought to be sold.[14]

Administrative unwillingness to encourage food crop marketing did not stem from lack of demand, for both Tanganyika's wage labor force and its eastern urban areas grew markedly during the first twenty-five years of British rule, despite temporary reversals during the Depression of the 1930s. The population of Dar es Salaam, for instance, nearly doubled between 1913 and 1939, while the number of wage earners in Tanganyika increased from 139,000 in 1912 to at least 244,000 in 1937.[15] Officials in Handeni were little interested, nevertheless, in the opportunities offered by growing urban markets, though one reason why they failed to see that food marketing might benefit farmers is that prices and profitability were depressed by monopsony control of grain in Handeni. The dozen families that composed the Gujarati community in Handeni managed to dominate its small maize market, not only because the Tanganyikan government was tolerant of monopsonistic crop-buyers (the Tanga Province administration did not shrink, for instance, from reporting that one buyer purchased all cotton in the province at a price only "slightly above" the government minimum[16]), but also because its failure to improve transportation, establish

13. Tour reports of 1928 and 1929 from Handeni District in the Tanga Province Book, TNA.

14. Minutes of August 12, 1933 in TNA 13709, v. 1.

15. J. E. G. Sutton, "Dar es Salaam: A Sketch of a Hundred Years," p. 19; Deborah Bryceson, *Food Insecurity and the Social Division of Labour in Tanzania 1919–1985*, p. 112; John Iliffe, *A Modern History of Tanganyika*, p. 305.

16. Tanganyika Territory, Department of Agriculture, Annual Report (1937, pt. 2), TNA. Evidence of the cotton monopsony in Tanga Province is also found in TNA 4/8/6, v. 1, especially letter of Beer and Thomas (Kwashemshi Estate) to Senior Agricultural Officer (Moshi), October 7, 1932. On the tendency of the British administration to support

market centers, and provide credit insured that the Gujarati families would face no competition. Connected by kinship, intermarriage, and business interests, these families were both the primary sources of credit in Handeni and the only traders in the district capable of purchasing and transporting grain in sizeable quantities. By making purchases and extending loans to farmers who pledged to repay in kind, they achieved control over the bulk of marketed maize and kept crop prices low.

The "Locust Famine" of 1932–1935

Many residents of Handeni District associate the calamitous famine of 1932–1935, the worst crisis in Uzigua since 1898–1900, with the deaths of parents, grandparents, siblings, and children. The severity of the "locust famine" persuaded some farmers, in fact, that *matambiko* were useless, for ancestors seemed incapable of protecting them from so terrible a disaster.[17] The sequence of events which transformed persistent food shortages into famine began in June and July 1932, when locust swarms ruined ripening grain in portions of eastern Uzigua. Shortages worsened after the failure of the short rains of 1932–1933 and turned into killing famine when drought extended through the long rains season of 1933. In late 1933 the short rains were again poor and locusts consumed crops in some places. Early 1934 was the worst period of famine; thereafter, conditions improved in most areas, though scarcity lingered throughout 1935 as drought and locusts continued to cause crop losses in some neighborhoods.[18]

While drought and locusts were responsible for heavy destruction of crops from 1932 to 1935, the extent of their impact is uncertain, and cannot easily be separated from the effects of the political changes, administrative impositions, and economic constraints that left cultivators ill-prepared for pestilence and the failure of rains. Rainfall, in fact, was not extraordinarily

---

monopsonies, see McCarthy, Chapter 7; Deborah Bryceson, "'The Tepid Backwater': Bagamoyo District and Its Marginal Commodity Production Within the Tanganyikan Colonial Economy, 1919–1961," pp. 4–5; Ralph Austen, "The Official Mind of Indirect Rule," p. 600.

17. Asumani Nyokka (Kwediboma, August 30, 1982).

18. Famine conditions are described in Mhonda Mission Journal, December 3, 1933; letters of Bishop of Zanzibar (December 16, 1933 and n.d. but probably October 1934, Kideleko) in USPG, UMCA Archives, Correspondence with Bishop of Zanzibar, S.F. 15, v. 8; Lee, "Famine in Zigualand," pp. 245–248; Tanganyika Territory, Department of Agriculture, Annual Report (1933), TNA; ARPC (1933), pp. 66–69 and (1934), pp. 56–57; J. L. Maddocks (Kideleko) to Padre Gibbons (December 11, 1933), TNA 13709, v. 1.

poor during the famine, for in 1932 and 1934 Handeni Town received average rains, and while its 591mm of rainfall in 1933 was much lower than the 49-year average of 847mm, it nevertheless remained well within the expectable range of precipitation there.[19] The impact of locust plagues is also difficult to assess, because although swarms were a dramatic spectacle that blackened the sky and ravaged plant life with astonishing speed, their damage was patchy.[20] Most of the swarms belonged to the great red locust (*Nomadacris septemfasciata*) plagues which, after breeding around Lakes Mweru and Rukwa in northern Zambia and southwestern Tanzania respectively, spread across eastern, central, and southern Africa in the 1930s.[21] Uzigua may also have been affected by the African migratory locust (*Locusta migratoria migratorioides*), whose plagues began in the Niger River valley in 1928 and reached East Africa in the early 1930s.[22] Although the causes of locust plagues are not well understood, one theory proceeds from the assumption that because locusts require dense vegetation for food and shelter as well as nearby bare ground where females can lay their eggs, permanent locust populations live in vegetation mosaics. These are areas of inherent instability where, because different vegetation types are competing for dominance, change may occur swiftly if drought or other climatic occurrence favors one form of vegetation. This line of reasoning suggests that the red locust plague may have begun when Lake Rukwa receded during drought, allowing the expansion of marshy lakeshore grassland where locusts breed, their rapid increase, and the formation of migratory swarms.[23]

Measuring the crop damage caused by locust plagues is guesswork, however, because, aside from the difficulty of collecting information on crop losses over enormous areas, only rough estimates have been made of

19. For monthly rainfall records, see Handeni District Book, v. 4, TNA and Tanga Integrated Rural Development Project, "Meteorological and Hydrological Data for the Tanga Region." Because these are not day-by-day records, however, they may conceal late rains and extended dry spells.

20. For descriptions of locust swarms, see Mhonda Mission Journal, January 4–8 and 19, November 21 and December 10 and 30, 1934, and Mandera Mission Journal, April 3, 1929 and January 3, 1934.

21. Sir Boris Uvarov, *Grasshoppers and Locusts: A Handbook of General Acridology*, 2: 476–495; V. Morant, "Migrations and Breeding of the Red Locust (*Nomadacris septemfasciata* Serv.) in Africa, 1927–1945."

22. Elizabeth Betts, "Outbreaks of the African Migratory Locust Since 1871."

23. D. F. Vesey-Fitzgerald, "The Vegetation of the Outbreak Areas of the Red Locust (*Nomadacris septemfasciata* Serv.) in Tanganyika and Northern Rhodesia," p. 13; R. C. Rainey, Z. Waloff and G. F. Burnett, "The Behaviour of the Red Locust (*Nomadacris septemfasciata* Serville) in Relation to the Topography, Meteorology and Vegetation of the Rukwa Rift Valley, Tanganyika"; R. F. Chapman, *A Biology of Locusts*, p. 50.

the area covered by an average swarm and the number of locusts which it contains. Studies of locust plagues produce staggering but imprecise estimates of the vegetation consumed by a swarm (between 400 and 2000 tons daily, according to one author).[24] Little is known, moreover, about the distribution and movement of swarms, although evidence from Uzigua during the 1930s indicates that locusts caused widely varying amounts of crop damage and struck neighboring villages at different times. A settlement might escape locust depredations altogether while its neighbors sustained heavy losses, and might be passed over several times before a swarm attacked its crops. At Mandera, for example, locusts did not appear until 1934, yet nearby areas were affected by the plague of 1932.[25]

Because their impact was uneven, locusts and drought left neighborhoods and settlements with different amounts of food. The Magamba area of central Handeni seemed to be in desperate straits during December 1933 and January 1934, for instance, yet the adjacent "chiefdoms" of Mazingara and Kwamsisi harvested plentiful maize. The relatively secure circumstances of some Nguu highlanders, moreover, enabled them to evade government trade prohibitions and send foodstuffs to the famine- and drought-stricken Uzigua lowlands in 1933, where they found "ready markets for sale of their surplus supplies to their needy neighbors."[26] Nevertheless, government restrictions on crop movements continued to discourage traders, particularly the Gujarati community, from attempting to bring foodstuffs into hungry villages.

Just as villages and neighborhoods sustained varying amounts of crop damage, the differences between households and individuals were also considerable, particularly because while men were able to leave Uzigua in search of work, women, the elderly, and the very young who remained at home often subsisted on wild tubers and other undomesticated foods. "During the past two months," wrote the Anglican missionary J. L. Maddocks in December 1933, "I have seen the most pitiable cases of starvation from time to time amongst old people and women, and numbers

24. Chapman, *Biology of Locusts*, pp. 23–24.

25. Mandera Mission Journal, June 28, 1932 and October 15, 1933. If, as Spiritan missionaries claimed, elderly Mhonda residents had not seen locusts before the 1930s, this would testify to the uneven pattern of their destructiveness because they must have lived in neighborhoods untouched by the plagues of the 1890s.

26. Quote is from A.D.O. (Handeni) to P.C. (Tanga), August 31, 1933, TNA 4/1161/1, v. 4. Also, Mhonda Mission Journal, December 3, 1933; ARPC (1933), p. 69; D.O. (Handeni) to P.C. (Tanga), April 6, 1934, TNA 13079, v. 2; A.D.O. (Handeni) to P.C. (Tanga), April 19 and 26, 1933, P.C. (Tanga) to Chief Secretary (Dar es Salaam), June 22, 1933 and correspondence from December 1933 and January 1934 in TNA 13079, v. 1.

of children who were reduced to little more than skin and bones, through prolonged starvation rations, if what they had eaten could be called rations at all."[27] Undoubtedly some of these cases resulted from the abandonment of wives and children, as would also happen during subsequent famines.[28] Yet in all parts of Handeni District, reported the administration in August 1933, even in the areas hardest hit by the famine, a few households, especially those headed by mission and government employees who received wages and rations, had sizeable food reserves. Indeed, particularly fortunate villagers actually expanded their livestock holdings during the famine by trading grain and cassava for the cattle and goats of indigent neighbors.[29]

While conditions in Handeni improved gradually after late 1934, farmers experienced food deficits through the rest of the decade. In early 1935, failure of the short rains brought acute shortages to southeastern Handeni, while in the Nguu highlands, where primary schools closed because weakened children could not attend, a teacher observed despairingly that "there is terrible, terrible hunger in this area."[30] In 1936, relieved administrators noted the return of residents who had fled during the years of famine and improvement in the "health and stamina of people," yet serious food shortages occurred once again around Mandera in 1937 and in Handeni District two years later.[31]

Surviving Famine Without Patronage

The combination of lack of patronage and absence of marketing opportunities left most cultivators to face famine in small, isolated groups during 1925 and from 1932 to 1935. Their strategies for survival were marked by resilience and deeply felt responsibility for dependents, but they also reveal the reduced scale of cooperating groups and the frequent resort, for want

27. Letter of J. L. Maddocks (December 11, 1933), TNA 13709, v. 1.
28. As local court records show: Handeni District Files M5/1, "Complaints" and 2/6, "Chanika: Legal." Court records from the 1930s have not survived.
29. Hamza Mlingo, Mswaki; Mandera Mission Journal, December 11, 1933; ARPC (1933), p. 65; A.D.O. (Handeni) to P.C. (Tanga), August 8, 1933, TNA 4/1161/1, v. 4; D.O. (Handeni) to P.C. (Tanga), August 1, 1935, TNA 4/1161/1. v. 7. The differences between men and women, young and old, wage-earners and non-wage earning farmers are very similar to those that emerged in Malawi during the 1949 famine: Megan Vaughan, *The Story of an African Famine* and "Famine Analysis and Family Relations: 1949 in Nyasaland," pp. 177–205.
30. Mgera Primary School Journal, January 28 and February 20, 1935.
31. Tanganyika Territory, Department of Agriculture, Annual Report (1936), TNA; Mandera Mission Journal, February 26 and July 6, 1937; ARPC (1939), p. 89.

of alternatives, to migration, a response which deepened environmental difficulties by reducing the number of farmers available to manage vegetation. Migrants often left Uzigua permanently for more promising areas such as Tanga or Arusha. Yet many men tried, nevertheless, to maintain their farms while traveling short and long distances to seek temporary employment.

A pattern of migration and short-term labor that would become typical of hungry seasons in interwar Uzigua developed in southern Nguu during January 1919, when migrants worked four or five days clearing and hoeing the fields of peasants before returning home with loads of cassava. In February 1922, hundreds of laborers once again came to Mhonda from the Uzigua lowlands and Wami Valley for this purpose.[32] Migration from eastern Uzigua to both the Nguu Mountains and coastal areas became even more widespread in the 1930s. "All Turiani district is crowded," reported a Spiritan from southern Nguu in 1933, "with strangers from Handeni, Kibindu and Mandera, all seeking cassava."[33] Touring the eastern Handeni "chiefdom" of Mazingara in 1935, Handeni's District Officer found that villagers supplemented a diet of gathered pumpkins, wild roots, and fruits with cassava and maize brought from other districts by men

> who have been working on other natives' shambas [fields] in return for a small load of foodstuffs. There is a constant stream backwards and forwards of people of this sort and they seldom stay at home longer than two or three days between each trip. By this means the people are able to fend off actual starvation and to carry on cultivation at home.[34]

Other men, adopting the habit that had developed in the German period, worked for peasants who lived near the Pangani Valley sisal plantations, sometimes in rotations, so that while one man was absent, others remained at home to farm.[35] The demand for casual labor in the Pangani

---

32. Lugoba Mission Journal: January 22 and May 26, 1919, February 26, April 3,4,5, May 28, 1922, January 12, 1924.

33. Mhonda Mission Journal, December 3, 1933.

34. Quote from D. O. (Handeni) to P. C. (Tanga), March 12, 1935, TNA 13079, v. 2. Also, P. C. (Tanga) to Chief Secretary (Dar es Salaam), February 28, 1935 in the same file.

35. Pogwa Rashidi, Handeni; Asumani Nyokka (Kwediboma, August 30, 1982 and March 29, 1983); Mohamedi Saidi Nyange, Kwediboma; Rajabu Sefu Mwenkumba, Kwa Mkono; Abedi Juma and others, Manga; Mohamedi Semsambia, Kilwa; Msulwa Mbega and Ramadhani Semndili (Gombero, September 20–21, 1983); ARPC (1933), p. 65 and (1935), p. 77; letter of J. L. Maddocks (December 11, 1933), P. C. (Tanga) to Chief Secretary (Dar es Salaam), December 19, 1933 and P. C. (Tanga) to Chief Secretary (Dar es Salaam), January 12, 1934 in TNA 13709, v. 1; D. O. (Handeni) to P. C. (Tanga), March 12, 1935, TNA 13709, v. 2; Lee, "Famine in Zigualand," pp. 247–248.

Valley declined, however, just as the great famine of the mid-1930s was taking hold in Uzigua, because the market for foodstuffs among sisal workers dwindled as plantations responded to Depression conditions by cutting wages and reducing the labor force.[36]

Although work under peasant employers became scarcer during the Depression, it remained preferable to plantation labor, which involved lengthy service, unfamiliar procedures, and low wages. A plantation worker received no pay until he had completed thirty days' tasks, a term which many men from Handeni, inexperienced in sisal work and perhaps weakened by hunger, needed six weeks to complete. This was far too long to leave dependents on their own resources, particularly because men had little chance of earning enough after-tax income to afford substantial food purchases. Low wages, of course, had kept men away from the sisal fields long before the 1930s, but during the Depression wages became even less attractive as they fell from a maximum of thirty shillings in 1929 to a maximum of fifteen shillings per thirty days by 1933. After the estates had made deductions for rations, moreover, a worker would be fortunate to have two shillings after five weeks of work. Hence plantation employment was no solution for men who were likely to be pressed upon their return home for ten shillings in tax (since the administration insistently pursued tax collection throughout the 1932–1935 famine[37]), as well as reimbursement for any government famine relief taken by their dependents. Men contemplating sisal work also had to wonder whether the government might make direct deductions from their pay, as the Handeni chiefs' council recommended in 1933.[38] Peasant employers, on the other hand, offered brief work terms that allowed laborers to return home frequently with provisions for

36. On agriculture in the Pangani Valley during the 1930s, see Helen P. Mhando, "Capitalist Penetration and the Growth of Peasant Agriculture in Korogwe District, 1920–1975," pp. 75–76, and letter of Rev. A. R. Jones (Mkuzi) to Longland (August 25, 1933), TNA 4/401. On the reduction of sisal wages during the Depression, see Anse Tambila, "A History of the Tanga Sisal Labour Force, 1936–1964," pp. 35, 74. The sisal workers who came from areas outside Tanga Province were the laborers most likely to be dependent upon purchases of food from local peasants. Their numbers declined from 11,000 in 1927 to 1800 in 1934: F. Longland, "Report on Labour Matters in Sisal Areas," no. 1 (March 29, 1936), TNA 23544.

37. Tax revenue from Tanga Province, Annual Reports (1932–1934), TNA; D.O. (Handeni) to P. C. (Tanga), September 6, 1932 and P. C. (Tanga) to Chief Secretary (Dar es Salaam), January 25, 1934 in TNA 4/1161/1, v. 4.

38. On wages, see Tanga Province, Annual Report (1927), TNA; Lee, "Famine in Zigualand," p. 247 and TNA 23544. On the disadvantages of plantation labor during the famine, see Lee, "Famine in Zigualand," p. 247; ARPC (1933), p. 66; letter of J. L. Maddocks (December 11, 1933), A.P.C. (Tanga) to Chief Secretary (Dar es Salaam), September 17, 1933, P. C. (Tanga) to Chief Secretary (Dar es Salaam), January 12, 1934 and letter of D. O. (Handeni), March 12, 1935 in TNA 13709, v. 1.

dependents, and paid cassava and other foodstuffs that permitted migrants to avoid costly food purchases. Short-term farm labor became so common that British officials regarded it as one of the Zigua "tribal customs."[39] Its advantages, however, rather than the force of custom, explain why farmers preferred it to work on European plantations.

Aside from short-term labor, trade with famine-free regions was the favorite resort of men such as the Nguu highlanders who in 1933–1934 walked some 150 miles westward with goats and pressed cakes of tobacco to buy grain and cassava in Kondoa-Irangi. Brothers and friends arranged to meet en route so that men returning eastward with food could exchange their loads for more tobacco and livestock.[40] A form of trade which evaporated in the mid-1930s, however, was sales of livestock, for relatively heavy marketing and low demand drove down prices. While grain prices were doubling in 1933, the price of a goat fell from about seven to less than one shilling, the average price for one cow declined from Shs. 70 to less than Shs. 20, and by December 1933, cattle and goats were "unsalable."[41] Hence a seller of livestock in 1933 obtained only one-quarter to one-third the amount of maize that he would have received in 1925.[42]

Although men traveled far to work and trade, women lacked these opportunities and were paid less than men, for the few wage-paying jobs available close to home. The interwar period was particularly difficult not only for the women who were abandoned during famines of the 1920s and 1930s, but also for the victims of an earlier wave of divorce stemming, it seems, from impoverishment and the long separations caused by labor conscription during the First World War. Some women found a rare postwar opportunity to earn cloth and money at the Spiritan missions, even though Spiritans—such as the evangelist who mournfully observed women and girls carrying sand for a construction project at Mhonda in September 1920—thought that women were unsuited for many jobs. Indeed, conceptions of both European and African men about what

39. Handeni District File 1/14, "Agricultural and Marketing: General," Report of Agricultural Field Officer (Kwakonje, February 8, 1955).

40. Ramadhani Kikobo (Kwediboma, August 12, 1982); Salimu Machaku and Mohamedi Rashidi, Kwediboma; Mohamedi Saidi Nyange, Kwediboma; Mohamedi Chambo and Mdoe Nyange, Kiberashi; M. A. Mavullah and others, Balanga; Saidi Hatibu, Mkonde; Elders of Gitu; Lee, "Famine in Zigualand," p. 246 and A.D.O. (Handeni) to P. C. (Tanga), April 19, 1933, TNA 13709, v. 1.

41. Letter of J. L. Maddocks (December 11, 1933), TNA 13709, v. 1; prices from Lee, "Famine in Zigualand," p. 246 and A.D.O. (Handeni) to P. C. (Tanga), April 19, 1933, TNA 13709, v. 1; also, Rajabu Sefu Mwenkumba, Kwa Mkono.

42. ARPC (1933), p. 66; also, letter of J. L. Maddocks (December 11, 1933) and P. C. (Tanga) to Chief Secretary (Dar es Salaam), January 12, 1934 in TNA 13709, v. 1.

constituted the proper work of women placed female casual laborers at a disadvantage, for the Spiritans often limited women to what they regarded as appropriate tasks and paid less for those types of work than for the labor done by men. The pay for women's weeding at the Mhonda mission, for example, was only half what men were paid for clearing bush from plots.[43]

Neither men nor women found casual labor to be an adequate substitute for patronage, because it failed to provide long-term entitlement to resources. Hence, it is not surprising that the outstanding cultural movement of the period, the postwar growth of Islam, responded to the need for new forms of mutual obligation and cooperation. The *Mrima* towns of Pangani, Tanga, and Bagamoyo were the principal sources of postwar Islamic influence, for their Qur'anic schools sent teachers to Uzigua to win conversions and encourage Muslims to undertake advanced study. The spearhead of the Islamic movement in the 1920s was the Qadiriyya brotherhood led by Shaykh Ramiya, a teacher and political notable who built up a patronage network among former slaves at Bagamoyo. Ramiya's success in forging relationships with disciples by providing material assistance (at Mandera he paid taxes for Islamic converts) and the spiritual benefits of his teaching in return for acceptance of Islam and labor on his plantations, was a model for Qadiriyya proselytizers who established similar relationships when they opened a "cooperative farm" in Handeni Town and attracted students to work in their fields at Mswaki, Kwa Mkono, and elsewhere. Ultimately, however, Shaykh Ramiya and other Qadiriyya teachers were no more successful than Zigua-speaking and Gujarati entrepreneurs in overcoming administrative obstacles to trade, market production, and employment of wage labor.[44]

43. Mhonda Mission Journal, June 29, 1918, January 22 and July 31, 1919, May 17, June 24, September 27, November 27–30, 1920, February 9, 1922; Maskati Mission Journal, July 1918, October 5, 1919; Lugoba Mission Journal, January 22, 1919; François X. Vogt, "Apostolisches Vikariat Bagamoyo," p. 75.

44. On the spread of Islam: Mohamedi Mjewe (Kwediboma, September 20, 1982); Haji Luwambo (Kwediboma, September 30, 1982); Rajabu Sefu Mwenkumba, Kwa Mkono; Mwalimu James Kibwana, Kwa Mkono; Omali Gumbo, Kwinji; Elders of Magamba; Mandera Mission Journal, June 26 and October 5, 1920, September 12–13, 1924, February 16, September 1 and October 10, 1925, April 11, 1926; Mhonda Mission Journal, August 5, 1920, February 1, 1921, June 5 and July 8, 1922, January 23 and July 19–23, 1926; Maskati Mission Journal, July 1920, May 23 and 29, July 9, 1922; Lugoba Mission Journal, September 8 and October 4, 1922; *BC* 28: 281 and 284; USPG, UMCA Archives, letter of Petro Limo to Travers (Kwa Maizi, April 12, 1922), Box A.5; Frank Zanzibar, "In Zigualand," p. 196; J. L. Maddocks, "A Christian Festival in a Mohammedan Land," p. 266; John Saidi, "Islam in Zigualand," p. 246; Pangani District, Annual Report (1921), TNA; August H. Nimtz, Jr., "The Role of the Muslim Sufi Order in Political Change: An Overview and Micro-analysis from Tanzania," pp. 80 and 393ff. Nimtz suggested that Uzigua had adopted Islam much earlier,

Thus the majority of farmers struggled to survive in small groups usually composed, say Handeni residents who experienced the "locust famine," of at most a few households bound together by kinship, affinity, and proximity. Handeni residents do not speak, however, of broad-based cooperation or assistance from chiefs and patrons. Help, if the needy found any, came from close friends, spouses, siblings, children, parents, and parents' siblings. The few government and mission employees in Handeni, for example, sheltered their immediate kin and affines: "Nearly all our Christians earning wages, however small, are keeping their own and perhaps their wife's parents," wrote a missionary from central Handeni in 1933, "and in every house you will meet strangers, chiefly children of relatives adopted for this time of stress."[45]

Women who gathered undomesticated foods such as the wild roots *mdudu* and *ndiga* (*Dioscorea dumetorum*), leaves, fruits, nuts, and honey were the primary providers of subsistence during famines, because food purchases were beyond the means of most famine victims, particularly the women, children and elderly who were left behind by male labor migrants.[46] Even government famine relief, provided on credit at the rate of fourteen cents per kilo of maize, was exceedingly expensive at a time when cattle were fetching only twelve to twenty shillings per head, and in any case never satisfied demand, for only 3 percent of Handeni's population received food from the administration between 1932 and 1935. Appointed chiefs, anxious to stanch the flow of money for famine relief from the Native Treasuries under their control, discouraged women from applying for government assistance by threatening to conscript their husbands for plantation labor.[47] Women "hide their distress," commented an Anglican missionary in 1933, "in case their menfolk will be drafted to the coast for

probably in the 1880s, but the numerous sources showing that widespread conversions occurred mainly after 1914 include the Mandera Mission Journal from the 1920s. See Nimtz, *Islam and Politics in East Africa: The Sufi Order in Tanzania*, pp. 11, 67 and 129 (ftn.).

45. Lee, "Famine in Zigualand," p. 248.

46. Salimu Machaku and Mohamedi Rashidi, Kwediboma; Asumani Nyokka (Kwediboma, December 1, 1983); M. A. Mavullah and others, Balanga; Mandera Mission Journal, December 6, 1933; Lee, "Famine in Zigualand," p. 245; ARPC (1933), p. 66; A.D.O. (Handeni) to P. C. (Tanga), April 19, 1933 and P. C. (Tanga) to Chief Secretary (Dar es Salaam), December 19, 1933 in TNA 13079, v. 1. Famine foods are listed by Sumra, "An Analysis of Environmental and Social Problems."

47. Mandera Mission Journal, December 11, 1933; Lee, "Famine in Zigualand," p. 246; Tanganyika Territory, Department of Agriculture, Annual Report (1933), TNA; ARPC (1933), p. 65; P. C. (Tanga) to Treasurer (Dar es Salaam), March 23, 1934, A.P.C. (Tanga) to D. O. (Handeni), July 1, 1933, A.P.C. (Tanga) to Chief Secretary (Dar es Salaam), October 20, 1933, letter of J. L. Maddocks (December 11, 1933) and P. C. (Tanga) to Chief Secretary (Dar es Salaam), January 12, 1934 in TNA 13709, v. 1.

work on the plantations, and be delayed there indefinitely, and they will not see them again."[48]

Many of the farmers who faced these difficulties decided to leave Uzigua altogether. Indeed, the departure of relatives and neighbors and the decline of communities are among the most painful memories of the 1932–1935 famine.[49] One administrator reported in 1933 that "some of the villages are deserted, their people having gone off to more favored parts in search of wages and food," while in the following year refugees from Handeni eked out an existence in Pangani District "by theft of crops standing in the local shambas." In the Mazingara portion of Handeni District "it was seldom that any young able-bodied people were found and some villages were completely deserted."[50]

While there are no district-wide data from Handeni to provide a measure of depopulation during the 1932–1935 famine, a census of Mswaki "chiefdom" conducted in 1935 showed that its population fell from 2138 before the famine to 1322.[51] Touring government officials saw that Handeni District was very lightly populated in the mid- and late 1930s. An agricultural researcher who visited the district in 1935, for example, found few settlements worth mentioning in his detailed report and noted only occasionally the "infrequent cultivations of the district." Administrators proposed that because the eastern Nguu highlands, where the District Officer had noticed loss of population in 1929, appeared underpeopled, it ought to be occupied by cultivators from the drier lowlands.[52] Officials

48. Quote from Lee, "Famine in Zigualand," pp. 246–247; A.P.C. (Tanga) to Chief Secretary (Dar es Salaam), July 17, 1933, TNA 13709, v. 1.

49. For example, Pogwa Rashidi, Handeni.

50. Quotes are from letter of Bishop of Zanzibar (December 16, 1933), USPG, UMCA Archives, Correspondence with Bishop of Zanzibar, S.F. 15, v. 8 and D. O. (Pangani) to P. C. (Tanga), October 3, 1934, TNA 4/401. On migration during famine: Abedi Juma and others, Manga; Ramadhani Semndili, Gombero; Mohamedi Chambo, Kiberashi; Mohamedi Mjewe (Kwediboma, September 27, 1982); Mohamedi Saidi Nyange, Kwediboma; Pogwa Rashidi, Handeni; Saidi Hatibu, Mkonde; M. A. Mavullah and others, Balanga; Mandera Mission Journal, December 11, 1933; Lee, "Famine in Zigualand," p. 247; letter of J. L. Maddocks (December 11, 1933) and P. C. (Tanga) to Chief Secretary (Dar es Salaam), December 19, 1933 and January 12, 1934 in TNA 13709, v. 1; D. O. (Handeni) to P. C. (Tanga), March 12, 1935, TNA 13079, v. 2.

51. TNA 4/1161/1, v. 7.

52. C. H. Grierson, "Handeni District," notes of meeting of June 25, 1934, C. F. M. Swynnerton, "Preliminary Memorandum on the Position in Handeni" (July 23, 1934), and "Marginal notes" in TNA 11299, v. 1. The British estimated the population of Handeni District to be 56,000 in 1928; it was estimated to be 170,000 in 1975. German estimates had placed the population of the same area at about 53,500 from 1898 to 1905, but the fact that they take no account of the demographic consequences of the 1898–1900 famine indicates their unreliability: RKA 6467/296–298, 6478/135–136, 6479. For impressions of depopulation in

were also concerned about the small size of many settlements, for most appeared to contain no more than thirty inhabitants.[53]

The Consequence of Famine and Depopulation: Epizootic

In contrast to the last precolonial famine in 1884–1886, the crises of 1925 and 1932–1935 conformed to the pattern that had developed in the 1890s, because the interwar famines forced many villagers, who had neither patrons nor alternative sources of relief, to leave the region. The decline of the farming population not only disrupted agricultural production but also allowed the spread of vegetation, wildlife, and insects and led to the trypanosomiasis and theileriosis outbreaks that left few cattle in Handeni District by the late 1930s. Even before 1925, however, incidence of the bovine disease had already begun to increase, for during the First World War famine, labor conscription, flight from warring armies, crop requisitions, and theft of livestock impaired farmers' ability to contain vector and wildlife habitats. Tsetse spread along the Wami River during the war, both east and west of the old *Grenzwildnis* between the Lukigura River and Kidudwe, and caused trypanosomiasis outbreaks which claimed many cattle. Elsewhere, trypanosomiasis reduced the Mandera mission herd from 300 to 30 head in one year, ruined the dairy operation that had thrived before the war at the Maskati mission, and killed many horses of the British-South African force.[54]

In the wake of wartime famine and the influenza pandemic, most of Uzigua's population lived in small, dispersed communities, as an Anglican missionary visiting Handeni District observed in 1924. Between Korogwe

---

Handeni: Bishop of Zanzibar (Kideleko, n.d. but probably October 1934), USPG, UMCA Archives, Correspondence with Bishop of Zanzibar, S.F. 15, v. 8.

53. The quote is from G. Milne, "A Soil Reconaissance Journey through Parts of the Tanganyika Territory," p. 199. Average settlement size is based upon Swynnerton's estimate of ten "families" per village, and the average of 3.3 persons per adult male taxpayer derived from the 1928 census. In the rather unlikely event that German colonial estimates as well as Swynnerton's observations were reliable, a significant decline in average settlement size could be demonstrated between 1898 and the 1930s, because German officials estimated average settlement size in 1898 (before the 1898–1900 famine) to be 55 persons. See C. F. M. Swynnerton, *The Tsetse Flies of East Africa*, p. 348; C. H. Grierson, "Handeni District," (July 21, 1934) and notes of meeting of June 25, 1934 in TNA 11299, v. 1; the 1928 census in the Tanga Province Book, TNA, and RKA 6467/296–298.

54. Francis Brett Young, *Marching on Tanga*, pp. 237 and 261; Mandera Mission Journal, September 26, 1915; *BC* 26: 305 and 27: 100; Maskati Mission Journal, August 8, 1915 and January 3, 1917; Lugoba Mission Journal, January 6, 1919; Vogt, "Apostolisches Vikariat," p. 75, and "Une conversation avec Monseigneur Vogt," p. 53; Mrisho Kizenga, Kwediboma.

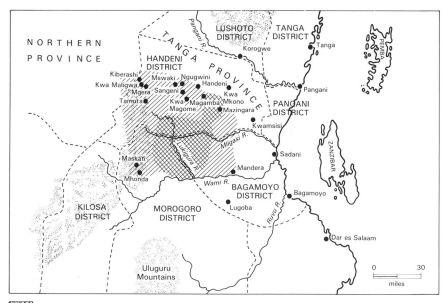

Map 4. Expansion of tsetse belts in Uzigua under Indirect Rule.

and Kwa Mkono, an area that before the war had contained several communities large enough to warrant missionary interest, he found only one village. Continuing on to Sangeni, a neighborhood of central Handeni District that had impressed European visitors of an earlier generation as a well-populated and relatively prosperous place, he saw "long stretches of uninhabited country" between villages. The contrast between prewar and postwar conditions was stronger still at Ngugwini, another neighborhood near Handeni Town, which in 1907 had contained about twenty villages, but which by 1924 was "merely jungle inhabited by buffaloes [the prime reservoir of theilerial infection], giraffes, and other big game."[55] Nowhere did the missionary find large villages like those that once had been ruled

55. The accounts of "Kwa Mkono," pp. 23–24 and "Kwa Maizi, and Its Daughter Parishes in Zigualand," pp. 240–243, may be compared with: USPG, UMCA Archives, letter of Hine (1907); Herbert Lister, "Letter" (Korogwe, March 1, 1892), pp. 68–69; W. H. Kisbey, "An Advance in Zigualand," pp. 64–66; Kisbey, "A Journey to Zigualand," pp. 172–175; Samwil Sehoza, "A Walk to Kwa Magome," pp. 160–163; and Oscar Baumann, *Usambara und seine Nachbargebiete*, p. 273.

by precolonial chieftains. Indeed, so many residents of the southern Nguu Mountains lived in remote hamlets, went the rumor heard by Spiritan missionaries at Mhonda, that the government was considering resettling them in large villages along motor roads. Even around the administrative and trading center at Handeni Town there were "not many farms."[56]

The scattered, shrunken farming settlements were unable to halt the colonization of formerly cleared land by bush and thicket, and consequently had great difficulty in protecting livestock from predatory wildlife and disease-bearing insects. Extensive formerly cultivated areas of Handeni District had reverted to bush by 1922, reported British authorities, and wildlife seemed to be roaming everywhere. Lions attacked livestock, while monkeys, baboons, and bush pigs [the major undomesticated trypanosomal reservoir in Handeni], "incredibly bold in their raids on native gardens," ravaged crops. With the regeneration of unmanaged vegetation and the advance of wildlife came tsetse, which one administrator realized was why trypanosomiasis outbreaks occurred in areas that had lost farmers. In Uzigua, he wrote, where "there had been diminution of population, bush crept over deserted lands and with the bush came tsetse."[57] Tick populations were undoubtedly growing as well, though there is no record of their increase because, as noted in an earlier chapter, aside from the occasional entomological or veterinary researcher, Europeans in Uzigua paid no attention to the tiny *Rhipicephalus appendiculatus* ticks that transmitted theileriosis.

Belts of tsetse infestation widened throughout postwar Uzigua, as the Spiritans of Mhonda discovered in 1920 when trypanosomiasis killed their cattle. In eastern Handeni District the administrative chief of Mazingara had to move his headquarters after tsetse invaded his home, and at Lugoba, just south of the Wami River, a Spiritan despondently recorded the decline of his herd from 120 to only nine cattle, which he attributed, along with the loss of his neighbors' "fine herds," to the appearance of tsetse.[58]

56. Francis Brett Young, *Marching on Tanga*, p. 190; also, Mhonda Mission Journal, August 18, 1920; *BC* 28: 327, and Maskati Mission Journal, July 1920.

57. Quote from Pangani District, Annual Report (1923), TNA; also, Pangani District, Annual Reports (1922, 1924) and Handeni Sub-District, Annual Report (1925), TNA; Francis Brett Young, *Marching on Tanga*, p. 237; USPG, UMCA Archives, Limo to Travers (Kwa Maizi, April 12, 1922); Charles Dundas, *African Crossroads*, p. 101. Lion attacks on humans and livestock are noted in Lugoba Mission Journal, May 7–8 and July 24–25, 1919, September 16 and October 17, 1924.

58. Mhonda Mission Journal, May 18, 1920; "Life of Zumbe Majugwe Mkumbe of Mazingara" (1949), TNA 4/6/5, v. 2; Lugoba Mission Journal, October 4, 24 and 27, November 16–17, 1920, August 26 and October 7, 1921, April 24 and July 26, 1922, August 1 and 5, 1923, September 21, October 5 and 17, 1924.

The expansion of tsetse zones was particularly well documented southwest of Handeni Town, where vegetation occupied formerly cultivated land on the margins of the uninhabited *Grenzwildnis* between the Lukigura and Mligasi rivers. As vegetation, wildlife, and vectors advanced to the northeast, farmers retreated toward Handeni, accompanied by Anglican missionaries who abandoned their station at Kwa Magome. Lions prowled northeastward close to Handeni Town, threatening livestock and their owners.[59]

Trypanosomiasis also reversed a postwar recovery of herds at Mandera in 1922, even though as late as May of that year cattle were exposed to *Glossina* only when they drank in the Wami River during the dry season, because tsetse were confined mainly to riverside vegetation. Over the next few months, however, tsetse spread rapidly and by August and September were unavoidable. The incidence of bovine trypanosomiasis increased, and at year's end the mission herd, 150 strong in January, had only 64 head. Tsetse occupied larger areas in succeeding years, forcing the missionaries to place their cattle in outlying stations and make long detours to avoid infested areas, just as their predecessors had done during post-rinderpest epizootics in the early years of the century.[60]

Tsetse infestation accelerated after each famine, as Handeni's District Officer learned in 1928–1929 when he reported that *Glossina* were occupying large tracts, particularly in the southwest reaches of the district. The neighborhood Kwa Mgumi, he wrote, "used to be a large cattle centre but fly has killed off all cattle," while further south, he continued, there were "plenty of tsetse although five years ago [that is, before the famine of 1925] this was a rich cattle country." At Ndwati, the District Officer again saw tsetse and deserted, formerly cultivated land, the signs of post-famine retreat before expanding fly belts.[61] Indeed, the rapidity of tsetse expansion during and after the famine of 1932–1935 finally prompted the government to undertake studies in Handeni District that confirmed the connection between epizootic and depopulation. An important spur to research was the British fear that despite the absence of human trypanosomiasis in Han-

59. Young, *Marching on Tanga*, p. 261; Maddocks, "Kwa Magome," pp. 69–70; Frank Zanzibar, "In Zigualand," p. 215; USPG, UMCA Archives, Limo to Travers (Kwa Maizi, April 12, 1922); Swynnerton to Chief Secretary (Dar es Salaam), November 14, 1926, TNA Early Secretariat File 2702, v. 4. Nineteenth-century evidence of this same *Grenzwildnis* is described in Chapter Two.

60. Mandera Mission Journal, May 1, 2, and 5, August 30, September 29, and December 31, 1922, June 12 and November 27, 1925; *BC* 28: 286.

61. J. E. G. Ransome, tour reports of January and October 1929, Tanga Province Book, TNA.

deni, spreading tsetse would infect migrant laborers who walked through the district from the Central Railway to the sisal plantations of the Pangani Valley.[62] The first study of tsetse infestation, trypanosomiasis, and settlement patterns was conducted in 1934 by C. F. M. Swynnerton, Tanganyika's Director of Tsetse Research, who, almost inexplicably in light of other evidence, concluded that tsetse were *not* spreading.[63] This was only one of several instances in which administrative personnel appeared reluctant to acknowledge the full severity of the Handeni situation.[64] Nevertheless, administrators did report fly belt expansion in the western Nguu highlands in 1935, and three years later the government commissioned another survey that showed that tsetse were becoming more widely distributed in the northwestern Nguu highlands, the Pangani Valley, and the Lukigura Valley, where trypanosomal infections were found in many cattle.[65]

Further research in 1939 and 1940 provided additional evidence of fly belt expansion and heavy incidence of bovine trypanosomiasis, and also demonstrated that depopulation resulting from the 1932–1935 famine had caused the spread of tsetse. At Kiberashi in northern Nguu, surveyors found that since 1934 *Glossina pallidipes* had infested thickets along watercourses, which is to say precisely the locations where farmers would have kept out tsetse had they not fled during the famine. *Glossina morsitans*, meanwhile, occupied valleys and the lower elevations of surrounding highlands that had been densely settled by precolonial communities. In his summary of the Kiberashi study, Swynnerton's successor as Director of Tsetse Research, H. E. Hornby, argued that the situation resulted from the post-1932 decline of farming and cattle populations. Bush, he concluded, was everywhere succeeding cultivation.[66]

62. Swynnerton to Chief Secretary (Dar es Salaam), November 14, 1926, TNA Early Secretariat File 2702, v. 4.

63. Swynnerton, "Preliminary Memorandum."

64. In the published report of his findings on Handeni, Swynnerton cast the situation in much more optimistic terms than he had used in his original, internal memorandum: Swynnerton, "Preliminary Memorandum" and *The Tsetse Flies*, p. 348. For another example of this tendency, compare J. E. G. Ransome, tour report of January 26, 1929, Tanga Province Book, and Tanga Province, Annual Reports (1928 and 1929), TNA. Government maps of tsetse distribution showed fly belts only in places where surveys had confirmed infestation. In areas where no surveys had been done (and this included most of Uzigua) tsetse belts were not marked, even if their existence was well known to administrators. See map appended to Tanganyika Territory, Department of Veterinary Science and Animal Husbandry, Annual Report (1925), TNA.

65. Tanganyika Territory, Department of Veterinary Science, Annual Reports (1935, 1938), TNA; Korogwe District, Annual Report (1938), TNA; Mohamedi Lusingo, Mafisa and Rajabu Sudi, Manga.

66. Notes on *baraza* at Kiberashi (January 19, 1939), TNA 26650, v. 1; correspondence, esp. H. E. Hornby to Chief Secretary (Dar es Salaam), October 11, 1940 in TNA 26650, v. 2.

A more comprehensive survey of Handeni District in 1940 revealed that the Kiberashi findings could be applied to the district as a whole. The survey indicated, in fact, that the tsetse situation was more serious in central Handeni than at Kiberashi. Once again this study cited depopulation during famine as the primary cause of tsetse expansion into formerly cultivated fields. The survey also implicated the abandoned German rubber plantations, which, as alienated property under government jurisdiction, could not be occupied by local residents. In their overgrown state they harbored wildlife and tsetse, a circumstance that was all the more troublesome because plantations had been laid out around scarce surface water where cattle had to drink. The solution, concluded Hornby, was increased cultivation and clearing of bush, particularly on the abandoned plantations; otherwise, he felt, no cattle would survive in central Handeni.[67]

The incidence of theileriosis increased in step with trypanosomiasis, meanwhile, just as it had before the First World War. A theileriosis epizootic during the 1932–1935 famine took a heavy toll of cattle in southern Uzigua and Bagamoyo District, and East Coast fever epizootics continued into the 1940s.[68] Indicative of the absence of bovine resistance to theileriosis were high death rates in calves, for during the mid-1930s outbreak, veterinarians reported a 50 percent mortality rate among calves, and in 1939–1940 they attributed about half of the deaths among calves at Kiberashi to East Coast fever.[69] Evidently calves were failing to acquire mild, resistance-building infections (and adults were failing to maintain resistance) not only because deaths caused by trypanosomiasis hindered the circulation of non-lethal theilerial strains through herds, but also because large tick populations and the proximity of buffalo and other undomesticated reservoirs of *Theileria* exposed cattle to intolerably heavy infections.

Here again, the decline of the cultivating population during the mid-1930s famine was responsible. Fewer farmers meant less clearing, less burning of grass and bush, less cattle browsing, and less hunting. As grasses grew long, ticks increased in neglected pastures, and as bush occupied former clearings, buffalo moved closer to villages. They became so numerous, in fact, that by the 1940s buffalo hunting would be one of the favorite ways for a young man to make money in Handeni. Wildlife near villages

67. P. C. (Tanga) to Chief Secretary (Dar es Salaam), April 12, 1940 and Report of H. E. Hornby to Chief Secretary (Dar es Salaam), September 24, 1940 in TNA 26650, v. 2.

68. Tanganyika Territory, Department of Veterinary Science, Annual Reports (1934, 1938), TNA; Hornby to Chief Secretary, September 24, 1940, TNA 26650, v. 2; ARPC (1941), p. 72. On theileriosis in the Uluguru Mountains, see Hutchins.

69. Tanganyika Territory, Department of Veterinary Science, Annual Report (1934), TNA; H. E. Hornby to Chief Secretary (Dar es Salaam), October 11, 1940, TNA 26650, v. 2.

made overgrown footpaths increasingly dangerous for children. "Since July and August 1944," wrote a school teacher at Mgera in northern Nguu during July 1945, "attendance has been bad because there are many lions. All of the children who live far from school encounter lions on the way to class."[70]

Considering that theileriosis was causing heavy cattle losses throughout Handeni, one discovery made by the veterinary researchers at Kiberashi was most puzzling: the Parakuyu Maasai pastoralists in the area had abandoned their practice of avoiding tick-filled pastures, and instead were keeping cattle in infested areas year-round. Although British researchers could find no explanation, Parakuyu residents of Kiberashi not only make sense of this behavior but also relate it to other developments—including the depopulation of Kiberashi and the roaming lions in nearby Mgera— though they do so with an assertion that initially seems absurd, even to pastoralists who live elsewhere. They say that lethal theileriosis, which they call "*ndigano*," came into existence at Kwa Maligwa, the neighborhood between Kiberashi and Mgera.

When precolonial Kwa Maligwa was still the densely populated home of slave-owning leaders and a rest stop on a major caravan route, pastoralists had found abundant dry-season pasturage there. Between the world wars, however, the area lost most of its population, primarily because of famines, and by the late 1930s it was overrun by thicket, uncropped grasses and wildlife, including the lions so frightening to schoolchildren. From the perspective of the Parakuyu pastoralists, therefore, it is perfectly reasonable to say that the fatal form of theileriosis began at Kwa Maligwa, because that is where, as the pastoralists made their customary seasonal return to a formerly well-managed environment, their cattle unexpectedly encountered many ticks and deadly illness. Cattle-keepers had no alternative to bringing their stock into dangerous dry-season grazing grounds, however, for shrunken farming communities had ceased tending grass and bush in many areas. Indeed, it was simply for lack of tick-free pastures, Parakuyu residents of Kiberashi recall, that *ndigano* killed many cattle during the interwar period.[71]

The experience of the Parakuyu pastoralists at Kwa Maligwa recapitulates the ecological history of Handeni District in the 1920s and 1930s. When Kwa Maligwa's population, lacking patronage and opportunities to trade, dispersed following successive famines, they abandoned the culti-

70. Mgera Primary School Journal, April, July and August 1945.
71. Leiluli Namania, Tangano Orleerewi, and Kari Orleerewi, Gitu.

Figure 6. Three generations of Parakuyu Maasai men at Kiberashi in 1983. Author's photograph.

vated fields and fire-managed pastures that had been ruled by precolonial chieftains. Once-cleared areas where cattle had found dry-season browsing were overgrown with bush and thicket, infested by ticks and tsetse, and visited by buffalo, bush pigs, and other wild reservoirs of *Theileria* and trypanosomes. Famine, the transformation of political authority, and government policies which drained resources from peasant communities had disrupted management of the environment. Thus the pastoralists of Kiberashi were left with no choice but to graze cattle in unhealthy pastures, for the system of land use and environmental control on which they depended had broken down.

Conclusion: Historical Interpretation and Ujamaa in Handeni District

When Handeni residents discussed their history in the early 1980s, they often commented guardedly about a highly sensitive issue from the recent past—Ujamaa villagization. They expressed regrets over homesteads and fields abandoned during forced resettlement in the 1970s and worries about the prospects of their new villages, where shortages of food and other necessities persisted. These recent experiences seemed to exert considerable influence on their thinking about the more distant past, for while their views remained grounded in orally transmitted knowledge organized around episodes such as the career of Mhelamwana, the execution of Mtunte, and compulsory cultivation under "Bwana" Pienaar, they drew conclusions about political authority and scarcity that were the basis of cautious, and indeed sometimes only implicit, criticisms of Ujamaa.

Political Authority and Scarcity

The accounts of Handeni residents complement written sources in showing that political authority determined the demographic and environmental impact of precolonial and colonial famine in Uzigua. In late precolonial society, political leaders who served as patrons provided farmers with food reserves, seed, arable land and livestock, thus enabling the majority of farmers to remain in their homes, work the land, and maintain a healthy disease environment despite periodic drought. Hence environmental stability depended on two interwoven processes: accumulation by patrons who employed dependent labor and redistribution to the clients who persuaded patrons to fulfill their responsibilities. In the precolonial politics of environmental control, therefore, the primary source of tension was the restraint imposed on individual ambition by norms of mutual obligation.

The power of patrons was broken by German colonialism, a development symbolized in Handeni by the dramatic execution of Mtunte. With their capacity to furnish patronage diminished by reorientation of trade, colonial taxation, the abolition of the slave trade, and military aggression, chieftains and other leaders transformed long-term clientage into temporary casual labor. By refusing claims on their resources, however, patrons left many dependents without access to food reserves and forced them to disperse in search of provisions during famines. Thus, because they stopped managing the bush, thicket, and grasses that harbored disease-carrying wildlife and insects, their departure led to epizootics of trypanosomiasis and theileriosis.

German administrators were succeeded by the British who introduced Indirect Rule, a system of administration based on the appointment of chiefs who derived their power almost entirely from the state, and who rarely fulfilled the responsibilities for redistribution and public health that had been held by precolonial leaders. Indirect Rule helped perpetuate scarcity and epizootics because administrators, captivated by their vision of self-sufficient tribes, villages, and households, restricted trade and employment of labor, blocked large-scale agricultural production, and required smallholder cultivation of cassava and cotton. At the same time they insisted that impoverished farmers continue to pay taxes, even if they had to earn tax money through migrant labor. Thus the interwar British administration not only reduced the diversity of crops and exchange relations that had provided precolonial insurance against scarcity, but also prevented farming communities from replacing patronage with new forms of accumulation and redistribution.

Ujamaa: A Return to Colonial Policies[1]

Had restrictive government policies, a crop buying monopsony, and inadequate transportation not stood in their way, entrepreneurial peasants would have swiftly integrated interwar Handeni into colonial markets, just as an earlier generation had seized the opportunity to enter Zanzibari commercial networks, for Handeni farmers were neither oriented toward self-sufficiency nor inhibited by values that discouraged market involvement. Widespread interest in market production and trade persisted, in

1. Comments on Ujamaa in Handeni are based on conversations and observations in the district during 1982–1983, records of the Handeni District and Tanga Region administrations, Maingwa Kallabaka, "The March Towards Ujamaa," and Michaela Von Freyhold, *Ujamaa Villages in Tanzania*.

fact, not only during the period of increased marketing in the 1950s and 1960s but also in the 1970s, when the government resettled many farmers in what it hoped would become self-sufficient Ujamaa villages. Handeni residents resisted villagization, however, and remained highly critical of it a decade later, but not because they wished to remain outside the national economy. Instead, they blamed the government for depriving them of opportunities to trade, hire labor, and find employment, and they appealed for better marketing and transport facilities, tractors, and credit. It is indeed ironic that in Handeni, a district long reputed to be resistant to progress, many peasants opposed state-imposed communal agriculture because it reduced opportunities for crop sales and wage employment.

Although the Tanzanian government intended Ujamaa villagization and associated policies to remove the vestiges of neo-colonial dependence, in Handeni such policies reintroduced some of the most disliked aspects of interwar colonial administration.[2] Like their British predecessors, administrators in the 1970s restricted trade within and beyond Handeni's boundaries, prohibited sales of foodstuffs, and banned employment of wage labor. At gunpoint, moreover, they forced many farmers to move into new settlements while police and soldiers burned their homes. The government expected Ujamaa settlements to be self-sufficient, but because uprooted villagers lacked cleared fields, food reserves, and seed, they often relied on government assistance and regarded labor in the supposedly communal village fields as nothing more than a way of staking claim to government patronage.[3] The administration encouraged this attitude by making receipt of famine relief conditional upon work in what became known as the "government fields." The government not only failed to provide famine relief to more than a relatively few villagers, however, but also compounded the problems of cotton and tobacco growers by reneging on payments for crops delivered to its buying agencies. At the same time it deprived Handeni and other regions of the advantage of proximity to Dar es Salaam and other cities, for in accordance with the policy of "pan-territorial pricing," its crop-buying agencies offered the same price throughout Tanzania regardless of producers' distance from urban markets.[4]

These policies prevented Ujamaa settlers from taking advantage of the

---

2. For parallels between interwar colonial administration and Ujamaa policies in Handeni, see James Giblin, "Peasant Self-Sufficiency in Tanzania: Precolonial Legacy or Colonial Imposition?" *Sustainable Agriculture in Africa.*

3. Von Freyhold, *Ujamaa Villages in Tanzania: Analysis of a Social Experiment,* pp. 79, 127, 130, 147, 153, esp. 155.

4. See Phil Raikes, "Eating the Carrot and Wielding the Stick: The Agricultural Sector in Tanzania," in *Tanzania: Crisis and Struggle for Survival,* pp. 122–123.

opportunities created by villagization to increase cattle keeping and expand employment of wage labor. Many displaced farmers who depended
on day-to-day earnings and occasional government famine relief would
have welcomed steady wage labor and could have cleared large areas
around the new settlements had they been employed in coordinated agricultural production. Because peasants could not obtain credit and circum-
vent government restrictions on wage employment and crop marketing,
however, villagers not only were unable to hire labor, but were also
prevented from accumulating wealth of any sort. Consequently, in the
early 1980s cattle holdings were confined to a mere handful of individuals
in most villages; in the entire district of Handeni there were only a
few privately-owned motor vehicles; and even the wealthiest villagers
rarely laid cement floors or made other improvements that would have
distinguished their homes from those of their neighbors. Few peasants
cultivated as much as four hectares, and while many farmers hired small
numbers of laborers for brief terms, employers often remunerated their
workers in cassava rather than cash. Those farmers who did manage to
accumulate wealth frequently invested it not in expanded agricultural production but in the education of children who were expected to find urban
employment in the state bureaucracy and in parastatals that distributed
scarce goods.

Just as Ujamaa policies squandered the opportunity to increase wage
employment, they also failed to reestablish control over the bovine disease
environment because they left many farmers without the means to purchase cattle, fostered weak village leadership, and directly interfered with
burning and clearing. Weak settlement leaders could do little about villagers who refused to work in communal fields, or about farmers who dis-
regarded orders to situate their plots contiguously and keep idle plots free
of bush and thicket. The result was that interspersed among cultivated
plots were overgrown fields which, because they harbored bush pigs, often
provoked quarrels between neighbors. Although village officers might
threaten negligent farmers with confiscation of untended plots, they were
unlikely to carry out their threats. Thus, while in some respects the combination of household plots and communal fields in Ujamaa villages
looked a good deal like the mixture of individual farms and large chieftains' fields in precolonial settlements, a major difference was that the
leaders of Ujamaa settlements had relatively little power. In particular,
village officers lacked resources which they could threaten to withhold
from redistribution, a deficiency that they sometimes tried to overcome by

distributing maize from communal fields on a selective basis. More often, however, fearful of violating the crop-buying monopsony held by government agencies, they sold the harvests of village fields at low official prices. Hence they actually resembled the appointed chiefs of Indirect Rule more than precolonial leaders, for their authority stemmed from their ability to act, in this and other ways, as intermediaries with the state.

The efforts of some village heads to engage in health-related activities were impeded, moreover, by the lowest-level representatives of the national government, the ward secretaries who supervised several villages. In one western Handeni village, for example, the village chairman engaged in divining, invited itinerant witch detectors to visit the settlement, and supervised bush burning. Because the ward secretary denounced or prohibited these actions, however, the chairman had to conceal his involvement. Hence, when villagers broke conservation rules by burning bush and thicket around the settlement, the chairman spent much of his time answering the ward secretary's angry summonses and feigning ignorance about the identity of those who were setting the fires. The arrival of touring witch detectors heightened frictions because the village chairman not only arranged their visits but also lodged them in his house. During one such visit, the ward secretary retreated from the village to district headquarters after his house was stoned late at night and remained there for several days while the witch detecting proceeded. He returned just in time to reassert his authority by petulantly canceling a celebration to mark the completion of the detector's treatment. In other instances, however, ward secretaries prevented witch detectors from practicing altogether.

Thus, despite the possibility that the large Ujamaa villages might have cleared disease-carrying insects from sizeable areas, government policies precluded the reestablishment of conditions that would have allowed livestock to regain resistance to trypanosomiasis and theileriosis. Instead, the bovine disease situation of the 1980s supported John Ford in his argument that wherever economic conditions prevent the environmental transformation necessary to eradicate disease-carrying insects and fail to guarantee access to imported drugs, immunological resistance remains a better safeguard against epidemic than pharmaceuticals. During the 1950s, 1960s, and 1970s, Handeni farmers had protected the health of their cattle with imported trypanicides and acaricides, but when Tanzania's foreign exchange crisis cut off drug supplies in the 1980s, bovine mortality increased markedly because Handeni's cattle, which lived in vector-infested areas, lacked immunological defenses.

Peasant History and Opposition to Ujamaa

Because coercive and restrictive state initiatives touched every household during the 1970s, intense resentment of the government prevailed throughout Handeni in the following decade. Although all villages were otherwise divided by numerous and overlapping conflicts between men and women, office holders and ordinary citizens, and various political factions, most peasants shared the belief that the government was largely responsible for their difficulties. This attitude was certainly not confined to frustrated entrepreneurs, for nearly-destitute men and women were as likely as their more secure neighbors to criticize a government which not only obstructed trade and accumulation but also made finding a wage-paying job virtually impossible. Under these conditions, peasant historians who chafed under restrictions on trade and wage labor and remained deeply indignant about forced resettlement (some punctuated their comments by pointing to the charred corrugated roofing that had been saved from homes burned by soldiers) spoke often about precolonial leaders who engaged in trade, provided patronage, and mediated with ancestors. They also described the diversity of exchange relations available to precolonial communities and criticized hindrances to trade raised by colonial and independent governments. In addition, they discussed changed relationships with ancestors by contrasting the centrality of *matambiko* in precolonial society with their disappearance under colonial rule.

Relations between the living and dead became a source of contention during Ujamaa villagization, in fact, when government officials reported that farmers resisted leaving their homes for fear that they would lose contact with ancestors.[5] Although administrators had difficulty in understanding such objections as anything except atavistic superstition, the villagers' views stemmed from the perception that both relations with ancestors and community welfare were related to political authority. Certainly relocation was not in itself unthinkable, as historical evidence of frequent changes in residence demonstrates. Farmers understood that moving to a new settlement need not disrupt relations with ancestors if they found leaders whose ability to serve as intermediaries with the dead was affirmed by their success in providing prosperity. They apparently did not expect to find such leadership in the Ujamaa villages, however, and therefore invoked their concerns about ancestors not because leaving

---

5. Von Freyhold, *Ujamaa Villages in Tanzania*, pp. 66–67, esp. 143; Kallabaka, "The March Toward Ujamaa," Chapter 3.

tambiko sites and burial places was utterly unacceptable, but because they believed that the government that instituted villagization would fail to provide the security and prosperity ensured by proper relations with ancestors.

Confronted with Ujamaa's failures, peasant historians contemplated the qualities which distinguished beneficent from harmful authority. Convinced that villagization had improved few lives, and frustrated by government obstruction of trade and market production, peasants speaking about their history implicitly contrasted past and present. By emphasizing the past importance of accumulating, trading leaders who responded to dependents' needs and bestowed the protection of ancestors, they developed an interpretation of their history that rejected administrators' conceptions of egalitarian, self-enclosed, and self-sufficient villages.

Sources

CITED INTERVIEWS IN HANDENI DISTRICT

AT BALANGA VILLAGE:

M. A. Mavullah, Hasani Bakari and other elders, May 23, 1983.

AT GITU VILLAGE:

Leiluli Namania, Tangano Orleerewi and Kari Orleerewi, Juma Ali Matebe, Salimu Mkunda, Mohamedi Saidi Gota, Ramadhani Mswagala, Mwenjuma Mdachi and Omali Mohamedi Gumbo, June 24, 1983.

AT GOMBERO VILLAGE:

Omali Maligwa Kidiza and Ramadhani Semndili, September 20, 1983.
Msulwa Mbega and Iddi Samshehiri, September 21, 1983.
Martin Mnyendo, September 22, 1983.

AT HANDENI TOWN (CHANIKA):

Pogwa Rashidi, August 14, 1982.
Ali Bakari Kimonje, Nassoro Ali Kajeze, Saidi Mdoe and Athumani Sevingi Magati, April 28, 1983.

AT KIBERASHI VILLAGE:

Mwejuma Mbwego, Athumani Mwegango, Mdoe Nyange, Mohamedi Chambo and Asumani Kilule, May 17, 1983.

AT KILWA VILLAGE:

Rashidi Mwenjuma Manyagala and Mohamedi Semsambia, September 11, 1983.
Nyangasi Mohamedi Munga, September 12, 1983.

AT KISANGASA VILLAGE:

Group interview with elders, September 17, 1982.

AT KWA DUNDWA VILLAGE:

Abdala Hamani Msede and Ali Omali Kipande, September 12, 1983.

AT KWA MALIGWA VILLAGE:

Salimu Kisailo, May 19, 1983.

AT KWA MASAKA VILLAGE:

Ernest Mkomwa, September 29, 1983.

AT KWA MKONO VILLAGE:

Rajabu Sefu Mwenkumba and Ramadhani Maingwa, December 21, 1982.
Selemani Kidanga, Ibrahimu Mohamedi Mkwayu, and Salimu Muhando, December 21 and 23, 1982.
Saidi Mohamedi Mwakilinga and Ali Mlimbo, December 23, 1982.
Shehe Bakari Ruhizo and Sankole Mhandeni, December 28, 1982.
Antoni Mhina, December 29, 1982.
James Kibwana and Leonard Kilua, December 30, 1982.

AT KWEDIBOMA VILLAGE:

Athumani Abdalla Mkomwa, August 9, 11–12, and 24, 1982.
Ramadhani Kikobo, August 12, 1982.
Salimu Machaku and Mohamedi Rashidi, August 18, 1982.
Haji Luwambo, August 18, 26–27 and September 30, 1982.
Fundi Asumani Nyokka, August 18 and 30, 1982; March 29, May 11, November 23, December 1, 1983.
Ali S. Sambuguma, August 26 and September 10, 1982.
Mzee Samzimba, September 1, 1982.
Pogwa Rashidi, September 2, 1982.
Mohamedi Saidi Nyange, September 5, 1982.
Mohamedi Mjewe, September 16, 19–21, 27, 1982 and February 8 and 26, 1983.
Mrisho Kizenga, September 22, 1982.

Kombo Sabo, September 26, 1982.
Mzee Samgome, February 25, 1983.
Mzee Sekiteke, March 8, 1983.
Ismaili Sumra, November 27, 1983.
Mzee Maguruti, November 29, 1983.

AT KWINJI VILLAGE:

Omali Gumbo, May 5, 1983.

AT MAFISA VILLAGE:

Mohamedi Lusingo, Mohamedi Mkande, Ibrahim Kigobwa and Mzee Ndege,
    July 1, 1983.
Asumani Mwanamauka and Omali Mwanamauka, July 1 and 2, 1983.

AT MAGAMBA VILLAGE:

Group interview with elders, September 30, 1983.

AT MANGA VILLAGE:

Abedi Juma, Mohamedi Nasoro, Idi Sefu, Yusufu Selemani, Rajabu Sudi and
    Mohamedi Waziri, October 10, 1983.

AT MGERA VILLAGE:

Ali Mohamedi Masomo and group interview with elders, August 19, 1982.

AT MKONDE VILLAGE:

Saidi Hatibu, May 29, 1983.

AT MSWAKI VILLAGE:

Hamza Mlingo, May 28, 1983.
Yusufu Kaberwa, May 28–29, 1983.

AT MUHEZA-HEGONGO (MUHEZA DISTRICT):

Paul Nkanyemka, August 18, 1983.

ARCHIVAL SOURCES AND GOVERNMENT REPORTS CITED IN
MORE THAN ONE CHAPTER

German Democratic Republic. Central State Archives (Potsdam). Reichs-
kolonialamt.
Germany. *Berichte über Land- und Forstwirtschaft in Deutsch Ostafrika*, 1902–1911.
———. *Die Deutsche Schutzgebiete in Afrika und der Südsee*, 1909/1910–1912/1913.
———. *Jahresbericht über die Entwicklung der Deutschen Schutzgebiete*, 1894/1895–
1908/1909.
———. *Medizinal-Berichte über die Deutschen Schutzgebiete*, 1903/1904–1911/1912.
Great Britain. Foreign Office. *Commercial Reports Received at the Foreign Office from
Her Majesty's Consuls* and *Diplomatic and Consular Reports on Trade and Fi-
nance* (Zanzibar).
Hamburgisches Museum für Völkerkunde und Vorgeschichte. A77 Nachlass Au-
gust Fonck.
Handeni District Headquarters (Handeni). Handeni District Files.
Mgera Primary School Journal, 1934–1956.
Rhodes House. Micr. Afr. 480. Kohler, J. "Beantwortung des Fragebogens über
die Rechte der Eingeborenen in der deutsche Kolonien."
Spiritan Archives U.S.A., Congregation of the Holy Ghost, Bethel Park, Pennsylvania. Journals of the Missions at Lugoba, Mandera, Maskati, and Mhonda
(microfilm). (Originals of the Mandera and Mhonda journals were obtained
at the Residence of the Bishop of Morogoro and the Bagamoyo Mission
respectively.)
Staatsarchiv der Freien und Hansestadt Hamburg, Bestand 622-2. Wissenschaft-
liche Nachlässe des Dr. Franz Stuhlmann, B.I., part 2: "Reise von Bagamoyo
nach Usegua und Unguu" (1888).
TIRDEP. "Meteorological and Hydrological Data for the Tanga Region." Tanga,
August 1977 (mimeographed).
Tanganyika Territory. Annual Reports of the Provincial Commissioners on Native
Administration, 1929–1959.
———. Department of Agriculture. Annual Reports, 1925–1961.
———. ———. "Agriculture in Tanganyika." Dar es Salaam: Government Printer,
1945.
———. Handeni District. Annual Reports, 1948–1958.
———. Handeni Sub-District. Annual Report, 1925.
———. Korogwe District. Annual Reports, 1937–1945.
———. Pangani District. Annual Reports, 1921–1925.
———. Tanga District. Annual Report, 1925.
———. Tanga Province. Annual Reports, 1927–1934.
Tanzania. Ministry of Water, Energy and Minerals. *Tanga Water Master Plan.* 5 vols.
Essen, 1976.

———. Tanga Region. Regional Planning Office. "Handeni District Development Strategy: First Draft." Tanga: mimeographed, October 1983.

Tanzania National Archives:

Morogoro and Tanga Province Books.

Bagamoyo, Handeni, Morogoro and Pangani District Books.

Early Secretariat File 11299, vol. 1: "Tsetse Reclamation and Sleeping Sickness Measures, Singida, Mkalama and Handeni Districts."

Native Affairs Files:

13079, vols. 1–3: "Shortages of Foodstuffs in Tanga Province."

23544: "Labour on Sisal Estates."

Tanga Region Records:

4/6/5, vols. 1 and 2: "Native Administration: Handeni District."

4/8/6, vol. 1: "Agriculture: Cotton Growing."

4/1161/1, vols. 1–7: "Native Tax."

USPG, UMCA Archives. Letter of Bishop John Hine (Korogwe, February 10, 1907). Box A.1 (XIII), Folio 699.

BOOKS, ARTICLES, UNPUBLISHED THESES, AND PAPERS

Abdalahe, Musa Sefu. "Habari za Wazigua." In possession of Mwalimu W. Mguhi of Kwa Mkono Primary School. Typewritten.

Acland, J. D. *East African Crops: An Introduction to the Production of Field and Plantation Crops in Kenya, Tanzania, and Uganda.* London: Longman for FAO, 1971.

Albrand, F. "Extrait d'un mémoire sur Zanzibar et sur Quiloa." *Bulletin de la Société de Géographie de Paris* 10 (1838): 65–84.

Alpers, Edward A. "State, Merchant Capital, and Gender Relations in Southern Mozambique to the End of the Nineteenth Century: Some Tentative Hypotheses." *African Economic History* 13 (1984): 23–55.

———. "The Story of Swema: Female Vulnerability in Nineteenth-Century East Africa." In *Women and Slavery in Africa*, pp. 185–219. Edited by Claire C. Robertson and Martin A. Klein. Madison: University of Wisconsin Press, 1983.

Ambler, Charles H. *Kenyan Communities in the Age of Imperialism: The Central Region in the Late Nineteenth Century.* New Haven and London: Yale University Press, 1988.

Arnold, David. *Famine: Social Crisis and Historical Change.* Oxford: B. Blackwell, 1988.

"Aus dem Bezirk Pangani." *DKb* 13 (1902): 257–259.

Austen, Ralph A. "The Official Mind of Indirect Rule: British Policy in Tanganyika, 1916–1939." In *Britain and Germany in Africa: Imperial Rivalry and Colonial Rule*, pp. 577–606. Edited by Prosser Gifford and W. Roger Louis. New Haven, Conn.: Yale University Press, 1967.

Ballard, Charles. "Drought and Economic Distress: South Africa in the 1800s." *Journal of Interdisciplinary History* 17, 2 (1986): 359–378.

Barnes, Sandra T. *Patrons and Power: Creating a Political Community in Metropolitan Lagos*. Bloomington: Indiana University Press with the International African Institute, London, 1986.

Bates, Margaret L. "Tanganyika Under British Administration, 1920–1955." Ph.D. dissertation, Oxford University, 1957.

Baumann, Oscar. "Der Unterlauf des Pangani-Flusses." *Petermanns Geographische Mitteilungen* 42 (1896): 59–62.

———. *Usambara und seine Nachbargebiete*. Berlin, 1891.

Baur, Étienne. "Dans l'Oudoé et l'Ouzigoua." In *À Travers le Zanguebar*, pp. 9–110. Edited by Étienne Baur and Alexandre Le Roy. Tours: Mame et Fils, 1893.

———. "Lettre." *LMC* 2 (1873): 62–63; 327–329.

———. "Lettre." *LMC* 7 (1875): 521–522.

———. "Lettre." *LMC* 14 (1882): 194–195; 342–344.

———. "Lettre." *APF* 54 (1882): 354–373.

———. "Lettre." *AOSE* 34 (1883): 107–115.

———. "Lettre." *AOSE* 35 (1884): 328–341.

Becker, C. H. "Materialien zur Kenntnis des Islam in Deutsch-Ostafrika." *Der Islam* 2 (1911): 1–48.

Beidelman, Thomas O. "The Baraguyu." *Tanganyika Notes and Records* 55 (September 1960): 244–278.

———. *Colonial Evangelism*. Bloomington: Indiana University Press, 1982.

———. "Kaguru Descent Groups (East-Central Tanzania)." *Anthropos* 66 (1971): 373–396.

———. "Kaguru Oral Literature: Discussion (Tanzania)." *Anthropos* 74 (1979): 497–529.

———. *Moral Imagination in Kaguru Modes of Thought*. Bloomington: Indiana University Press, 1986.

———. "A Note on Baraguyu House-Types and Baraguyu Economy." *Tanganyika Notes and Records* 56 (March 1961): 56–66.

———. "Witchcraft in Ukaguru." In *Witchcraft and Sorcery in East Africa*, pp. 57–98. Edited by John Middleton and E. H. Winter. New York: Praeger, 1963.

Beinart, William, and Colin Bundy, eds. *Hidden Struggles in Rural South Africa: Politics and Popular Movements in the Transkei and Eastern Cape, 1890–1930*. London: J. Currey, 1987.

Bennett, Norman R. *A History of the Arab State of Zanzibar*. London: Methuen, 1978.

Bennett, Norman R. and George E. Brooks, Jr., eds. *New England Merchants in Africa: A History Through Documents, 1802 to 1865*. Brookline, Mass.: Boston University Press, 1965.

"Bericht des Kompagnie-führers Leue über die Expedition nach Mhonda." *DKb* 4 (1893): 246–249.

Berntsen, John L. "Pastoralism, Raiding and Prophets: Maasailand in the Nineteenth Century." Ph.D. dissertation, University of Wisconsin-Madison, 1979.

Berry, L., ed. *Tanzania in Maps*. London: University of London Press, 1971.

Berry, Sara S. "The Food Crisis and Agrarian Change in Africa: A Review Essay." *African Studies Review* 27, 2 (1984): 1–109.

Betts, Elizabeth. "Outbreaks of the African Migratory Locust Since 1871." *Anti Locust Memoir* no. 6 (1961).

"Der Bezirk Pangani in Jahre 1909." *DOAR* 3, 93 (November 28, 1910).

Bloyet, A. "À la Station de Kondoa." *Bulletin de la Société de Géographie de Paris* (1890): 350–364.

Boaler, S. B. and K. C. Sciwale. "Ecology of a Miombo Site, Lupa North Forest Reserve Tanzania. III: Effects on the Vegetation of Local Cultivation Practices." *Journal of Ecology* 54 (1966): 577–587.

Boswell, John. *The Kindness of Strangers: The Abandonment of Children in Western Europe from Late Antiquity to the Renaissance.* New York: Pantheon, 1988.

Boteler, Thomas. *Narrative of a Voyage of Discovery to Africa and Arabia.* 2 vols. London: Bentley, 1835.

Brokensha, David. "Handeni Revisited." *African Affairs* 70, 279 (April 1971): 159–168.

Brooke, Clarke. "Types of Food Shortages in Tanzania." *Geographical Review* 57, 3 (1967): 333–357.

Brouardel, Paul Camille Hippolyte. *L'Infanticide.* Paris: Baillière, 1897.

Bryceson, Deborah Fahy. *Food Insecurity and the Social Division of Labour in Tanzania, 1919–1985.* Houndmills and London: St. Martin's Press, 1990.

———. "Peasant Cash Cropping Versus Self-Sufficiency in Tanzania: A Historical Perspective." *IDS Bulletin* 19, 2 (1988): 37–46.

———. "'The Tepid Backwater': Bagamoyo District and Its Marginal Commodity Production Within the Tanganyikan Colonial Economy, 1919–1961." *Transafrican Journal of History* 11 (1982): 1–25.

Bulletin de la Congrégation du Saint-Esprit, vols. 14–28 (1887/1888–1923/1924).

Bundy, Colin. *The Rise and Fall of the South African Peasantry.* Berkeley and Los Angeles: University of California Press, 1979.

Bunker, Stephen. *Peasants Against the State: The Politics of Market Control in Bugisu, Uganda, 1900–1983.* Urbana and Chicago: University of Illinois Press, 1987.

Bursian, Alexander. *Die Häuser- und Hüttensteuer in Deutsch-Ostafrika.* Jena: Abhandlungen des Staatswissenschaftlichen Seminars zu Jena, 1910.

Burton, Richard F. *The Lake Regions of Central Africa.* 2 vols. London: Longmans, 1860.

———. "The Lakes Regions of Central Equatorial Africa." *Journal of the Royal Geographical Society* 29 (1859): 1–464.

———. *Zanzibar: City, Island and Coast.* 2 vols. London: J. Murray, 1872.

Burton, Richard F. and J. H. Speke. "A Coasting Voyage from Mombasa to the Pangani River." *Journal of the Royal Geographical Society* 28 (1858): 188–226.

Burtt, B. D. "Some East African Vegetation Communities." *Journal of Ecology* 30 (1942): 65–140.

Cameron, Sir Donald. *My Tanganyika Service and Some Nigeria.* London: Allen and Unwin, 1939.

Cassanelli, Lee. *The Shaping of Somali Society: Reconstructing the History of a Pastoral People, 1600–1900.* Philadelphia: University of Pennsylvania Press, 1982.

———. "Social Construction on the Somali Frontier: Bantu Former Slave Communities in the Nineteenth Century." In *The African Frontier: The Repro-*

duction of Traditional African Societies, pp. 216–238. Edited by Igor Kopytoff. Bloomington and Indianapolis: Indiana University Press, 1987.

Celander, Nils. *Miombo Woodlands in Africa: Distribution, Ecology and Patterns of Land Use*. Swedish University of Agricultural Sciences, International Rural Development Centre, Working Paper no. 16. Uppsala, 1983.

Central Africa 31 (April 1913): 108. Untitled note.

Chambers, Robert, Richard Longhurst and Arnold Pacey, eds. *Seasonal Dimensions to Rural Poverty*. Montclair, N.J.: Allanheld, Osmun, 1981.

Chapman, R. F. *A Biology of Locusts*. London: Edward Arnold, 1976.

Cheater, Angela P. *Idioms of Accumulation: Rural Development and Class Formation Among Freeholders in Zimbabwe*. Gweru, Zimbabwe, 1984.

Christie, James. *Cholera Epidemics in East Africa*. London: Macmillan and Co., 1876.

Christopher, William. "Extract from a Journal by Lt. W. Christopher, Commanding the H. C. Brig of War *Tigris*, on the E. Coast of Africa. Dated 8th May 1843." *Journal of the Royal Geographical Society* 14 (1844): 76–103.

Cohen, David William and E. S. Atieno Odhiambo. *Siaya: The Historical Anthropology of an African Landscape*. London: J. Currey, 1989.

Comaroff, Jean. *Body of Power, Spirit of Resistance: The Culture and History of a South African People*. Chicago and London: University of Chicago Press, 1985.

Conyers, D., et al. "Agro-Economic Zones of North-Eastern Tanzania." University of Dar es Salaam, BRALUP Research Report no. 13. Dar es Salaam, 1970.

Cooper, Frederick. "Peasants, Capitalists, and Historians: A Review Article." *Journal of Southern African Studies* 7, 2 (1981): 284–314.

———. *Plantation Slavery on the East Coast of Africa*. New Haven and London: Yale University Press, 1977.

Coulbois, François. "Seconde tournée dans le vicariat apostolique du Zanguebar." *LMC* 18 (1886): 594–597.

———. "Le Sultanat du Zanguebar." *LMC* 18 (1886): 382–384; 393–395; 412–414.

———. "Une tournée dans le vicariat apostolique de Zanguebar, Oct.–Nov., 1884." *LMC* 17 (1885): 462–466; 485–489; 497–502; 512–515; 521–525; 536–538; 545–548.

Coulson, Andrew. *Tanzania: A Political Economy*. Oxford: Clarendon Press, 1982.

Courmont, Raoul de. "Lettre." *AOSE* 36 (1885): 316–339.

———. "Lettre." *AOSE* 38 (1887): 91–107.

———. "Lettre," *AA* 11 (1896): 67–71.

———. "Rapport." *APF* 61 (1889): 47–63.

———. "Rapport." *AA* 9 (1894): 81–96.

Cranefield, Paul. *Science and Empire: East Coast Fever in Rhodesia and Transvaal*. Cambridge: Cambridge University Press, 1991.

Dale, Godfrey. "An Account of the Principal Customs and Habits of the Natives Inhabiting the Bondei Country." *Journal of the Anthropological Institute* 25 (1896): 181–239.

Daly, Martin and Margo Wilson. "A Sociobiological Analysis of Human Infanticide." In *Infanticide: Comparative and Evolutionary Perspectives*, pp. 487–502. Edited by Glenn Hausfater and Sarah Blaffer Hrdy. New York: Aldine, 1984.

Dawson, Marc Harry. "Socio-Economic and Epidemiological Change in Kenya, 1880–1925." Ph.D. dissertation, University of Wisconsin-Madison, 1983.

Decken, Carl Claus van der. *Reisen in Ostafrika.* 2 vols. Leipzig and Heidelberg: Winter'sche Verlagshandlung, 1869.

De Waal, Alexander. *Famine That Kills: Darfur, Sudan, 1984–1985.* Oxford: Clarendon Press, 1989.

Dias, Jill R. "Famine and Disease in the History of Angola ca. 1830–1930." *Journal of African History* 22 (1981): 349–378.

Dobson, E. B. "Land Tenure of the Wasambaa." *Tanganyika Notes and Records* 10 (1940): 19–20.

Dolan, T. T. "Theileriosis: A Comprehensive Review." *Revue Scientifique et Technique (International Office of Epizootics)* 8, 1 (1989): 11–36.

Douglas, Rev. G. W. "The Archdeaconry of Zigualand." *Central Africa* 44 (October 1926): 213–217.

Dundas, Charles. *African Crossroads.* London: Greenwood Press, 1955.

———. "Native Laws of Some Bantu Tribes of East Africa." *Journal of the Royal Anthropological Institute* 51 (1921): 217–278.

Durrill, Wayne K. "Atrocious Misery: The African Origins of Famine in Northern Somalia, 1839–1884." *American Historical Review* 91, 2 (April 1986): 287–306.

Dussercle, Roger. *Du Kilima-ndjaro au Cameroun: Monseigneur F.-X. Vogt (1870–1943).* Paris, 1954.

"Einem Berichte des Bezirksamtmanns v. Rode über seine Betheiligung an dem Zuge des Oberführers Freiherrn v. Manteuffel." *Deutsches Kolonialblatt* 4, 15 (August 1, 1893): 375–380.

Eisenstadt, S. N., and L. Roniger. *Patrons, Clients and Friends: Interpersonal Relations and the Structure of Trust in Society.* Cambridge: Cambridge University Press, 1984.

Eldredge, Elizabeth A. "Drought, Famine and Disease in Nineteenth-Century Lesotho." *African Economic History* no. 16 (1987): 61–93.

Emouet, T. R. P. "Nouvelles de la Mission du Sacre-Coeur de Mhonda," *L'Echo* 1, 1 (January 1884): 35–40.

Engel, Alois. *Die Missionsmethode der Missionare v. Heiligen Geist auf dem Afrikanischen Festland.* Knechtsteden: Druck und Verlag der Missionsdruckerei Knechtsteden, 1932.

Farler, J. P. Letter from Magila, Low Sunday, 1877. USPG, Central Africa Mission, *Occasional Papers* (1877).

———. "Native Routes in East Africa from Pangani to the Masai Country and the Victoria Nyanza." *PRGS* N.S. 4 (1882): 730–746.

Feierman, Steven. *Peasant Intellectuals: Anthropology and History in Tanzania.* Madison: University of Wisconsin Press, 1990.

———. *The Shambaa Kingdom: A History.* Madison: University of Wisconsin Press, 1974.

Fields, Karen E. *Revival and Rebellion in Colonial Central Africa: Revisions to the Theory of Indirect Rule.* Princeton, N.J.: Princeton University Press, 1985.

Fischer, G. A. *Das Masai-Land.* Hamburg, 1885.

Ford, John. *The Role of the Trypanosomiases in African Ecology: A Study of the Tsetse Fly Problem.* Oxford: Clarendon Press, 1971.

Freyhold, Michaela von. *Rural Development Through Ujamaa*. Vol. 2: *Case Studies From Handeni*. University of Dar es Salaam: Typewritten, 1971.

———. *Ujamaa Villages in Tanzania: Analysis of a Social Experiment*. New York: Monthly Review Press, 1979.

Ganzenmüller, Dr. K. "Usegura und Usaramo, Ukhutu, Usagara und Ugogo." *Mitteilungen der Saechisch-Thuringischen Verein für Erdkunde (Halle)* 9 (1886): 94–124.

Germain, A. "Notes sur Zanzibar et la Côte orientale d'Afrique." *Bulletin de la Société de Géographie de Paris* 5 (1868): 530–559.

Giblin, James L. "East Coast Fever in Socio-Historical Context: A Case Study from Tanzania." *International Journal of African Historical Studies* 23, 3 (1990): 401–421.

———. "Peasant Self-Sufficiency in Tanzania: Precolonial Legacy or Colonial Imposition?" In *Sustainable Agriculture in Africa*, pp. 257–272. Edited by E. Ann McDougall. Trenton, NJ: Africa World Press, Inc., 1990.

———. "Trypanosomiasis Control in African History: An Evaded Issue?" *Journal of African History* 31 (1990): 59–80.

Gommenginger, Charles. "Lettre." *APF* 61 (1889): 333–353.

Graham, James D. "Indirect Rule: The Establishment of 'Chiefs' and 'Tribes' in Cameron's Tanganyika." *Tanzania Notes and Records* 77–78 (1976): 1–9.

Grohs, Elisabeth. *Kisazi: Reiferiten der Mädchen bei den Zigua und Ngulu Ost Tanzanias*. Berlin: Dietrich Reimer Verlag, 1980.

Grottanelli, Vinigi L. "The Peopling of the Horn of Africa." In *East Africa and the Orient: Cultural Syntheses in Pre-Colonial Times*, pp. 44–75. Edited by H. Neville Chittick and Robert I. Rotberg. New York and London: Africana Publishing Co., 1975.

Grunder, Horst. *Christliche Mission und Deutscher Imperialismus, 1884–1914*. Paderborn: Ferdinand Schöningh, 1982.

Guillain, Charles. "Côte de Zanguebar et Mascate, 1841." *Revue Coloniale* (1843): 520–563.

———. *Documents sur l'histoire, la géographie et le commerce de la côte orientale d'Afrique*. 3 vols. Paris: Arthus Bertrand, 1856.

Halfani, M.S. "Some Luguru Clan Histories, Utani Relationships, Ancestor Propitiation, and Ownership: A Case Study of Langali Community in Mgeta." University of Dar es Salaam, 1974. Typewritten.

Harms, Robert. *Games Against Nature: an Eco-Cultural History of the Nunu of Equatorial Africa*. Cambridge: Cambridge University Press, 1987.

Hathout, S. A. and S. Sumra. "Rainfall and Soil Suitability Index for Maize Cropping in Handeni District." University of Dar es Salaam, BRALUP Research Report no. 12. Dar es Salaam, 1974.

Henderson, W. O. "German East Africa, 1884–1918." In *History of East Africa* 2:123–162. Edited by Vincent Harlow and E. M. Chilver. Oxford: Clarendon Press, 1965.

Herlehy, Thomas J. "Historical Dimensions of the Food Crisis in Africa: Surviving Famines Along the Kenya Coast, 1880–1980." Boston University, African Studies Center Working Paper no. 87, 1984.

Hine, Bishop John. "Work in the Zigua Country." *Central Africa* 25 (1907): 115–124.

Hodges, Geoffrey. *The Carrier Corps: Military Labor in the East African Campaign, 1914–1918*. New York, Westport, Conn., and London: Greenwood Press, 1986.

Höhnel, Ludwig von. *Discovery of Lakes Rudolf and Stefanie*. Trans. Nancy Bell. London: Frank Cass, 1968.

Hordern, Charles, comp. *Military Operations: East Africa*. In *History of the Great War Based on Official Documents*, vol. 1. London: H. M. Stationery Office, 1941.

Horner, Anton. "De Bagamoyo à Mhonda (Oussigoua)." *LMC* 10 (1878): 177–179; 189–191; 202–208.

———. "De Bagamoyo à l'Oukami." *Bulletin de la Société de Géographie, Paris* 6 (1873): 125–139.

———. "Lettre." *AOSE* 17 (1865): 48–56; 121–129.

———. "Lettre." *AOSE* 20 (1868): 382–392.

———. "Lettre." *LMC* 1 (1868): 65–67.

———. "Lettre." *APF* 42 (1870): 29–55.

———. "Lettre." *LMC* 5 (1873): 62–63; 74–75; 164; 295; 327–329; 339–348; 388.

———. "Lettre." *LMC* 6 (1874): 426.

———. "Lettre," *AOSE* 31 (1880): 27–47.

———. "Lettre." *LMC* 14 (1882): 194–195.

———. "L'Oukami (Afrique Orientale) I." *LMC* 5 (1873): 584–586.

———. "L'Oukami (Afrique Orientale) II." *LMC* 5 (1873): 596–598.

———. "L'Oukami (Afrique Orientale) IV." *LMC* 5 (1873): 622–624.

———. "L'Oukami (Afrique Orientale) VI." *LMC* 6 (1874): 20–21; 33–34; 44–45.

———. "Voyage dans L'Oukami." *LMC* 4 (1871–1872): 414–416.

Hück, Th. P. *Ludwig Karl Gommenginger: Erlebnisse und Arbeiten eines Afrikanischen Missionärs*. Rixheim, 1890.

Hyden, Goran. *Beyond Ujamaa in Tanzania: Underdevelopment and an Uncaptured Peasantry*. Berkeley: University of California Press, 1980.

Iliffe, John. *A Modern History of Tanganyika*. Cambridge: Cambridge University Press, 1979.

Ingham, Kenneth. "Tanganyika: The Mandate and Cameron, 1919–1931." In *History of East Africa* 2: 543–593. Edited by Vincent Harlow and E. M. Chilver. Oxford: Clarendon Press, 1965.

Irvin, A. D. and W. D. Morrison. "Immunopathology, Immunology, and Immunoprophylaxis of Theileria Infections." In *Immune Responses in Parasitic Infections: Immunology, Immunopathology, and Immunoprophylaxis*, vol. 3: *Protozoa*, pp. 223–274. Edited by E. J. L. Soulsby. Boca Raton, Fl.: CRC Press, 1987.

Isaacman, Allen. "Peasants and Rural Social Protest in Africa." *African Studies Review* 33, 2 (September, 1990): 1–120.

Johnston, Alexander Keith. "Notes of a Trip from Zanzibar to Usambara in February and March 1879." *PRGS* N.S. 1 (1879): 545–558.

Johnston, Harry Hamilton. *The Kilimanjaro Expedition*. London: Kegan Paul, 1886.

Kaerger, Karl. *Tangaland und die Kolonisation Deutsch Ostafrikas*. Berlin: H. Walther, 1892.

Kallabaka, Maingwa W. J. "The March Towards Ujamaa: Ten Years After. Evaluation of the Ujamaa Program at the Local Community Level." M.A. thesis, University of Dar es Salaam, 1978.

Karst, Joseph. "Lettre." *APF* 63 (1891): 33–43.

Kaya, Hassan Omari. *Problems of Regional Development in Tanzania*. Saarbrucken and Fort Lauderdale, 1985.

Kimambo, I. N. *A Political History of the Pare of Tanzania*. Nairobi: East African Publishing House, 1969.

"Kindermord unter den Wadoe- u. Wasegua Stammen." *Katholischen Missionen* 24 (1896): 23.

Kisbey, W. H. "An Advance in Zigualand." *Central Africa* 19 (April 1901): 64–66.

———. "A Journey in Zigualand." *Central Africa* 18 (1900): 172–175.

———. "Through Zigua to Ngulu." *Central Africa* 26 (October 1908): 264–265.

———. "A Tour in the Zigua Country." *Central Africa* 22 (October 1904): 203–206.

———. "The Work at Korogwe." *Central Africa* 24 (February 1906): 33–38.

———. *Zigula-English Dictionary*. London, 1906.

Kjekshus, Helge. *Ecology Control and Economic Development in East African History: The Case of Tanganyika, 1850–1950*. Berkeley: University of California Press, 1977.

Klamroth, M. *Der Islam in Deutsch Ostafrika*. Berlin, 1912.

Klein, Martin A., ed. *Peasants in Africa: Historical and Contemporary Perspectives*. Beverly Hills and London: Sage, 1980.

Koloniales Jahrbuch. 1895.

Koponen, Juhani. *People and Production in Late Precolonial Tanzania: History and Structures*. Helsinki: Finnish Society for Development Studies, 1988.

Krapf, Johann Ludwig. *Reisen in Ostafrika*. 2 vols. Stuttgart, 1858; reprinted Stuttgart: F. A. Brockhaus Abt Antiquarium, 1964.

Kremer, Eduard. *Die Unperiodischen Schwankungen der Niederschläge und die Hungersnöte in Deutsch-Ostafrika*. Altenburg, 1910.

Krenzler, Eugen. *Ein Jahr in Ostafrika*. Ulm, 1888.

Kuper, Adam. *Wives for Cattle: Bridewealth and Marriage in Southern Africa*. London: Routledge and Kegan Paul, 1982.

"Kwa Maizi, and Its Daughter Parishes in Zigualand." *Central Africa* 42 (November 1924): 240–243.

"Kwa Mkono." *Central Africa* 42 (February 1924): 23–24.

Lagercrantz, Selma. *A Contribution to the Study of Anomalous Dentition and Its Ritual Significance in Africa*. Stockholm: The Ethnographical Museum of Sweden, Smärre Meddelanden no. 16, 1939.

Lan, David. *Guns and Rain: Guerrillas and Spirit Mediums in Zimbabwe*. London, Berkeley and Los Angeles: University of California Press, 1985.

Langer, William L. "Infanticide: A Historical Survey." *History of Childhood Quarterly* 1 (1973): 353–365.

Langheld, Wilhelm. *Zwanzig Jahre in deutschen Kolonien*. Berlin: Weicher, 1909.

Last, James T. "A Journey into the Nguru Country from Mamboia, East Central Africa." *PRGS* N.S. 4, 3 (1882): 148–157.

———. "The Tribes on the Road to Mpwapwa." *The Church Missionary Intelligencer and Record* N.S. 4 (1879): 659–665.

———. "A Visit to the Masai People Living Beyond the Borders of the Nguru Country." *PRGS* N.S. 5 (1883): 517–543.

———. "A Visit to the Wa-Itumba Iron-workers and the Mangaheri, near Mamboia, in East Central Africa." *PRGS* N.S. 5 (1883): 581–592.

Lee, Grace Bridges. "Famine in Zigualand." *Central Africa* 51 (December 1933): 245–248.

Le Roy, Alexandre. "À la découverte," *LMC* 19 (1887): 293–296; 308–312; 320–322; 330–334; 341–344; 353–356; 365–367; 381.

———. "Au Kilimandjaro". *LMC* 25 (1893): 10–11; 16–20; 29–33; 54–58; 64–67; 76–80; 90–92; 101–104; 113–116; 124–128; 137–141; 148–152; 161–166; 173–179; 187–189; 193; 197–200; 209–212.

———. "Lettre." *AOSE* 34 (1883): 308–321.

———. "Lettre." *APF* 56 (1884): 42–59.

———. "Rapport," *APF* 58 (1886): 186–198.

———. *Sur terre et sur l'eau.* Tours: Alfred Mame et fils, 1898.

Leubuscher, Charlotte. *Tanganyika Territory: A Study of Economic Policy Under Mandate.* London: Oxford University Press, 1944.

Leue, A. "Nguru." *Deutsche Kolonialzeitung* 23 (1906): 276–277; 316; 333–334; 361–363.

———. "Die Sklaverei in Deutsch-Ostafrika." *Beiträge zur Kolonialpolitik und Kolonialwirtschaft* 2 (1900–1901): 617–625.

Lichtenheld, G. "Ergebnisse der von R. Koch Ausgeführten und Vorgezeichneten Forschungen über das Küstenfieber der Rinder in Deutsch-Ostafrika." *Zeitschrift für Hygiene und Infektionskrankheiten* 61 (1908): 261–272.

Lind, E. M. and M. E. S. Morrison. *East African Vegetation.* London: Books on Demand UMI, 1974.

Lister, Herbert. "Letter" (Korogwe, March 1, 1892). *Central Africa* 10 (1892): 68–69.

Lorenz. "Sitten und Gebräuche unserer Wanguru." *Echo aus Knechtsteden* 6 (1904–1905): 101–103, 245–246, 270–273.

Mackintosh, Maureen. *Gender, Class and Rural Transition: Agribusiness and the Food Crisis in Senegal.* London and Atlantic Highlands, N.J.: Zed Books, 1989.

Maddocks, J. L. "A Christian Festival in a Mohammedan Land." *Central Africa* 40 (December 1922): 266–267.

———. "Kwa Magome." *Central Africa* 46 (April 1928): 69–70.

———. "Report from Kwa Mkono." *Central Africa* 43 (September 1925): 200.

Maddox, Gregory H. "Leave, Wagogo, You Have No Food: Famine and Survival in Ugogo, Tanzania, 1916–1961." Ph.D. dissertation, Northwestern University, 1988.

Malaisse, F. "L'Homme dans la forêt claire zambézienne. Contribution à l'étude de l'écosystème forêt claire (miombo)." *African Economic History* 7 (Spring 1979): 38–64.

Manley, Rev. G. T. "Mohammedan Advance in Africa." *The Church Missionary Gleaner* 41 (February 2, 1914): 22–23.

Mariam, Mesfin Wolde. *Rural Vulnerability to Famine in Ethiopia, 1958–1977.* London: Intermediate Technology Publications, 1986.

Marno, Ernest. "Bericht über eine Excursion von Zanzibar (Saadani) nach Koa-Kiora." *Mittheilungen der Kaiserlichen und Königlichen Geographischen Gesellschaft in Wien* 21 (1878): 353–426.

McCann, James. *From Poverty to Famine in Northeast Ethiopia: A Rural History, 1900–1935.* Philadelphia: University of Pennsylvania Press, 1987.

McCarthy, D. M. P. *Colonial Bureaucracy and Creating Underdevelopment: Tanganyika, 1919–1940.* Ames: Iowa State University Press, 1982.

McVicar, Thomas. "Death Rites Among the Waluguru and Wanguru." *Primitive Man* 18, 1–2 (1945): 26–35.

———. "The Position of Woman Among the Wanguru." *Primitive Man* 7, 2 (1934): 17–22.

———. "Sibs and Names Among the Wanguru." *Primitive Man* 12, 4 (1939): 103–109.

———. "Wanguru Religion." *Primitive Man* 14, 1–2 (1941): 13–30.

Meinecke, Gustav. *Aus dem Lande des Suaheli.* Berlin, 1895.

———. "Pangani." *Deutsches Kolonialzeitung* 7 (1894): 154–155.

Mgaza, Simon. "Letter." *Muli* (Handeni) no. 25 (August 1953).

Mhando, Helen P. "Capitalist Penetration and the Growth of Peasant Agriculture in Korogwe District, 1920–1975." M.A. thesis, University of Dar es Salaam, 1977.

Mhina, A. K. "Agricultural Change in Korogwe District-Bungu Division." Dissertation paper, Department of History, University of Dar es Salaam, 1974.

Milne, G. "A Soil Reconnaissance Journey through Parts of Tanganyika Territory, December 1935 to February 1936." *Journal of Ecology* 35 (1947): 192–265.

"Mission de l'Immaculée-Conception, à Morogoro (Ouzigoua)." *L'Echo des Missions d'Afrique de la Congrégation du Saint-Esprit et du Saint Coeur de Marie* 1, 3 (July 1884): 114–120.

Mkomwa, Ernest L., and Godfrey Nkwileh. "Jadi, Mila, Desturi na Historia ya Wazigua." Handeni, Unpub. MSS, 1968.

Mochiwa, Anthony. *Habari za Wazigua.* London, 1954.

Mohamed, S. E. "Letter." *Muli* (Handeni), no. 10 (1952).

Morant, V. "Migrations and Breeding of the Red Locust (*Nomadacris septemfasciata* Serville) in Africa, 1927–1945." *Anti Locust Memoir*, no. 2 (1947).

Mortimore, Michael. *Adapting to Drought: Farmers, Famines and Desertification in West Africa.* Cambridge: Cambridge University Press, 1989.

Mtoro bin Mwenyi Bakari. "Meine Reise nach Udoe bis Uzigua." In *Schilderungen der Suahili*, pp. 138–197. Edited by Carl Velten. Göttingen, 1901.

Mullens, Joseph. "A New Route and New Mode of Travelling into Central Africa." *PRGS* 21 (1877): 233–248.

Müller, Fritz Ferdinand. *Deutschland-Zanzibar-Ostafrika.* Berlin: Rütten u. Loening, 1959.

Munro, J. Forbes. "British Rubber Companies in East Africa Before the First World War." *Journal of African History* 24 (1983): 369–379.

Musere, Jonathan. *African Sleeping Sickness: Political Ecology, Colonialism and Control in Uganda.* Lewiston N.Y.: Edwin Mellen Press, 1990.

Muya, Mwalumwambo A. O. M. "A Political Economy of Zigua Utani." In *Utani Relationships in Tanzania* 6:187–248. Edited by Stephen A. Lucas. University of Dar es Salaam, 1975. Mimeographed.

Ndagala, Daniel K. "Pastoral Livestock-Keeping and Rural Development in Tanzania: The Case of the Wakwavi." M.A. thesis, University of Dar es Salaam, 1980.

New, Charles. "Journey from the Pangani, via Wadigo, to Mombasa." *PRGS* 19, 5 (1874–1875): 317–323.

Newitt, M. D. D. "Drought in Mozambique, 1823–1831." *Journal of Southern African Studies* 15, 1 (1988): 15–35.

Nicholls, C. S. *The Swahili Coast.* London: Holmes and Meier, 1971.

Nicholson, Sharon Elaine. "A Climatic Chronology for Africa: Synthesis of Geological, Historical and Meteorological Information and Data." Ph.D. dissertation, University of Wisconsin-Madison, 1976.

Nimtz, August H. Jr. *Islam and Politics in East Africa: The Sufi Order in Tanzania.* Minneapolis: University of Minnesota Press, 1980.

———. "The Role of the Muslim Sufi Order in Political Change: An Overview and Micro-analysis from Tanzania." Ph.D. dissertation, Indiana University, 1973.

Norman, M. J. T., C. J. Pearson, and P. G. E. Searle. *The Ecology of Tropical Food Crops.* Cambridge: Cambridge University Press, 1984.

Nurse, Derek and Thomas Spear. *The Swahili.* Philadelphia: University of Pennsylvania Press, 1985.

Orde-Browne, G. St. J. "Witchcraft and British Colonial Law." *Africa* 8 (1935): 482–483.

Parker, Bishop. "Letter." *Church Missionary Intelligencer and Record* 12 (1887): 692–694.

Peires, J. B. *The Dead Will Arise: Nongqawuse and the Great Xhosa Cattle-Killing Movement of 1856–1857.* Bloomington: Indiana University Press, 1989.

Peters, Karl. *Gesammelte Schriften,* 3 vols. Munich and Berlin: C. H. Beck, 1943.

Pfeil, Graf Joachim von. "Beobachtungen während meiner letzten Reise in Ostafrika." *Petermanns Geographische Mitteilungen* 34 (1888): 1–9.

Picarda, Cado. "Autour de Mandera." *LMC* 18 (1886): 184–189, 197–201, 208–211, 225–228, 234–237, 246–249, 258–261, 269–274, 281–285, 294–297, 312–324, 332–334, 342–346, 356–357 and 365–369.

———. "Compte-Rendu de la Réunion des chefs du Miono et du Loupoungwi (Zanzibar)." *AOSE* 35 (1884): 400–413.

———. "Compte-Rendu de la Réunion des chefs du Miono et du Loupoungwi (Zanzibar)." *L'Echo des Missions d'Afrique de la Congrégation du Saint-Esprit et du Saint Coeur de Marie* 1, 4 (October 1884): 171–183.

———. "Rapport." *LMC* 16 (1884): 505–509.

————. "Les Wazigoua." *L'Echo des Missions d'Afrique de la Congrégation du Saint-Esprit et du Saint Coeur de Marie* 2, 8 (July 1885): 154–159.

Pottier, Johan P. "The Politics of Famine Prevention: Ecology, Regional Production and Food Complementarity in Western Rwanda." *African Affairs* 85, 339 (April 1986): 207–237.

Price, Roger. *Private Journal of the Reverend Roger Price*. London, 1878.

Pruen, Dr. "Slavery in East Africa." *Church Missionary Intelligencer and Record* N.S. 13 (1888): 661–665.

Raikes, Phil. "Eating the Carrot and Wielding the Stick: The Agricultural Sector in Tanzania." In *Tanzania: Crisis and Struggle for Survival*, pp. 105–141. Edited by Jannik Boesen, et al. Uppsala: Scandinavian Institute of African Studies; Stockholm: Almquist and Wiksell, 1986.

Rainey, R. C., Z. Waloff, and G. F. Burnett. "The Behaviour of the Red Locust (*Nomadacris septemfasciata* Serville) in Relation to the Topography, Meteorology and Vegetation of the Rukwa Rift Valley, Tanganyika." *Anti-Locust Bulletin* 26 (1957).

Ranger, Terence. "European Attitudes and African Realities: The Rise and Fall of the Matola Chiefs of South-East Tanzania." *Journal of African History* 20, 1 (1979): 63–82.

————. "Growing from the Roots: Reflections on Peasant Research in Central and Southern Africa." *Journal of Southern African Studies* 5, 1 (1978): 99–133.

————. "Religious Movements and Politics in Sub-Saharan Africa." *African Studies Review* 29, 2 (June 1986): 1–70.

"Rapport d'ensemble sur la Mission de Mandera." *AA* 1 (January 1886): 13–29.

Reichard, Paul. *Deutsch-Ostafrika: Das Land und seine Bewohner*. Leipzig: O. Spamer, 1891.

Rey, P. P. *Les Alliances de classes: sur l'articulation des modes de production*. Paris: Maspero, 1973.

————. *Colonialisme, néocolonialisme et transition au capitalisme: exemple de la 'Comilog' au Congo-Brazzaville*. Paris: Maspero, 1971.

Rigby, Peter. *Persistent Pastoralists: Nomadic Societies in Transition*. London: Zed Books, 1985.

Rubin, Deborah S. "People of Good Heart: Rural Response to Economic Crisis in Tanzania." Ph.D dissertation, Johns Hopkins University, 1986.

Sacleux, Charles. *Dictionnaire Français-Swahili*. Zanzibar and Paris: Mission des P. P. du St. Esprit, 1891.

Saidi, John. "Islam in Zigualand." *Central Africa* 41 (December 1923): 246.

"Salt Production among the Wasambaa." *Tanganyika Notes and Records* 8 (December 1939): 102–103.

Samatar, Abdi Ismail. *The State and Rural Transformation in Northern Somalia, 1884–1986*. Madison: University of Wisconsin Press, 1989.

Schmidt, Rochus. *Geschichte des Araberaufstandes in Ost-Afrika*. Frankfurt, 1892.

————. "Militärische Stützpunkte im Innern Ostafrikas." *Deutsche Kolonialzeitung* 5 (1892): 50–54.

Schneider, Theophil. "Missions-Korrespondenz." *Echo aus Afrika* 16 (1904): 53–54.

Schoeller, Max. *Mitteilungen über meine Reise nach Äquatorial-Ost-Afrika und Uganda, 1896–1897*. 3 vols. Berlin, 1901.

Scott, James C. *The Moral Economy of the Peasant: Rebellion and Subsistence in Southeast Asia*. New Haven and London: Yale University Press, 1976.

Scrimshaw, Susan C. M. "Infanticide in Human Populations: Societal and Individual Concerns." In *Infanticide: Comparative and Evolutionary Perspectives*, pp. 439–462. Edited by Glenn Hausfater and Sarah Blaffer Hrdy. New York: 1984.

Seavoy, Ronald E. *Famine in East Africa: Food Production and Food Policies*. New York: Greenwood Press, 1989.

Sehoza, Samwil. "A Walk to Kwa Magome." *Central Africa* 29 (June 1911): 160–163.

Sen, Amartya. *Poverty and Famines: An Essay on Entitlement and Deprivation*. Oxford: Clarendon Press, 1981.

Sender, John and Sheila Smith. *Poverty, Class and Gender in Rural Africa: A Tanzanian Case Study*. London and New York: Routledge, 1990.

Shenton, Robert W. *The Development of Capitalism in Northern Nigeria*. London: J. Currey, 1986.

Sheriff, Abdul M. H. *Slaves, Spices and Ivory in Zanzibar: Integration of an East African Commercial Empire into One World Economy, 1770–1873*. London: J. Currey, 1987.

Shorter, Aylward. *Chiefship in Western Tanzania: A Political History of the Kimbu*. Oxford: Clarendon Press, 1972.

Sigl, Bezirksamtmann. "Bezirksamt Pangani." *Material zur Beurteilung des Standes der Sklavenfrage in den deutschen Schutzgebieten, 1892–1904*. Pangani, n.d.

Sissons, Carol Jane. "Economic Prosperity in Ugogo, East Africa, 1860–1890." Ph.D. dissertation, University of Toronto, 1984.

Smee, Hardy, and Wingham. "Observations during a Voyage of Research." *Transactions of the Bombay Geographical Society* 6 (1844): 23–61.

Spear, Thomas T. *The Kaya Complex: A History of the Mijikenda Peoples of the Kenya Coast to 1900*. Nairobi: Kenya Literature Bureau, 1978.

Speke, J. H. *What Led to the Discovery of the Source of the Nile*. London: Blackwood, 1864.

"Station Petershöhe in Useguha." *Kolonial-Politische Korrespondenz* 2, 2 (October 16, 1886): 298–300.

Stuhlmann, Franz. "Beiträge zur Kenntnis der Tsetse-fliege." *Arbeiten aus dem Kaiserlichen Gesundheitsamte* 26 (1907): 301–383.

———. "Bericht über eine Reise durch Usegua und Unguu." *Mitteilungen der Geographischen Gesellschaft in Hamburg* 10 (1887–1888): 143–175.

———. *Mit Emin Pascha ins Herz von Afrika*. Berlin, 1894.

Sumra, Suleman Alarakhia. "An Analysis of Environmental and Social Problems Affecting Agricultural Development in Handeni District." M.A. thesis, University of Dar es Salaam, 1975.

———. "Primary Education and Transition to Socialism in Rural Tanzania: A Case Study of an Ujamaa Village in Mswaki, Handeni District." Ph.D. dissertation, Stanford University, 1986.

Sutton, J. E. G. "Dar es Salaam: A Sketch of a Hundred Years." *Tanzania Notes and Records* 71 (1970): 1–19.

Swantz, Marja-Liisa. *Ritual and Symbol in Transitional Zaramo Society with Special Reference to Women*. Uppsala: Scandinavian Institute of African Studies; New York: Africana Publishing, 1986.

Swynnerton, C. F. M. "Some Factors in the Replacement of Ancient East African Forests by Wooded Pastureland." *South African Journal of Science* 14 (1918): 493–518.

———. *The Tsetse Flies of East Africa*. London, 1936.

Tambila, Anse. "A History of the Tanga Sisal Labour Force, 1936–1964." M.A. thesis, University of Dar es Salaam, 1974.

Tooley, Michael. *Abortion and Infanticide*. Oxford: Clarendon Press, 1983.

Tschannerl, G. et al. "Handeni Water Supply: Preliminary Report and Design Criteria." University of Dar es Salaam, BRALUP Report no. 22. Dar es Salaam, 1971.

Tujifunze Lugha Yetu!:6. N.p., n.d.

Turshen, Meredeth. *The Political Ecology of Disease in Tanzania*. New Brunswick, N.J.: Rutgers University Press, 1984.

UNESCO/UNEP/FAO. *Tropical Forest Ecosystems*. Paris, 1978.

Usambara-Post, vols. 3–13 (1903–1914).

Uvarov, Boris. *Grasshoppers and Locusts: A Handbook of General Acridology*. 2 vols. London: Cambridge University Press, 1977.

Vassanji, Moyez G. *The Gunny Sack: Africa's Answer to "Midnight's Children."* London: Heinemann, 1989.

Vaughan, Megan. "Famine Analysis and Family Relations: 1949 in Nyasaland." *Past and Present* 108 (1985): 177–205.

———. *The Story of an African Famine: Gender and Famine in Twentieth-Century Malawi*. Cambridge: Cambridge University Press, 1987.

Vejmola, L. and N. Ngobei. "Water Supply and Range Management Improvements for the Nomadic Population and Livestock in the West Handeni Area." TIRDEP Library, Working Paper no. 29. Tanga, 1975.

Vesey-Fitzgerald, D. F. "The Vegetation of the Outbreak Areas of the Red Locust (*Nomadacris septemfasciata* Serville) in Tanganyika and Northern Rhodesia." *Anti-Locust Bulletin* 20 (1955).

Vogt, François X. "Apostolisches Vikariat Bagamoyo." *Echo aus Afrika* 33 (1921): 75–76.

———. "Aus dem Gebiete der Hungersnot." *Echo aus Afrika* 20 (1908): 111–112.

———. "Bericht." *Echo aus den Missionen der Kongregation vom Heiligen Geist* 14 (1913): 82–85.

———. "Une conversation avec Monseigneur Vogt." *AA* 38 (1922): 52–55.

———. "Jahresbericht." *Echo aus den Missionen der Kongregation vom Heiligen Geist* 9 (1907–1908): 79–84.

———. "Jahresbericht." *Echo aus den Missionen der Kongregation vom Heiligen Geist* 10 (1908–1909): 83–86.

———. "Missions Korrespondenz." *Echo aus Afrika* 21 (1909): 174–177.

————. "Reisebericht." *Echo aus Afrika* 22 (1910): 49–52.

Wagner, J. *Deutsch Ostafrika: Geschichte der Gesellschaft für deutsche Kolonisation und der Deutsch-Ostafrikanischen Gesellschaft*. Berlin, Mitocher und Röstell, 1886.

Waller, Richard. "Ecology, Migration, and Expansion in East Africa." *African Affairs* 84, 336 (July 1985): 347–370.

Watts, Michael. *Silent Violence: Food, Famine and Peasantry in Northern Nigeria*. Berkeley: University of California Press, 1983.

Weidner, Fritz. *Die Haussklaverei in Ostafrika*. Jena, 1915.

Welch, J. R. "Observation of Deciduous Woodland in the Eastern Province of Tanganyika Territory." *Journal of Ecology* 48 (1960): 557–573.

Werth, Dr. E. *Das Deutsch-Ostafrikanische Küstenland und die Vorgelagerten Inseln*. 2 vols. Berlin, 1915.

Wilson, Charles T. and R. W. Felkin. *Uganda and the Egyptian Soudan*. 2 vols. London, 1882.

Wright, Marcia. "East Africa, 1870–1905." In *The Cambridge History of Africa* 6: 539–591. Edited by J. D. Fage and Roland Oliver. Cambridge: Cambridge University Press, 1985.

Wylie, Diana. "The Changing Face of Hunger in Southern African History, 1880–1980." *Past and Present* 122 (February 1989): 159–199.

Yeoman, G. H. and Jane B. Walker. *The Ixodid Ticks of Tanzania*. London: CAB International, 1967.

Young, Francis Brett. *Marching on Tanga*. New York, 1927.

Young, Sherilynn. "What Have They Done With the Rain?" Paper presented to the Annual Meeting of the African Studies Association, Baltimore, November 1–4, 1978.

Zanzibar, Frank [Frank Weston]. "In Zigualand." *Central Africa* 31 (October–December 1921): 187–197, 212–216, 232–239.

Index

Agriculture, precolonial, 19–22; and farm size, 38; and seasonal tasks, 21–22

Akidas: appointment of, 114–15; and compulsory cotton cultivation, 92–93; and Islam, 115–16

Ancestor veneration, 158; and British-appointed chiefs, 140; disappearance of, 117–20; in historical interpretation, 182–83; and *si* communities, 75, 77; and Spiritan missionaries, 64–65

Bagamoyo Mission, 61

Bibi Mandaro, 111

Bondei, labor migration to, 100

Bridewealth: distributed to political leaders, 77; paid in livestock, 35–37

Bushiri, rebellion of, 65, 87; and Uzigua, 87

Bwana Hamadi, 47, 53

Bwana Heri, 87

Cameron, Sir Donald, 136–37, 141, 151

Caravan trade, 24–25, 46–49, 85–86; decline of, 87–90; routes of, 50–51

Cassava, 140, 149–50

Casual labor: in German period, 99–101, 128; in British period, 162–64; by women, 164–65

Cattle disease: and decline of patronage, 178; and famine, 168, 171–73; studies of, in Handeni, 171–74; and Ujamaa villagization, 180–81. *See also* Theileriosis; Trypanosomiasis; Tsetse flies; Vegetation management

Chiefs under British administration, 136–41; economic restrictions upon, 151; election of, 137–38; and environmental relations, 140–41; and famine relief, 166; and Islam, 140; and labor conscription, 146; and patronage, 139–41

Chiefs under German administration: appointment of, 113, 114, 117

Chieftains: and accusations of infanticide, 105–7, 111; alliances of, 50–52, 57–59; and caravan trade, 47–49, 58, 88–90; decline of, in German period, 88–90, 95–97, 111–13, 116–17; and famine of 1884–1886, 121–24; first-generation, 49–52; and German taxation, 90–92; settlements of, 56; and slave trade, 55–57; and tolls, 47–48, 49, 58; traditions of, 70–72, 74, 81. *See also* Bibi Mandaro; Kilo Mwanamachau; Kisabengo; Kolwa; Machaku; Mani; Mhelamwana; Pogwa Mnowowakala; Sedenga; Simbamwene; Sonyo

Clientage: benefits of, 37–38, 39–40; obligations of, 67–69

Clients: and constraints on patrons, 81; of Spiritan missionaries, 66–68

Cotton cultivation: compelled by British, 147–48; compelled by Germans, 92–93; and wage labor, 148

Crop pests, 117; in German period, 127. *See also* Locusts

Crops, precolonial, 20–22

Crop sales: and British taxation, 145; during British period, 149–50, 156–58; during famines, 125–26, 128, 155–56, 161

Crop yields, precolonial, 39

DOAG. *See* German East Africa Company

Drought, 9; as cause of famine, 9–10; and famine, 125–26, 158–59; in Handeni, 18–19

East Coast fever. *See* Theileriosis

Environmental history: and famine, 9–10; in Handeni District, 8–9; interpretation of, in Handeni District, 117–20, 182–83

Environments: and group identities, 17–18; trade between, 22–27; in Uzigua, 18–19

Epidemics, 128–129. *See also* Influenza pandemic; Smallpox

Famine: causes of, 9–10; and demographic change, 122–23, 125, 126–27, 167–68; pre-1880s, 40–41; of 1884–1886, 121–24; of 1894–1896, 124–25; of 1898–1900, 115, 125–27; and environmental history, 9–10; in Handeni District, 1, 11–12; of 1907–1910, 128; of 1916–1918, 153–55; of 1925, 155–56; of 1932–1935, 158–61; and patronage, 121–24, 125, 127; and settlement patterns, 122–24, 125, 127
Famine foods, 128, 166
Famine relief, 166–67
Fires: and disease control, 32–33; and theileriosis, 31; and trypanosomiasis, 30; and vegetation management, 22, 32–33
First World War: environmental effects of, 168; in Uzigua, 153–55
Fonck, August, 91–92
Ford, John, epidemiological theory of, 29–30, 32, 181

Gender division of labor, 22, 26
German administration: and accusations of infanticide, 102–4, 109–11; and appointment of Akidas, 114–15; and suppression of chieftains, 111–13
German East Africa Company, 86–87
Grenzwildnis: expansion of, 168–175; precolonial, 34, 36, 53

Handeni Chiefs' Council, ordinances of, 140–41
Handeni District: as part of Uzigua, 15; plantations in, 93–95, 143–146; population of, 1, 167–68 n.52; post-1940 conditions in, 12
Healers: and accusations of infanticide, 105–7, 109–11; and missionaries, 62–64; suppression of, 109–14
Hine, John (bishop of Zanzibar), 132
Hoffmann, A. W., 145–46
Holy Ghost Order. See Spiritan missionaries; Bagamoyo Mission; Lugoba Mission; Mandera Mission; Mhonda Mission; Picarda, Father Cado
Hornby, H. E., 172–73
Households: composition of, 79–80; and patrons, 78–80

Hunger: during German period, 124–29; during 1920s, 155–56; during 1930s, 158–61
Hunting: and control of theileriosis, 31; precolonial, 27–28
Hyden, Goran, 4, 6

Indian traders: and caravan trade, 45–46; as creditors, 156; and crop monopsony, 157–58; in Handeni during British period, 145, 151; in Handeni during German period, 89
Indirect Rule: chiefs appointed under, 136–41; and restrictions on rural accumulation, 150–52; and self-sufficiency, 141–42; and si traditions, 137; and "tribal" history, 136–37; and wage labor, 142–46
Infanticide: accusations of, 104–6, 107–11; in European history, 107 n.12
Influenza pandemic, 155
Iron wares, trade in, 27
Islam: and Akidas, 115–16; and British-appointed chiefs, 140; in British period, 165; in German period, 115–16
Ivory, trade in, 26–27, 28, 46, 48–49, 72, 87

Kaguru Mountains, 27; and si identities in, 73
Kiberashi Village, studies of cattle disease at, 172–74
Kidyakingo. See Famine, pre-1880s
Kigego. See Vigego
Kilo Mwanamachau, 55; murder of, 117
Kinship, idiom of, 50, 58, 97
Kisabengo, 53
Kiswahili. See Swahili language
Kizigua. See Zigua language
Kiwiri, 99–100
Kolwa, 57, 105, 124; and Spiritan missionaries, 65
Krepp, Adolph, 103–4
Kwa Luguru si, 76–77
Kwa Maligwa Village, cattle disease at, 174–175

Labor conscription: during First World War, 153–55; during German period, 92–93, 94–95
Labor migration: in British period, 162–64; in German period, 90–91, 100

Landholding: and chieftains, 56; conflict over, 74; in modern Handeni, 38–39 n.34; precolonial, 38–39; and *si* traditions, 74

Liebert, Governor Eduard von, 111

Livestock: and political authority, 35–37; and precolonial patronage, 35–38; and ritual, 37

Locusts: and causes of plagues, 159; and crop damage, 159–60; in 1898–1900, 125–26; in 1930s, 158–60

Lugala. See Famine, of 1884–1886

Lugoba Mission, and suppression of healers, 111

Maasai: chieftains' alliances with, 117; farmers' cooperation with, 35; in Handeni District, 16–17; and rinderpest, 129; trade with, 26–27, 35, 48, 54–55. *See also* Parakuyu Maasai

Machaku, 53–54

Magamba, 53, 76–77, 96–97; epidemic at, 128–29. *See also* Kwa Luguru *si.*

Mandera Mission, 112; and accusations of infanticide, 105–7; and cattle disease at, 130–31, 168, 171; and famine, 122, 124, 125–26, 128; foundation of, 62; and labor, 143–44, 145; political position of, 65; and population decline during German period, 127, 131

Mani, 53, 76–77

Markets: and monopsony in British period, 157–58; precolonial, 24, 26, 48

Matambiko. See Ancestor veneration

Mgera Village, 54; election at, 138; spread of wildlife at, 174–75

Mhelamwana, 49–50, 53, 70–72, 76

Mhonda Mission, 64–65; agriculture at, 67–68; and chieftains, 111–12; foundation of, 62; and healers, 111–12; patronage at, 67–68, 80, 91; political power of, 65, 96

Morogoro, 53; agriculture at, 68–69; patronage at, 68–69

Mpwapwa, and taxation, 90–92

Mrima coast, 23–25; and caravan trade, 46–47, 50, 53, 72, 85–88. *See also* Pangani; Sadani; Trade, with Swahili Coast

Mrima War of Resistance. *See* Bushiri, rebellion of

Mswaki Village, 53–54; census of, 167

Mtunte: and accusations of infanticide, 102–4; execution of, 102–3

Muheza, and labor migration to, 100

Ndorobo hunter-gatherers, 17, 26; trade with, 48

Nguu Mountains, 17, 18, 20, 22, 23–24, 26; chieftains of, 54–55; food exports from, 23–24, 46–47; *si* traditions from, 73–74; trading camps in, 46–48, 86, 87

Nkumuwlwa Pogwa, 113–14

Pangani, 23, 24; and caravan trade, 46, 50–52, 54; and its decline, 88

Pangani Valley, 18, 20, 22, 24, 26, 49; caravan trade in, 50–52, 54; cattle in, 33; and labor migration to, 100, 162–64; slave plantations in, 86

Parakuyu Maasai: and attempt to expel from Handeni, 141–42; and cattle disease at Kiberashi, 174–75; in Handeni District, 17

Patronage: in colonial period, 177–78; disappearance of, 95–97, 104, 111–12, 116–17, 156–57, 177–78; and disease control, 69; and famine, 40–41, 121–23, 124–29, 161–68; in Handeni's history, 8–9, 177–78; and households, 78–81; norms of, 81; and Ujamaa villagization, 180–81

Patrons: and German taxation, 90–91; and labor of clients, 67–69; obligations of, 8, 37–39, 67–69, 77

Pawning, 66; and German taxation, 90

Peasants: in historical literature, 3–6; market and subsistence tendencies among, 3–7

Pemba, clove production at, 85

Peters, Karl, 86

Picarda, Father Cado: and accusations of infanticide, 105–7, 109; and Mandera mission, 65, 105–7, 109

Pienaar, E., 135–36, 149

Plantation labor in Handeni, 93–95, 142–46, 162–64

Pogwa Mnowowakala, 54–55

Political leaders, precolonial: and environmental relations, 117–20, 177; duties of, 62–69

Population of Uzigua: changes in, 131, 168–170; decline in, and famine, 155, 167–68; decline in, and cattle disease, 168–75. *See also* Handeni District, population of

Qadiriyya brotherhood, 165

Rainfall in Handeni, 9, 18–19, 158–59
Relations of production: changes in, 99–101; outside the household, 10–11, 67–69, 80; and patronage, 67–69, 80
Rinderpest, 129–31; and Kilo Mwanamachau, 117
Rubber plantations in Handeni, 93–95; and cattle disease, 173
Rukorongwe, 52–53

Sadani, 23; and caravan trade, 50, 54; and its decline, 88
Scarcity in Handeni: attitudes about, 7, 117–20, 182–83; causes of, 8–10
Sedenga, 116
Self-sufficiency: and Indirect Rule, 141–42; and Ujamaa villagization, 2–3, 179–80
Settlement patterns: and cattle disease, 168–75; change in, 130–31, 155, 167–70; and chieftains, 56; and famine, 122–24, 125, 127; precolonial, 19–20, 30–31, 33–34
Settlements, manner of naming, 75
Shaykh Ramiya, 165
Si communities, 51–54; defined, 73–75; and interpretation of history in Handeni, 75; Mhelamwana's membership in, 71; and patronage, 74–75, 77–78; and political authority, 75–78, 119; and precolonial politics, 73–78; and ritual, 75, 77–79, 117–20; rivalries between, 78–79; traditions of, 73–74; traditions of, and Indirect Rule 137. See also *Rukorongwe*; *Wakinaluma*
Simbamwene, 69, 80
Si names, 54, 73–74, 77
Sisal plantation labor, 100, 144–45, 162–64
Slavery: and agriculture, 46–47; decline of, 95–99; and manumission, 97–98; and property rights, 99
Slave trade, 23–27, 40–41, 48, 50, 55–57, 80, 86; decline of, 87; and famine, 40–41; and Mhelamwana, 72. See also Spiritan missionaries, and the slave trade

Sleeping Sickness. *See* Trypanosomiasis, human
Smallpox, 64, 127, 129
Sonyo, 53, 103; appointment of, as administrative chief, 113; decline of, in German period, 96–97; and Kilo Mwanamachau, 117; and precolonial politics, 76–77
Spiritan missionaries (Holy Ghost Order): and accusations of cannibalism, 108–9; and accusations of infanticide, 105–11; and ancestor veneration, 64–65; and cattle disease, 130–31; and decline of patronage, 91; and evangelical strategy, 60–66; and famine of 1894–1896, 124–25; and healers, 62–64, 105–7, 109–12; and patronage, 66–68, 80, 90, 96, 106–7; political authority of, 62–68; and the slave trade, 61, 66; trade of, 66; and wage labor, 143–44
Spirit possession, 101
Swahili language, 24
Swynnerton, C. F. M., 172

Tamota Estate, 145–46
Taxation: British, 139; and Akidas, 114–15; and crop sales, 148–49, 155–57; and famine, 125–26, 128, 155–56, 163; German, 90–92; and labor recruitment, 143–46
Theileria, 31–32
Theileriosis: in German period, 130–32; loss of bovine resistance to, 130–32, 173–74; in 1930s, 173–75; in precolonial Uzigua, 32–34; transmission of, 31–32
Trade, 22–28; early-colonial changes in, 87–90; goods used in, 23–28; "inter-tribal," prohibition of, 141–42; of livestock, 34–35, 88, 152, 164; during the 1930s, 151–52, 164; precolonial, 22–28, 48–49; restrictions on, 91, 142; routes of, 50–51, 88–89; with Swahili Coast, 22–27, 34, 46–49, 72
"Tribal" characteristics, 23, 108–9
Trypanosomiasis, bovine: during First World War, 168; in precolonial Uzigua, 32–34; in German period, 130–32; in 1920s, 168–71; in 1930s, 171–75; transmission of, 29–32. *See also* Tsetse flies
Trypanosomiasis, human 30 n.2
Tsetse flies (*Glossina* spp.): spread of, 130–31, 168, 170–73; and trypanosomiasis, 29–31

Ujamaa villagization, 2, 7, 177; agricultural policies associated with, 2–3, 178–180; attitudes about, in Handeni, 182; and cattle disease, 181; opposition to, in Handeni, 179, 182–83
Uzaramo, famine of 1898–1900 in, 125–26
Uzigua: and caravan trade, 46–49; as part of northeastern Tanzania, 15

Vegetation management: decline of, 130–31, 168–75; and disease control, 30–33; in 1980s, 180–81; precolonial, 22
Vigego, 70, 72 n.2, 104; and accusations of infanticide, 105–06, 108–09

Waganga. See Healers
Wage labor in Handeni, shortage of, 142–46
Wages of plantation laborers, 94, 98, 144–45, 163
Wakinaluma, 51
Wami Valley, 20–21, 24; cattle in, 33–34; chieftains of, 50

Wegazi, 75, 77–80; and missionaries, 64; and si traditions, 75
Wildlife: in German period, 127, 130–31; during 1920s, 169–71; during 1930s, 173–74
Witch detection, 140, 181
Women: and casual labor, 164–65; condition of, in British period, 164–67; and economic independence, 80; and famine of 1932–1935, 160–61; in households, 80; and precolonial agricultural labor, 22; and precolonial political authority, 80. See also Bibi Mandaro; Gender division of labor; Simbamwene

Yusufu Kaberwa, 53–54, 116–17

Zanzibar, 25; and caravan trade, 86–87; clove economy of, 45; decline of Uzigua's trade with, 87–88; Omani government of, 47, 85–86
Zigua language, 15–16

University of Pennsylvania Press
ETHNOHISTORY SERIES

Lee V. Cassanelli, Juan A. Villamarin, and Judith E. Villamarin, Editors

Christopher Boehm. *Blood Revenge: The Enactment and Management of Conflict in Montenegro and Other Tribal Societies*. 1987.

Lee V. Cassanelli. *The Shaping of Somali Society: Reconstructing the History of a Pastoral People, 1600–1900*. 1982.

James L. Giblin. *The Politics of Environmental Control in Northeastern Tanzania, 1840–1940*. 1992.

Robert M. Hill, II and John Monaghan. *Continuities in Highland Maya Social Organization: Ethnohistory in Sacapulas, Guatemala*. 1987.

James McCann. *From Poverty to Famine in Northeast Ethiopia: A Rural History, 1900–1935*. 1987.

Derek Nurse and Thomas Spear. *The Swahili: Reconstructing the History and Language of an African Society, 800–1500*. 1985.

James A. Quirin. *The Evolution of the Ethiopian Jews: A History of the Beta Israel to the 1920's*. 1992.

Norman B. Schwartz. *Forest Society: A Social History of Petén, Guatemala*. 1990.

Lawrence J. Taylor. *Dutchmen on the Bay: The Ethnohistory of a Contractual Community*. 1983.

This book has been set in Linotron Galliard. Galliard was designed for Mergenthaler in 1978 by Matthew Carter. Galliard retains many of the features of a sixteenth-century typeface cut by Robert Granjon but has some modifications that give it a more contemporary look.

Printed on acid-free paper.